SYNTAX OF THE MOODS AND TENSES IN NEW TESTAMENT GREEK

SYNTAX

OF THE

MOODS AND TENSES

IN

NEW TESTAMENT GREEK

BY

ERNEST DE WITT BURTON

KREGEL PUBLICATIONS
Grand Rapids, Michigan 49501

Syntax of the Moods and Tenses in New Testament Greek published by Kregel Publications, a division of Kregel, Inc. Reprint of the Third Edition, Copyright © 1900 by Ernest D. Burton, published by The University of Chicago Press, Chicago, Illinois.

Kregel Publications edition 1976
Second Printing 1978

Library of Congress Catalog Card Number 76-25360
ISBN 0-8254-2256-6

PREFACE

THE first edition of this work appeared as a pamphlet in
1888. In issuing this revised and enlarged edition, it seems
desirable to state somewhat more fully than was done in the
former preface the purpose which it is hoped the book will
serve. Classified according to its intent, it belongs among the
aids to the interpretation of the New Testament. It is de-
signed to assist English-speaking students in the task of
translating the Greek New Testament into English forms of
thought and expression. The work has not been undertaken
under the impression that grammar is an end in itself, or that
a knowledge of it is the sole qualification for successful interpretation, but in the conviction that grammar is one of
the indispensable auxiliaries of interpretation. The book is
written, therefore, in the interest not of historical but of
exegetical grammar, not of philology as such, but of philology
as an auxiliary of interpretation. If it has any value for
historical grammar, this is incidental. Its main purpose is
to contribute to the interpretation of the New Testament by
the exposition of the functions of the verb in New Testament
Greek, so far as those functions are expressed by the distinctions of mood and tense.

The student of the New Testament who would interpret it
with accuracy and clearness must possess — along with other
qualifications for his work — a knowledge of the distinctions
of thought which are marked by the different moods and
tenses of the Greek verb. If he would acquire facility in the
work of interpretation, he must have an easy familiarity with
the leading uses of each mood and tense. It is not enough

that he have at hand for reference an encyclopedic treatise on
the subject. He must acquire, as a personal mental possession, a knowledge of the leading functions of the several
forms of the Greek verb, and of the forms which express
those functions in English. For this purpose he needs a book
which, availing itself of the assured results of comparative
and historical grammar, and applying to the interpretation of
the Greek verb the principles of grammar and logic, the laws
both of Greek and of English speech, shall enumerate the
various functions of each mood and tense, exhibit in some
degree their relative importance, and define each clearly.
The definitions should be scientifically accurate, but they
should at the same time be constructed with reference to the
point of view of the interpreter. For the English-speaking
student English usage must be constantly considered and
must frequently be defined and compared with Greek usage.
If such a book does not solve all the problems of New
Testament grammar, it should, by its treatment of those which
it discusses, illustrate to the student the right method of
investigation and so suggest the course which he must pursue
in solving for himself those problems which the book leaves
unsolved. My aim has been to provide a book fulfilling these
conditions.

The aim of the book has determined the method of its construction. The usages which are of most frequent occurrence,
or otherwise of especial importance, have been emphasized by
being set in the largest type, with a title in bold-faced type.
The table of contents also has been so constructed as to make
prominent a conspectus of the leading uses. It may be well to
require of students who use the book as a text-book that they
be able to name and define these leading usages of each mood
and tense; if they also commit to memory one of the Greek
examples under each of these prominent usages, they will do
still better.

The matter printed in smaller type consists partly of fuller
exposition of the usages defined in the more prominently

printed sections, partly of enumeration and definition of the
less frequent usages. The portions in smallest type are
chiefly discussions of the rarer or more difficult usages. They
are an addition to the text-book proper, and are intended to
give the work, to a limited extent, the character of a book of
reference. The occasional discussions of English usage would
of course have no place in a work on Greek grammar pure
and simple, but to the end which this book is intended to
serve they are as really germane as any discussions of the
force of a Greek tense. One often fails to apprehend accurately a thought expressed in Greek quite as much through
inexact knowledge of one's own language as through ignorance
of Greek usage.

As concerns the extent to which I have used the work of
others, little need be added to the testimony which the pages
of the book themselves bear. While gathering information
or suggestion from all accessible sources, I have aimed to
make no statement concerning New Testament usage which I
have not myself proved by personal examination of the passages. Respecting classical usage and pre-classical origins, I
have relied upon those authorities which are recognized as
most trustworthy.

On a subsequent page is added a list of books and authors
referred to by abbreviations in the body of the book. To all
of the works there enumerated, as well as to those mentioned
by full title in the body of the book, I am under obligation for
assistance or suggestion. It is a pleasure also to acknowledge
the valuable assistance privately given by various friends.
Prominent among these, though not completing the list, are
Professor W. G. Hale of the University of Chicago, Profes-
sors M. L. D'Ooge and W. W. Beman of the University of
Michigan, my brother, Professor Henry F. Burton of the
University of Rochester, and Professor George W. Gilmore
of Brooklyn, N.Y. But I am chiefly indebted to Professor
William Arnold Stevens of the Rochester Theological Semi-
nary, under whose instructions I first became interested in the

subject of this book, and to whom my obligations in many directions are larger than can be acknowledged here.

In quoting examples from the New Testament I have followed the Greek text of Westcott and Hort as that which perhaps most nearly represents the original text, but have intended to note any important variations of Tischendorf's eighth edition or of Tregelles in a matter affecting the point under discussion. The word *text* designates the preferred reading of the editor referred to, as distinguished from the marginal reading. In the English translation of the examples I have preferred to follow the Revised Version of 1881 rather than to construct entirely independent translations. Yet in not a few passages it has seemed necessary to depart from this standard either because the revisers followed a Greek text different from that of Westcott and Hort, or because their translation obscured the value of the passage as an illustration of the grammatical principle under discussion, or occasionally because I was unwilling even to seem to approve what I regarded as unquestionably an error of translation.

While I have given all diligence to make the book correct in statement and in type, I dare not hope that it has altogether escaped either typographical errors or those of a more serious character. I shall welcome most cordially criticisms, suggestions, or corrections from any teacher or student into whose hands the book may fall.

ERNEST D. BURTON

CHICAGO, September, 1893.

NOTE TO THE THIRD EDITION.—It having become necessary to send the plates of this book to the press again, I have availed myself of the opportunity to correct such errors, typographical and other, as have come to my attention, and to make a few alterations of statement which use of the book has convinced me are desirable. The chief changes are in §§ 67 Rem. 1, 98, 120, 137, 142-145, 153, 189, 195, 198, 200 Rem., 202, 225, 235, 236, 318, 325-328, 344 Rem. 2, 352 Rem., 406, 407, 485.

CHICAGO, June, 1898.   E. D. B.

CONTENTS

——•◦•——

The Aorist Indicative

The Future Indicative

The Perfect Indicative

CONTENTS xiii

Moods in Concessive Sentences

Moods in Relative Clauses

I. DEFINITE RELATIVE CLAUSES

II. CONDITIONAL RELATIVE SENTENCES

III. RELATIVE CLAUSES EXPRESSING PURPOSE

IV. RELATIVE CLAUSES INTRODUCED BY WORDS MEANING UNTIL, WHILE, AND BEFORE

Moods in Indirect Discourse

Construction after Καὶ ἐγένετο

xvi   CONTENTS

THE INFINITIVE

SECTION   PAGE

361–363.   Origin, and Classification of Uses   143–145

The Infinitive without the Article

364, 365.   IMPERATIVE INFINITIVE   146
366, 367.   INFINITIVE OF PURPOSE   146
368.   INFINITIVE AS AN INDIRECT OBJECT   147
369–371.   INFINITIVE OF RESULT   147–150
372–374.   Exceptional usages   150
375.   INFINITIVE DEFINING CONTENT OF A PREVIOUS VERB
          OR NOUN 150, 151
376, 377.   INFINITIVE LIMITING ADJECTIVES AND ADVERBS . .   151
378, 379.   INFINITIVE LIMITING NOUNS 151, 152
380–382.   INFINITIVE AFTER πρίν or πρίν ἤ   152
383.   INFINITIVE USED ABSOLUTELY   153
384, 385.   INFINITIVE AS SUBJECT   153
386.   INFINITIVE AS APPOSITIVE   153
387–389.   INFINITIVE AS OBJECT. 153, 154
390.   Infinitive in Indirect Discourse 154, 155
391.   Infinitive after verbs of *hoping, promising, swearing, commanding*, etc.   155

The Infinitive with the Article

392.   General Use of Infinitive with the Article .   155, 156
393.   INFINITIVE WITH τό AS SUBJECT   156
394.   INFINITIVE WITH τό AS OBJECT   156
395.   INFINITIVE WITH THE ARTICLE, IN APPOSITION . .   156, 157
396.   INFINITIVE WITH τῷ   157
397.   INFINITIVE OF PURPOSE WITH τοῦ.   157
398.   INFINITIVE OF RESULT WITH τοῦ 157, 158
399.   INFINITIVE WITH τοῦ AFTER ADJECTIVES   158
400.   INFINITIVE WITH τοῦ AFTER NOUNS   158
401.   INFINITIVE WITH τοῦ AFTER VERBS THAT TAKE THE
          GENITIVE 158, 159
402, 403.   Various constructions after Verbs of *hindering*   159
404, 405.   INFINITIVE WITH τοῦ AS SUBJECT OR OBJECT. . .   159, 160
406–417.   INFINITIVE WITH THE ARTICLE GOVERNED BY PREPOSITIONS   160–163

THE PARTICIPLE

NEGATIVES WITH THE INFINITIVE AND PARTICIPLE

LIST OF WORKS AND AUTHORS

A.J.P. . . . . American Journal of Philology.

Alf. . . . . . . *Henry Alford*, The Greek New Testament. 4 vols. London.

A.V. . . . . . Authorized Version of the New Testament.

B. . . . . *Alexander Buttmann*, A Grammar of the New Testament Greek. Translated by J. H. Thayer. Andover, 1873.

Bib. Sac. . . . Bibliotheca Sacra.

Br. . . . . . . *Karl Brugmann*, Griechische Grammatik, in Iwan Müller's Handbuch der klassischen Altertumswissenschaft, vol. II. Second Edition. München, 1890.

Cl. Rev. . . . . Classical Review.

Del. . . . . . . *B. Delbrück*, Syntaktische Forschungen. Halle, 1871–1888.

Ev. Pet. . . . . Apocryphal Gospel of Peter. (Verses according to the edition of Harnack, Leipzig, 1893.)

G. . . . . *W. W. Goodwin*, A Greek Grammar. Revised Edition. Boston, 1892.

Gild. . . . . . *Basil L. Gildersleeve*, various papers in *A.J.P.* and *T.A.P.A.*

*G.*MT. . . . . *W. W. Goodwin*, Syntax of the Moods and Tenses of the Greek Verb. Revised and enlarged. Boston, 1889.

Gr. . . . . . . *Thomas Sheldon Green*, A Treatise on the Grammar of the New Testament. New Edition. London, 1862.

HA. . . . . . . *James Hadley*, A Greek Grammar for Schools and Colleges. Revised by F. D. Allen. New York, 1884.

Hr. . . . . . . *W. R. Harper*, Elements of Hebrew Syntax. New York, 1888.

J. . . . . *W. E. Jelf*, A Grammar of the Greek Language. Third Edition. 2 vols. Oxford and London, 1861.

J.B.L. . . . . Journal of the Society of Biblical Literature and Exegesis.

K. . . . . *Raphael Kühner*, Grammatik der Griechischen Sprache. Hanover, 1869–1872.

Ka. . . . . . . *E. Kautzsch*, Grammatik des Biblisch-Aramäischen. Leipzig, 1884.

L. and S. . . . *Liddell and Scott,* Greek-English Lexicon, etc. Seventh Edition. New York, 1882.

Ltft. . . . . . . *J. B. Lightfoot,* Commentaries on Galatians, on Philippians, and on Colossians and Philemon.

Mart. Polyc. . Martyrium Polycarpi. (See any edition of the Apostolic Fathers.)

Meist. . . . . . *K. Meisterhans,* Grammatik der Attischen Inschriften. Berlin, 1885.

Mey. . . . . . *H. A. W. Meyer,* Kommentar über das Neue Testament. Göttingen, 1867–1876. English Translation, Edinburgh, 1873–1880.

Ps. Sol. . . . . The Psalms of Solomon. (Recent edition by Ryle and James, Cambridge, 1891.)

R.V. . . . . . The New Testament in the Revised Version of 1881.

S. . . . . *W. H. Simcox,* The Language of the New Testament. London and New York, 1889.

Th. . . . . . . *J. H. Thayer,* A Greek-English Lexicon of the New Testament: Being Grimm's Wilke's Clavis Novi Testamenti, translated, revised, and enlarged. New York, 1886.

Tisch. . . . . . *Constantinus Tischendorf,* Novum Testamentum Graece. Eighth Edition. 2 vols. Leipzig, 1869–72.

Treg. . . . . . *S. P. Tregelles,* The Greek New Testament. London, 1857–79.

T.A.P.A. . . . Transactions of the American Philological Association.

W. . . . . . . *G. B. Winer.* See *WM.* and *WT.*

WH. . . . . . *Westcott and Hort,* The New Testament in the Original Greek, the text revised by B. F. Westcott and F. J. A. Hort. 2 vols. Cambridge and New York, 1881.

WM. . . . . . *G. B. Winer,* A Treatise on the Grammar of New Testament Greek. Translated by W. F. Moulton. Third Edition. Edinburgh, 1882.

WT. . . . . . *G. B. Winer,* A Grammar of the Idiom of the New Testament. Seventh Edition, enlarged and improved by Gottlieb Lünemann. Revised and authorized Translation by J. H. Thayer. Andover, 1869.

WS. . . . . . *G. B. Winer's* Grammatik des neutestamentlichen Sprachidioms, Achte Auflage, neu bearbeitet von *D.* Paul Wilh. Schmiedel, Göttingen, 1894– (in process of publication).

For classical and Scripture writers the ordinary abbreviations are used. References to the Old Testament are to the Septuagint Version, unless otherwise indicated.

SYNTAX

OF THE

MOODS AND TENSES IN NEW TESTAMENT GREEK

————

INTRODUCTORY

1. FORM AND FUNCTION. The following pages deal with
the various functions of the various verb-forms of the Greek
of the New Testament, so far as respects their mood and
tense. It is important that the nature of the relation between
form and function be clearly held in mind. It is by no means
the case that each form has but one function, and that each
function can be discharged by but one form. Forms of various
origin may be associated together under one name and perform
the same function, or group of functions. Compare, *e.g.*, the
Aorist Active Infinitives, λῦσαι and εἰπεῖν: these forms are of
quite diverse origin; in function they have become entirely
assimilated. The same is true of the Aorist Active Indicatives,
ἔδειξα and ἔστην. Forms also which still have different names,
and usually perform different functions, may have certain
functions in common. Compare the Aorist Subjunctive and
the Future Indicative in clauses of purpose (197, 198). On
the other hand, and to an even greater extent, we find that a
given form, or a given group of forms bearing a common name,
performs various distinct functions. Observe, *e.g.*, the various
functions of the Aorist Indicative (38–48).

1

The name of a given form, or group of forms, is usually derived from some prominent function of the form or group. Thus the term Aorist reflects the fact that the forms thus designated most frequently represent an action indefinitely without reference to its progress. The name Present suggests that the forms thus designated denote present time, which is true, however, of the smaller part only of those that bear the name, and of none of them invariably. The name Optative again reminds us that one function of the forms so named is to express a wish. While, therefore, the names of the forms were originally intended to designate their respective functions, they cannot now be regarded as descriptive of the actual functions, but must be taken as conventional, and to a considerable extent arbitrary, names of the forms. The functions must be learned, not from the names, but from observation of the actual usage.

2. The Interpreter's Relation to Grammar. Both the grammarian as such and the interpreter deal with grammar, but from very different points of view. The distinction between these points of view should be clearly recognized by the interpreter. It may be conveniently represented by the terms historical grammar and exegetical grammar. Historical grammar deals with the development of both form and function through the various periods of the history of the language, and does this in purely objective fashion. Exegetical grammar, on the other hand, takes the forms as it finds them, and defines the functions which at a given period each form discharged, and does this from the point of view of the interpreter, for the purpose of enabling him to reproduce the thought conveyed by the form. To investigate the process by which the several forms were built up, to determine the earliest function of each such form, to show how out of this earliest function others were developed, and how forms of different origin, and presumably at first of different function, became associated, discharging the same function and eventually coming to bear the same name — all this belongs to historical grammar. To reproduce in the mind of the interpreter, and to express as nearly as may be in his own tongue, the exact thought which a given form was in the period in question capable of expressing — this is the task of exegetical grammar. Historical grammar views its problem wholly from the point of view of the language under investigation, without reference to the language of the grammarian. Exegetical grammar is necessarily concerned both with the language under investigation and with that in which the interpreter thinks and speaks, since its problem is to aid in reproducing in the latter tongue thought expressed in the former.

The results of historical grammar are of the greatest interest and value to exegetical grammar. Our interpretation of the phenomena of language in its later periods can hardly fail to be affected by a knowledge of the earlier history. Strictly speaking, however, it is with the results only of the processes of historical grammar that the interpreter is concerned. If the paradigm has been rightly constructed, so that forms of diverse origin perhaps, but completely assimilated in function, bear a common name, exegetical grammar is concerned only to know what are the functions which each group of forms bearing a common name is capable of discharging. Thus, the diversity of origin of the two Aorists, ἔλυσα and ἔλιπον, does not immediately concern the interpreter, if it is an assured result of historical grammar that these two forms are completely assimilated in function. Nor does it concern him that the αι at the end of the Infinitives, δεῖξαι and ἰέναι, is the mark of the Dative case, and that the earliest use of such infinitives was as a verbal noun in the Dative case, except as this fact of historical grammar aids him in the interpretation of the phenomena of that period of the language with which he is dealing. The one question of exegetical grammar to which all other questions are subsidiary is, What function did this form, or group of forms, discharge at the period with which we are dealing? What, *e.g.*, in the New Testament, are the functions of the Present Indicative? What are the uses of the Aorist Subjunctive?

For practical convenience forms are grouped together, and the significance of each of the distinctions made by inflection discussed by itself. The present work confines itself to the discussion of mood and tense, and discusses these as far as possible separately. Its question therefore is, What in the New Testament are the functions of each tense and of each mood? These various functions must be defined first of all from the point of view of the Greek language itself. Since, however, the interpreter whom in the present instance it is sought to serve thinks in English, and seeks to express in English the thought of the Greek, reference must be had also to the functions of the English forms as related to those of the Greek forms. Since, moreover, distinctions of function in the two languages do not always correspond, that is, since what in Greek is one function of a given form may be in English subdivided into several functions performed by several forms, it becomes necessary not only to enumerate and define the functions of a given form purely from the point of view of Greek, but to subdivide the one Greek function into those several functions which in English are recognized and marked by the employment of different forms. An enumeration of the uses of a given Greek tense made for the use of an English interpreter may therefore properly include certain titles which would not occur in a list made for one to whom Greek was the language of

ordinary speech and thought. The Aorist for the English
Perfect, and the Aorist for the English Pluperfect (46, 48)
furnish a pertinent illustration. The interests of the English
interpreter require that they be clearly recognized. Fidelity
to Greek usage requires that they be recognized as, strictly
speaking, true Historical Aorists.

3. The Greek verb has four moods, — the Indicative, the
Subjunctive, the Optative, and the Imperative. With these
are associated in the study of Syntax the Infinitive, which is,
strictly speaking, a verbal noun, and the Participle, which is
a verbal adjective.

The Subjunctive, Optative, Imperative, and Infinitive are
often called dependent moods.

REM. The term *dependent* is not strictly applicable to these moods,
and least of all to the Imperative, which almost always stands as a principal verb. It has, however, become an established term, and is retained
as a matter of convenience.

4. There are seven tenses in the Greek, — the Present,
Imperfect, Aorist, Future, Perfect, Pluperfect, and Future
Perfect.

Those tenses which denote present or future time are called
Primary tenses. Those tenses which denote past time are
called Secondary tenses. Since the time denoted by a tense
varies with the particular use of the tense, no fixed line of
division can be drawn between the two classes of tenses. In
the Indicative the Present and Perfect are usually, and the
Future and Future Perfect are always, Primary tenses; the
Imperfect, Aorist, and Pluperfect are usually Secondary
tenses.

THE TENSES

5. The action denoted by a verb may be defined by the tense of the verb

(*a*) As respects its *progress.* Thus it may be represented as *in progress,* or as *completed,* or *indefinitely,* i.e. as *a simple event* without reference to progress or completion.

(*b*) As respects its time, as *past, present,* or *future.*

The tenses of the Indicative mood in general define the action of the verb in both these respects.

The tenses of the other moods in general define the action of the verb only as respects its progress. *HA.* 821; *G.* 1249.

REM. The *chief* function of a Greek tense is thus not to denote time, but progress. This latter function belongs to the tense-forms of all the moods, the former to those of the Indicative only.

TENSES OF THE INDICATIVE MOOD

6. The significance of the tenses of the Indicative mood may be stated *in general* as follows : —

As respects progress: The Present and Imperfect denote action in progress ; the Perfect, Pluperfect, and Future Perfect denote completed action ; the Aorist represents the action indefinitely as an event or single fact ; the Future is used either of action in progress like the Present, or indefinitely like the Aorist.

As respects time: The Present and Perfect denote present time ; the Imperfect, Aorist, and Pluperfect denote past time ; the Future and Future Perfect denote future time.

6

7. The tenses of the Indicative in general denote time relative to that of speaking. Most exceptions to this rule are apparent or rhetorical rather than real and grammatical. In indirect discourse the point of view, as respects time, of the original speaking or thinking is retained. Cf. 351. Of two verbs of past time, one may refer to an action antecedent to the other, but this fact of antecedence is implied in the context, not expressed in the tense. Cf. 29 and 48. By prolepsis also a verb of past time may refer to or include events to take place after the time of speaking, but before a point of future time spoken of in the context. Cf. 50. In conditional sentences of the second form, the tenses are properly timeless. Cf. 248. See *Br.* 154 (p. 180).

THE PRESENT INDICATIVE

8. The Progressive Present. The Present Indicative is used of action in progress in present time. *HA.* 824; *G.* 1250, 1.

Matt. 25 : 8; αἱ λαμπάδες ἡμῶν σβέννυνται, *our lamps are going out.* Gal. 1 : 6; θαυμάζω ὅτι οὕτως ταχέως μετατίθεσθε ἀπὸ τοῦ καλέσαντος ὑμᾶς, *I marvel that ye are so quickly removing from him that called you.*

9. The most constant characteristic of the Present Indicative is that it denotes action in progress. It probably had originally no reference to present time (see *Br.* 156). But since, in the historical periods of the language, action in progress in past time is expressed by the Imperfect, and the Future is used both as a progressive and as an aoristic tense for future time, it results that the Present Indicative is chiefly used to express action in progress in present time. Hence in deciding upon the significance of any given instance of the Present Indicative in the New Testament as well as in classical Greek, the interpreter may consider that there is, at least in the majority of words, a certain presumption in favor of the Progressive Present rather than any of the other uses mentioned below.

10. The Progressive Present in Greek is not always best translated by what is commonly called in English the "Progressive Form." Some English verbs themselves suggest action in progress, and do not, except when there is strong emphasis on the progressive idea, use the progressive form. Thus the verb θαυμάζω, in Gal. 1 : 6, is a Progressive Present, but is best translated *I marvel*, the verb itself sufficiently suggesting the idea of action in progress.

11. THE CONATIVE PRESENT. The Present Indicative is occasionally used of action attempted, but not accomplished. *HA.* 825; *G.* 1255. This use is, however, not to be regarded as a distinct function of the tense. The Conative Present is merely a species of the Progressive Present. A verb which of itself suggests effort, when used in a tense which implies action in progress, and hence incomplete, naturally suggests the idea of attempt. All the verb-forms of the Present system are equally, with the Present, capable of expressing attempted action, since they all denote action in progress. John 10 : 32, λιθάζετε, and Gal. 5 : 4, δικαιοῦσθε, illustrate this usage in the Present. Similar is the use of the Present in Rom. 2 : 4, ἄγει, *leadeth*, i.e. such is its tendency.

For examples of the Imperfect see 23. Respecting the resultative force of such verbs in the Aorist see 42.

12. The General or Gnomic Present. The Present Indicative is used to express customary actions and general truths. *HA.* 824, *a*; *G.* 1253, 1291.

Matt. 7 : 17; πᾶν δένδρον ἀγαθὸν καρποὺς καλοὺς ποιεῖ, *every good tree bringeth forth good fruit.*

2 Cor. 9:7; ἱλαρὸν γὰρ δότην ἀγαπᾷ ὁ θεός, *for God loveth a cheerful giver.*

13. The Aoristic Present. The Present Indicative is sometimes used of an action or event coincident in time with the act of speaking, and conceived of as a simple event. Most frequently the action denoted by the verb is identical with the act of speaking itself, or takes place in that act.

Acts 16:18; παραγγέλλω σοι ἐν ὀνόματι Ἰησοῦ Χριστοῦ, *I command thee in the name of Jesus Christ.* See also Mark 2:5, ἀφίενται; Acts 9:34, ἰᾶται; 26:1, ἐπιτρέπεται; Gal. 1:11, γνωρίζω, and the numerous instances of λέγω in the gospels.

Rem. This usage is a distinct departure from the prevailing use of the Present tense to denote action in progress (cf. 9). There being in the Indicative no tense which represents an event as a simple fact without at the same time assigning it either to the past or the future, the Present is used for those instances (rare as compared with the cases of the Progressive Present), in which an action of present time is conceived of without reference to its progress.

14. The Historical Present. The Present Indicative is used to describe vividly a past event in the presence of which the speaker conceives himself to be. *HA.* 828; *G.* 1252.

Mark 11:27; καὶ ἔρχονται πάλιν εἰς Ἱεροσόλυμα, *and they come again to Jerusalem.* See also Luke 8:49, ἔρχεται; John 18:28, ἄγουσιν. This use is very frequent in the gospels.

15. The Present for the Future. In a similar way the Present Indicative may be used to describe vividly a future event.

Mark 9:31; ὁ υἱὸς τοῦ ἀνθρώπου παραδίδοται εἰς χεῖρας ἀνθρώπων, *the Son of man is delivered into the hands of men.* See also Matt. 26:18, ποιῶ; 27:63, ἐγείρομαι; Luke 3:9, ἐκκόπτεται.

REM. The term "Present for Future" is sometimes objected to, but without good reason. The arguments of Buttmann, pp. 203 f., and Winer, *WT.* pp. 265 ff. ; *WM.* pp. 331 ff., are valid only against the theory of an arbitrary interchange of tenses. It is indeed not to be supposed that Greek writers confused the Present and the Future tenses, or used them indiscriminately. But that the form which customarily denoted an act in progress at the time of speaking was sometimes, for the sake of vividness, used with reference to a fact still in the future, is recognized by all grammarians. See, *e.g.*, *J.* 397 ; *K.* 382, 5 ; *G.*MT. 32. The whole force of the idiom is derived from the unusualness of the tense employed.

16. The Present form ἥκω means *I have come* (John 2 : 4; 4 : 47; etc.). Similarly πάρειμι (*I am present*) sometimes means *I have arrived* (Acts 17 : 6; etc.). This, however, is not a Present for the Perfect of the same verb, but a Present equivalent to the Perfect of another verb. The use of ἀκούω meaning *I am informed* (cf. similar use of English *hear, see, learn*) is more nearly a proper Present for Perfect (1 Cor. 11 : 18; 2 Thess. 3 : 11). Such use of the Present belongs to a very few verbs. *HA.* 827 ; *G.* 1256.

17. The Present of past Action still in Progress. The Present Indicative, accompanied by an adverbial expression denoting duration and referring to past time, is sometimes used in Greek, as in German, to describe an action which, beginning in past time, is still in progress at the time of speaking. English idiom requires the use of the Perfect in such cases. *HA.* 826 ; *G.* 1258.

Acts 15 : 21 ; Μωυσῆς γὰρ ἐκ γενεῶν ἀρχαίων κατὰ πόλιν τοὺς κηρύσσοντας αὐτὸν ἔχει, *for Moses from generations of old has had in every city them that preached him.* See also Luke 13 : 7, ἔρχομαι; 15 : 29, δουλεύω; John 5 : 6, ἔχει; 2 Tim. 3 : 15, οἶδας. This Present is almost always incorrectly rendered in R. V.

REM. Cf. *Br.* 156, "Das Präsens in Verbindung mit πάρος, πάλαι, ποτέ wurde seit Homer gebraucht, um eine Handlung auszudrücken, die sich durch die Vergangenheit bis zur Zeit des Sprechens hinzieht." In the New Testament examples definite expressions of past time occur in place of the adverbs πάρος, etc.

18. The Aorist Indicative, limited by an expression meaning *up to this time,* may also be used of acts beginning in past time and continuing to the time of speaking. Matt. 27 : 8; 28 : 15. Cf. 46, and 52.

19. Verbs in indirect discourse retain the point of view, as respects time, of the original statement; a Progressive Present in indirect discourse accordingly denotes action going on at the time, not of the quotation of the words, but of the original utterance of them. English usage in indirect discourse is different, and from this difference it results that a Greek Present Indicative standing in indirect discourse after a verb of past time must often be rendered by a verb of past time. These cases, however, involve no special use of the Greek tense, and should not be confused with those of the Historical Present. Cf. 351–356.

20. PERIPHRASTIC FORM OF THE PRESENT. One of the clearly marked peculiarities of the Greek of the New Testament is the frequency with which periphrastic forms composed of a Present or Perfect Participle (Luke 23 : 19 is quite exceptional in its use of the *Aorist* Participle; cf. Ev. Pet. 23), and the Present, Imperfect, or Future Indicative, or the Present Subjunctive, Imperative, Infinitive, and even participle, of the verb εἰμί (rarely also ὑπάρχω), are used instead of the usual simple forms. Cf. 431, and see the full discussion with examples in *B.* pp. 308–313, and the list (not quite complete) in *S.* pp. 131 ff.

Instances of the periphrastic Present Indicative are, however, few. The clear instances belong under the head of the General Present.

Matt. 27 : 33; εἰς τόπον λεγόμενον Γολγοθά, ὅ ἐστιν Κρανίου Τόπος λεγόμενος, *unto a place called Golgotha, which is called Place of a Skull.* See also Matt. 1 : 23; Mark 5 : 41; 2 Cor. 2 : 17; 9 : 12.

THE IMPERFECT INDICATIVE

21. The Progressive Imperfect. The Imperfect is used of action in progress in past time. *HA.* 829; *G.* 1250, 2.

Mark 12 : 41 ; καὶ πολλοὶ πλούσιοι ἔβαλλον πολλά, *and many that were rich were casting in much.*

Luke 1 : 66 ; καὶ γὰρ χεὶρ κυρίου ἦν μετ' αὐτοῦ, *for the hand of the Lord was with him.*

John 11 : 36 ; ἴδε πῶς ἐφίλει αὐτόν, *behold how he loved him.*

22. The statement respecting the translation of the Progressive Present (cf. 10), applies to the Imperfect also. Notice the third example above, and see also Luke 2 : 51, *his mother kept* [διετήρει] *all these things in her heart;* in Luke 24 : 32, A.V., *did not our heart burn within us,* is better than R.V., *was not our heart burning within us.* Though the verb is a periphrastic Imperfect, καιομένη ἦν, the English form *did burn* sufficiently suggests action in progress to render it adequately.

23. THE CONATIVE IMPERFECT. The Progressive Imperfect is sometimes used of action attempted, but not accomplished. Cf. 11. *HA.* 832; *G.* 1255.

Matt. 3 : 14 ; ὁ δὲ διεκώλυεν αὐτόν, *but he would have hindered him.* See also Luke 1 : 59, ἐκάλουν; 15 : 16, ἐδίδου; Acts 7 : 26, συνήλλασσεν; 26 : 11, ἠνάγκαζον.

24. The Imperfect of Repeated Action. The Imperfect is used of customary or repeated action in past time. *HA.* 830; *G.* 1253, 2

Acts 3 : 2 ; ὃν ἐτίθουν καθ' ἡμέραν πρὸς τὴν θύραν τοῦ ἱεροῦ, *whom they used to lay daily at the gate of the temple.*

25. For the use of the Imperfect, Aorist, or Pluperfect in a condition contrary to fact, or its apodosis, see 248, 249.

26. The Imperfect and Aorist with ἄν are used in classical Greek to denote a customary past action taking place under certain circumstances. In the New Testament this usage never occurs in principal clauses. The use of the Imperfect and Aorist with ἄν in conditional relative clauses is possibly a remnant of the usage. Cf. 315.

27. The Imperfect and Aorist are used in a clause expressing an unattained wish having reference to the present or past. The Imperfect denotes action in progress. The Aorist represents the action indefinitely as a simple event. Either tense may refer to either present or past time. All the New Testament instances seem to refer to present time.

Rev. 3 : 15; ὄφελον ψυχρὸς ἦς ἢ ζεστός, *I would that thou wert cold or hot.* See also 1 Cor. 4 : 8 (Aor.) ; 2 Cor. 11 : 1 (Imperf.).

REM. 1. In classical Greek unattainable wishes are expressed by εἴθε or εἰ γάρ with the Indicative (*HA.* 871 ; *G.* 1511) or ὤφελον with the Infinitive. In Callimachus, 260 B.C., ὤφελον is found with the Indicative (*L.* & *S.*, ὀφείλω II. 3. *fin.*). In the New Testament εἰ γάρ (in this sense) and εἴθε do not occur, but ὄφελον, shortened form of ὤφελον, is used (as an uninflected particle) with the Imperfect and Aorist Indicative. *WM.* p. 377 ; *WT.* p. 301, N. 2.

REM. 2. In Gal. 5 : 12 ὄφελον is followed by the Future, but the wish is probably not conceived of as unattainable.

28. When an Imperfect refers to an action not separated from the time of speaking by a recognized interval, it is best translated into English by the Perfect, using preferably the progressive form, unless the verb itself suggests action in progress.

1 John 2 : 7 ; ἦν εἴχετε ἀπ᾽ ἀρχῆς, *which ye have had from the beginning.*
See also Luke 2 : 49 ; Rom. 15 : 22 ; Rev. 3 : 2 (cited by *Weymouth*
in *Theological Monthly,* IV. 42, who also quotes examples from classical authors). Cf. 52.

29. When an action denoted by an Imperfect evidently preceded an event already mentioned, such Imperfect is sometimes
best translated into English by the Pluperfect. From the
point of view of Greek, however, this, like the preceding
usage, is an ordinary Progressive Imperfect or Imperfect of
Repeated Action. Cf. 52.

Matt. 14:4; ἔλεγεν γὰρ ὁ Ἰωάνης αὐτῷ, Οὐκ ἔξεστίν σοι ἔχειν αὐτήν,
for John had been saying to him, It is not lawful for you to have her.
See also Luke 8 : 27 ; Acts 9 : 39.

30. The Imperfect of verbs denoting obligation or possibility, when used to affirm that a certain thing should or
could have been done, *i.e.* was required or possible under the
circumstances related, is a true affirmative Imperfect. It is
incorrect in this case to speak of an omitted ἄν, since though
it is frequently the case that the necessary or possible deed
did not take place, the past necessity or possibility was actual,
not hypothetical or "contrary to fact." Here belong Matt.
18:33; 23:23; 25:27; Acts 24:19; 26:32; 27:21; 2 Cor.
2:3, etc.

The Imperfect is also used of a past necessity or obligation
when the necessary deed did take place. Here also, of course,
the Imperfect has its usual force. Luke 13:16; 24:26;
John 4:4; Acts 1:16; 17:3.

31. Buttmann, pp. 216 f., 225 f., describes correctly the class of cases
in which the past obligation or possibility was actual, but in which the
required or possible deed did not take place, but wrongly includes in
his list several passages in which not only the fact but the obligation
or ability is hypothetical. Such are John 9 : 33 ; 1 Cor. 5 : 10 ; Heb. 9 : 26,
which are to be explained in accordance with 249. The distinction

between these two classes of cases is not always easily marked in English translation, since the English forms *could*, *should*, etc., are used both for actual and for hypothetical obligation or ability. Cf. *He could have gone, if he had been well,* and *He could have gone, but did not wish to go.*

32. Through a dimming of the distinction between the ideas of present and past obligation (which has occurred also in English in the case of the word *ought*), the Imperfect without ἄν is sometimes used to express a present obligation. The Infinitive after such an Imperfect is always in the Present tense. In accordance with this usage we are probably to explain Acts 22 : 22; Eph. 5 : 4; Col. 3 : 18; cf. *Ltft.* on Col. *loc. cit.* and *G.*MT. 416.

On these several uses of the Imperfect of verbs of obligation, etc., see *G.*MT. 413–423.

33. The Imperfect of verbs of wishing, without ἄν, is best explained as a true Progressive Imperfect, describing a desire which the speaker for a time felt, without affirming that he actually cherishes it at the time of his present utterance. This is especially clear in Philem. 13, 14, where the apostle states in one clause what his desire — his personal preference — was (ἐβουλόμην), and in the next his actual decision (ἠθέλησα), as over against his preference. The reason for describing the desire as past is not always, however, that it has been put aside. Failure to realize the desire, or the perception that it cannot be realized, or reluctance to express a positive and deliberate choice may lead the speaker to use the Imperfect rather than the Present. Similarly we sometimes say in colloquial English, *I was wishing that such a thing might happen,* or even more commonly, *I have sometimes wished.* Nearly the same meaning may be conveyed in English by the more usual potential form, *I should like, I would* *that,* or *I could wish.*   In Acts 25 : 22 the use of the Imperfect ἐβουλόμην rather than a Present softens the request for polite-ness' sake, and may well be rendered *I should like.*   In Gal. 4 : 20 it is probably the impossibility of realizing the wish that leads to the use of the Imperfect, and ἤθελον παρεῖναι may be rendered, *I would that I were present.*   In Rom. 9 : 3 ηὐχόμην may have been chosen because the apostle shrank from expressing a deliberate choice in regard to so solemn a matter, or because he thought of it as beyond the control or influence of his wish.   *I could pray* expresses the meaning with approximate accuracy.   In all these cases, however, what is strictly stated in the Greek is merely the past existence of a state of desire; the context alone implies what the present state of mind is.   Cf. *G*.MT. 425.

34. PERIPHRASTIC FORM OF THE IMPERFECT.   Periphras-tic Imperfects, formed by adding a Present Participle to the Imperfect of the verb εἰμί, are frequent in the New Testament, especially in the historical books.   The large majority of these forms denote continued action.

Mark 10 : 32; καὶ ἦν προάγων αὐτοὺς ὁ Ἰησοῦς, *and Jesus was going before them.*   So also Luke 1 : 10, 22; John 13 : 23; and probably Mark 2 : 18.   In a few instances repeated action is referred to, as Luke 5 : 16; 19 : 47; Gal. 1 : 23.   Cf. 431.

THE AORIST INDICATIVE

35. The constant characteristic of the Aorist tense in all of its moods, including the participle, is that it represents the action denoted by it indefinitely; *i.e.* simply as an event, neither on the one hand picturing it in progress, nor on the other affirming the existence of its result.   The name *indefi-nite* as thus understood is therefore applicable to the tense in all of its uses.

As respects the point of view from which the action is looked at, however, we may distinguish three functions of the tense common to all of its moods.

First, it may be used to describe an action or event in its entirety. This use of the tense, since it is by far the most frequent, may be called by pre-eminence the Indefinite Aorist. In the Indicative it may be called the Historical Aorist. The Aorist of any verb may be used in this sense; thus εἰπεῖν, to say; διακονῆσαι, to serve.

Secondly, it may be used to denote the inception of a state. The Aorist thus used may be called the Inceptive Aorist. It belongs to verbs which in the Present and Imperfect denote the continuance of a state; thus σιγᾶν, to be silent; σιγῆσαι, to become silent.

Thirdly, it may be used to denote the success of an effort. The Aorist thus used may be called the Resultative Aorist. It belongs to verbs which in the Presènt and Imperfect denote effort or attempt; thus κωλύειν, to hinder, obstruct; κωλῦσαι, to prevent.

The genetic relation of these three functions of the Aorist tense has not been satisfactorily defined. In the Greek, both of the classical and the New Testament periods, however, they appear side by side as co-ordinate uses. Br. 159; Del. iv., pp. 100 f.

REM. Respecting the force of the Indefinite Aorist, compare Brugmann's statement concerning the Aorist forms: "Am häufigsten wurden diese Formen so gebraucht, dass man sich die Handlung in einen ungeteilten Denkakt ganz und vollständig, in sich abgeschlossen, absolut vorstellen sollte. Das Factum wurde einfach constatiert ohne Rücksicht auf Zeitdauer." Br. 159.

36. In addition to these uses which belong to the Aorist in all its moods, the Aorist Indicative has three uses, instances of which are comparatively infrequent. These are the Gnomic Aorist, the Epistolaŕy Aorist, and the Dramatic Aorist.

The Aorist for the Perfect and the Aorist for the Pluperfect are, as explained below (52), not distinct functions of the
Aorist, but merely special cases of the Historical, Inceptive,
or Resultative Aorist.

37. The distinction between the Indefinite, the Inceptive,
and the Resultative functions of the Aorist is often ignored,
or its legitimacy denied. It is true that there are cases in
which it is not possible to decide certainly whether a given
verb refers to the inception of an action only, or to its entire
extent, and others in which there is a similar difficulty in
deciding whether the reference is to the action as a whole or
to its result only. It is true also that the genetic relation of
these three uses of the tense is not a matter of entire certainty, and that it is possible that, historically speaking, they
are but varying types of one usage. Especially must it be
regarded as doubtful whether the Resultative Aorist is anything else than the Indefinite Aorist of verbs denoting effort.
The matter of importance to the interpreter, however, is
that, whatever the genesis of the fact, of the Aorists of the
New Testament some denote a past act in its undivided
entirety, others denote merely or chiefly the inception of an
action, and others still affirm as a past fact the accomplishment of an act attempted. These distinctions, which from the
exegetical point of view it is often important to mark, are
conveniently indicated by the terms *indefinite, inceptive,* and
resultative. With reference to the validity of this distinction,
see *Br.* 159.

The Inceptive Aorist is illustrated in Acts 15 : 13, *and after
they had become silent* [μετὰ τὸ σιγῆσαι] *James answered.* It
is evident that the Infinitive must refer to the becoming
silent, not to the whole period of silence, since in the latter
case James must have been silent while the others were silent,

and have begun to speak when their silence had ended.   In
2 Cor. 8 : 9, we must read not *being rich he was poor*, but *being
rich he became poor; ἐπτώχευσεν* is manifestly inceptive.   So
also in Luke 2 : 44, *supposing him to be in the company, they
went a day's journey*, it was not the holding of the opinion that
he was in the company that preceded the day's journey, but
the forming of it, and the participle *νομίσαντες* is inceptive.
Contrast Acts 16 : 27.   See other examples under 41.

Illustrations of the resultative sense are less numerous and
less clear.   In Acts 7 : 36, however, *this man led them forth,
having wrought wonders and signs in Egypt and in the Red Sea,
and in the wilderness forty years*, the verb *ἐξήγαγεν* seems to
refer only to the result, since the signs wrought in the Red
Sea and the wilderness would otherwise have been represented
as accompanying the bringing out, and instead of *ποιήσας* we
should have had *ποιῶν*.   See also 42.[1]

38. The Historical Aorist.   The Aorist Indicative is
most frequently used to express a past event viewed in its
entirety, simply as an event or a single fact.   It has no
reference to the progress of the event, or to any existing
result of it.   *HA*. 836 ; *G*. 1250, 5.

John 1 : 11 ; *εἰς τὰ ἴδια ἦλθεν, καὶ οἱ ἴδιοι αὐτὸν οὐ παρέλαβον, he came
unto his own and they that were his own received him not.*

39.   Since any past event without reference to its duration
or complexity may be conceived of as a single fact, the Historical Aorist may be used to describe

(a) A momentary action.

Acts 5 : 5 ; *ἐξέψυξεν, he gave up the ghost.*
Matt. 8 : 3 ; *καὶ ἐκτείνας τὴν χεῖρα ἥψατο αὐτοῦ, and having stretched
forth his hand he touched him.*

---

[1] Cf. Mart. Polyc. 8 : 2, 3, where both *ἔπειθον; were persuading*, **and**
ἀποτυχόντες τοῦ πεῖσαι, failing to persuade, refer to the **same event.**

(b) An extended act or state, however prolonged in time, if viewed as constituting a single fact without reference to its progress.

Acts 28 : 30 ; ἐνέμεινεν δὲ διετίαν ὅλην ἐν ἰδίῳ μισθώματι, *and he abode two whole years in his own hired dwelling.*

Eph. 2 : 4 ; διὰ τὴν πολλὴν ἀγάπην αὐτοῦ ἣν ἠγάπησεν ἡμᾶς, *because of his great love wherewith he loved us.*

(c) A series or aggregate of acts viewed as constituting a single fact.

Matt. 22 : 28 ; πάντες γὰρ ἔσχον αὐτήν, *for they all had her.*

2 Cor. 11 : 25 ; τρὶς ἐναυάγησα, *thrice I suffered shipwreck.*

40. These three uses of the Historical Aorist may for convenience be designated as the Momentary Aorist, the Comprehensive Aorist, and the Collective Aorist. But it should be clearly observed that these terms do not mark distinctions in the functions of the tense. An Historical Aorist, whatever the nature of the fact affirmed, affirms it simply as a past fact. The writer may or may not have in mind that the act was single and momentary, or extended, or a series of acts, but the tense does not express or suggest the distinction. The purpose of the subdivision into momentary, comprehensive, and collective is not to define the force of the tense-form, but to discriminate more precisely the nature of the facts to which it is applied as shown by the context or the circumstances. Cf. *G.*MT. 56.

REM. The term *Historical Aorist* is applied to the use of the Aorist here described only by pre-eminence. In strictness the Inceptive and Resultative Aorists are also Historical. Compare what is said concerning the term *Indefinite* under 35.

41. The Inceptive Aorist. The Aorist of a verb whose Present denotes a state or condition, commonly denotes the beginning of that state. *HA.* 841 ; *G.* 1260.

2 Cor. 8 : 9; δι' ὑμᾶς ἐπτώχευσεν πλούσιος ὤν, *though he was rich, for your sakes he became poor.* See also Luke 15 : 32; John 4 : 52; Acts 7 : 60; Rom. 14 : 9.

Rem. The Aorist of such verbs is not, however, necessarily inceptive. The same form may be in one sentence inceptive and in another historical. Cf. Luke 9 : 36 with Acts 15 : 12, the verb ἐσίγησα being in the former historical, in the latter probably inceptive.

42. The Resultative Aorist. The Aorist of a verb whose Present implies effort or intention, commonly denotes the success of the effort. Cf. 11, 23. *Br.* 159.

Acts 27 : 43; ὁ δὲ ἑκατοντάρχης ... ἐκώλυσεν αὐτοὺς τοῦ βουλήματος, *but the centurion ... prevented them from their purpose.* See also Matt. 27 : 20; Acts 7 : 36.

43. The Gnomic Aorist. The Aorist is used in proverbs and comparisons where the English commonly uses a General Present. *HA.* 840; *G.* 1292; *G.*MT. 154–161; *B.* pp. 201 ff.; *WM.* pp. 346 f.; *WT.* p. 277; *Br.* 160.

1 Pet. 1 : 24; ἐξηράνθη ὁ χόρτος, καὶ τὸ ἄνθος ἐξέπεσεν, *the grass withereth and the flower falleth.* See also Luke 7 : 35; John 15 : 6; Jas. 1 : 11, 24.

Rem. Winer's contention (*WT.* p. 277; *WM.* p. 346) that the Gnomic Aorist does not occur in the New Testament does not seem defensible. The passages cited above are entirely similar to the classical examples of this ancient and well-established idiom.

44. The Epistolary Aorist. The writer of a letter sometimes puts himself in the place of his reader and describes as past that which is to himself present, but which will be past to his reader. *HA.* 838.

Eph. 6 : 22; ὃν ἔπεμψα πρὸς ὑμᾶς εἰς αὐτὸ τοῦτο, *whom I send to you for this very purpose.* See also Acts 23 : 30; 1 Cor. 5 : 11; Phil. 2 : 28; Col. 4 : 8; Philem. 11.

45. The Dramatic Aorist. The Aorist Indicative is sometimes used of a state of mind just reached, or of an act expressive of it. The effect is to give to the statement greater vividness than is given by the more usual Present. *HA.* 842; *G*.MT. 60; *K.* 386, 9; *Br.* 160.

Luke 16 : 4.; ἔγνων τί ποιήσω, *I know* [lit. *I knew*, or *I perceived*] *what I shall do.*

Rem. This usage is in classical Greek mainly poetical and is found chiefly in dialogue. It is sometimes called "Aoristus tragicus." Brugmann thus describes it: "Nicht selten wurde der Aorist von dem gebraucht, was soeben eingetreten ist, besonders von einer Stimmung, die soeben über einen gekommen ist, oder von einem Urteil, das man sich soeben gebildet hat." See numerous examples in K. 386, 9.

46. The Aorist for the (English) Perfect. The Aorist is frequently used in Greek where the English idiom requires a Perfect. *G*.MT. 58; *HA.* 837; *B.* pp. 197, 198.

Luke 19 : 9; σήμερον σωτηρία τῷ οἴκῳ τούτῳ ἐγένετο, *to-day is salvation come to this house.*

Matt. 5 : 21; ἠκούσατε ὅτι ἐρρέθη τοῖς ἀρχαίοις, *ye have heard that it was said to them of old time.*

Phil. 4 : 11; ἐγὼ γὰρ ἔμαθον ἐν οἷς εἰμὶ αὐτάρκης εἶναι, *for I have learned in whatsoever state I am therein to be content.* See also under 52.

47. The Aorist Indicative of a few verbs is used in the New Testament to denote a present state, the result of a past act, hence with the proper force of a Greek Perfect. Cf. 75, 86. So the Aorists ἀπέθανον (cf. Mark 5 : 35 with Luke 8 : 49, and see John 8 : 52 *et al.*), ἐξέστην (Mark 3 : 21; 2 Cor. 5 : 13), and possibly ἔγνων (John 7 : 26; cf. 1 Macc. 6 : 13). All these Aorists may also be used as simple historical Aorists.

48. The Aorist for the (English) Pluperfect. The Aorist Indicative is frequently used in narrative passages of a past event which precedes another past event mentioned or implied in the context. In English it is common in such a case to indicate the real order of the events by the use of a Pluperfect for the earlier event. Cf. 52, 53. *HA*. 837; *G*.MT. 58; *B*. pp. 199 f.

John 19 : 30; ὅτε οὖν ἔλαβεν τὸ ὄξος ὁ Ἰησοῦς εἶπεν, Τετέλεσται, *when therefore Jesus had received the vinegar, he said, It is finished.*

Matt. 14 : 3; ὁ γὰρ Ἡρῴδης κρατήσας τὸν Ἰωάνην ἔδησεν, *for Herod having laid hold on John had bound him.* See also Matt. 27 : 31; Mark 8 : 14; Luke 8 : 27; John 12 : 17; 13 : 12.

REM. It has been much disputed whether ἀπέστειλεν in John 18 : 24 is to be assigned to this head. The valid objection to this is not in any inappropriateness of the Aorist tense to express an event antecedent to one already mentioned, — the Aorist is the only form that can be used if the event is thought of simply as an event (cf. *Mey. ad loc., contra*), — but in the presence of οὖν, which is, in John especially, so constantly continuative, and in the absence of any intimation in the context that the events are related out of their chronological order.

49. From the general principles of indirect discourse in English and in Greek it results that an Aorist Indicative in indirect discourse after a verb of past time must usually be rendered into English by a Pluperfect. Cf. 353. These cases form a class entirely distinct from those that are included above under the term Aorist for the English Pluperfect.

50. Both the Aorist and the Perfect are sometimes used proleptically, but this is rather a rhetorical figure than a grammatical idiom. *WM*. pp. 341, 345, 347; *WT*. pp. 273, 277, 278.

1 Cor. 7 : 28; ἐὰν δὲ καὶ γαμήσῃς, οὐχ ἥμαρτες, *but even if thou shalt marry, thou hast not sinned.* See also John 15 : 8; Jas. 2 : 10.

51. For the Aorist in a condition contrary to fact, see 248. For the Aorist expressing an unattained wish, see 27.

52. ENGLISH EQUIVALENTS OF THE GREEK AORIST INDICATIVE. It should be observed that the Aorist for the Perfect and the Aorist for the Pluperfect are not variations from the normal use of the Greek Aorist. Viewed strictly from the point of view of Greek Grammar, these Aorists are simply Historical, Inceptive, or Resultative Aorists. The necessity for mentioning them arises merely from the difference between the English and the Greek idiom.

The Greek Aorist corresponds to the English simple Past (or Imperfect or Preterite, *loved, heard*, etc.) more nearly than to any other English tense. But it is not the precise equivalent of the English Past; nor is the Greek Perfect the precise equivalent of the English Perfect; nor the Greek Pluperfect of the English Pluperfect. This will appear distinctly if we place side by side the definitions of the tenses which in general correspond in the two languages.

The English Perfect is used of any past action between which and the time of speaking the speaker does not intend distinctly to interpose an interval.[1]

The Greek Perfect is used to represent an action as standing complete, *i.e.* as having an existing result, at the time of speaking.

The English Pluperfect is used to mark the fact that the event expressed by it preceded another past event indicated by the context, and this whether the earlier event is thought of as completed at the time of the later event, or only indefinitely as a simple occurrence preceding the later event.[1]

The Greek Pluperfect is used to represent an action as standing complete, *i.e.* as having an existing result, at a point of past time indicated by the context.

[1] The English Perfect and Pluperfect by their auxiliaries *have* and *had* distinctly suggest completed action in the proper sense, viz. the possession of a thing in the condition indicated by the participle, and substan-

The English Past is used of any past action between which and the moment of speaking an interval is thought of as existing. It affirms nothing respecting existing result.

The Greek Aorist is used of any past event which is conceived of simply as an event (or as entered upon, or as accomplished), regardless alike of the existence or non-existence of an interval between itself and the moment of speaking, and of the question whether it precedes or not some other past action. It affirms nothing respecting existing result.

It is evident from this comparison that the English Perfect has a larger range of use than the Greek Perfect.

tially this is the meaning often conveyed by these tenses. Thus, *I have learned my lesson*, differs but little in meaning from *I have my lesson learned*. But this is by no means the only use which may be made of these tenses in modern English. They have, in fact, ceased to be Perfect tenses in any proper sense of that word. Compare, *e.g.*, the Pasts and Perfects in the following examples: *The army arrived. The army has arrived. Many men fought for their country. Many men have fought for their country. He often visited Rome. He has often visited Rome.* Only in the first example is existing result suggested by the Perfect tense. In each pair the distinguishing mark between the two sentences is that while the Perfect tense places the event in the past time without defining whether or not an interval has elapsed since the event, the Past tense places it in the past time and suggests an interval.

Similarly, the English Pluperfect affirms only the antecedence of its event to the other past event, leaving it to the context or the nature of the fact to show whether at the past time referred to there were existing results or not. Thus in the sentence, *I showed him the work which I had done*, it is implied that the results of the doing remained at the time of the showing. But in the sentence, *He did not recognize the persons whom he had previously seen*, it is not implied that any result of the seeing remained at the time of the non-recognition.

Thus a past event between which and the time of speaking no interval is distinctly thought of may be expressed by the English Perfect, whether the result of the event is thought of as existing or not; but it can be expressed by the Greek Perfect only in case such result is thought of. So also the English Pluperfect has a wider range than the Greek Pluperfect. For while the Greek can use its Pluperfect for an event which preceded another past event only in case the result of the earlier event is thought of as existing at the time of the later event, the English freely uses its Pluperfect for all such doubly past events, without reference to the existence of the result of the earlier event at the time of the later one.

On the other hand, the Greek Aorist has a wider range than the English Past, since it performs precisely those functions which the Greek Perfect and Pluperfect refuse, but which in modern English are performed not by the Past but by the Perfect and Pluperfect. The Greek Aorist, therefore, in its ordinary use not only covers the ground of the English Past, but overlaps in part upon that of the English Perfect and Pluperfect. Hence arise the so-called Aorist for Perfect and Aorist for Pluperfect.

If the attempt be made to define more exactly the extent of this overlapping, it will appear that a simple past event which is conceived of without reference to an existing result, and between which and the time of speaking the speaker does not wish distinctly to suggest an interval, — the interval may be ever so long, in fact, — will be expressed in Greek by the Aorist, because the result is not thought of, and in English by the Perfect, because the interval is not thought of. Cases of this kind arise, e.g., when the event is said to continue up to the time of speaking, so that there is actually no interval [Matt. 27 : 8; διὸ ἐκλήθη ὁ ἀγρὸς ἐκεῖνος Ἀγρὸς Αἵματος

ἕως τῆς σήμερον, *therefore that field has been called Field of Blood
until this day.* See also Matt. 28:15; John 16:24]; or when the
event is so recent as to make the thought of an interval seem
unnatural [Luke 5:26; εἴδαμεν παράδοξα σήμερον, *we have seen
strange things to-day.* See also Mark 14:41; Acts 7:52, νῦν
... ἐγένεσθε]; or when the time of the event is entirely
indefinite [Matt. 19:4; οὐκ ἀνέγνωτε, *have ye not read?* See
also Rev. 17:12; exx. are frequent in the New Testament];
or when the verb refers to a series of events which extends
approximately or quite to the time of speaking [Matt. 5:21;
ἠκούσατε ὅτι ἐρρέθη τοῖς ἀρχαίοις, *ye have heard that it was said
to the ancients;* the reference is doubtless to the frequent
occasions on which they had heard such teachings in the
synagogue. See also 1 Esdr. 4:26, 27].

Instances of the Greek Aorist for the English Pluperfect
arise when a past event which is conceived of simply as an
event without reference to existing result is mentioned out
of its chronological order, or is expressed in a subordinate
clause. The Greek employs the Aorist, leaving the context
to suggest the order; the English usually suggests the order
by the use of a Pluperfect. See exx. under 48. Cf. *Beet*, The
Greek Aorist as used in the New Testament, in *Expositor*, xi.
191–201, 296–308, 372–385; *Weymouth*, The Rendering into
English of the Greek Aorist and Perfect, in *Theological
Monthly*, iv. 33–47, 162–180.

53. In many cases in which the Greek Aorist is used of
an event antecedent to another past event already referred to,
English idiom permits a simple Past. A Pluperfect is strictly
required only when the precedence in time is somewhat prominent. The Revisers of 1881 have used the Pluperfect spar-
ingly in such cases. It might better have been used also in
Matt. 9:25; Mark 8:14; John 12:18 (*had heard*).

54. An Aorist which is equivalent to an English Perfect or Pluperfect may be either an *historical*, or an *inceptive*, or a *Resultative* Aorist. If historical, it may be either *momentary*, *comprehensive*, or *collective*.

In Luke 15 : 32, ἔζησεν, and in 1 Cor. 4 : 8, ἐπλουτήσατε, are inceptive Aorists which may be properly rendered by the English Perfect ; probably also ἐβασίλευσας, in Rev. 11 : 17, should be rendered, *thou hast become king.*

In Rom. 3 : 23, ἥμαρτον is evidently intended to sum up the aggregate of the evil deeds of men, of which the apostle has been speaking in the preceding paragraphs (1 : 18 — 3 : 20). It is therefore a collective historical Aorist. But since that series of evil deeds extends even to the moment of speaking, as is indeed directly affirmed in the πάντες, it is impossible to think of an interval between the fact stated and this statement of it. It must therefore be expressed in English by the Perfect tense, and be classed with Matt. 5 : 21 as a collective Aorist for (English) Perfect. Of similar force is the same form in Rom. 2 : 12. From the point of view from which the apostle is speaking, the sin of each offender is simply a past fact, and the sin of all a series or aggregate of facts together constituting a past fact. But inasmuch as this series is not separated from the time of speaking, we must, as in 3 : 23, employ an English Perfect in translation. This is upon the supposition that the verb ἥμαρτον takes its point of view from the time of speaking, and the apostle accordingly speaks here only of sin then past, leaving it to be inferred that the same principle would apply to subsequent sin. It is possible, however, that by a sort of prolepsis ἥμαρτον is uttered from the point of view of the future judgment [κριθήσονται], and refers to all sin that will then be past. In this case the Future Perfect, *shall have sinned*, may be used in translation, or again the Perfect, common in subordinate clauses in English as an abbreviation of the Future Perfect. Whether the same form in Rom. 5 : 12 shall be rendered in the same way or by the English Past depends upon whether it is, like the other cases, a collective Aorist, representing a series of acts between which and the time of speaking no interval is interposed, or refers to a deed or deeds in the remote past in which the "all" in some way participated. So far as the tense-form is concerned there is no presumption in favor of one or the other of these interpretations, both uses of the tense being equally legitimate. The nature of the argument or the author's thought, as learned from sources outside the sentence itself, must furnish the main evidence by which to decide.

55. The Aorist εὐδόκησα in Matt. 3 : 17 ; 17 : 5 ; Mark 1 : 11 ; Luke 3 : 22 ; 2 Pet. 1 : 17, may be explained — (*a*) as a Historical Aorist having reference to a specific event as its basis. *I was well pleased with thee,* *e.g.* for receiving baptism. If all the instances were in connection with the baptism, this would be the most natural explanation. But for those that occur in connection with the account of the transfiguration this explanation fails, and is probably therefore not the true explanation of any of the instances. (*b*) as a comprehensive Historical Aorist covering the period of Christ's preïncarnate existence. Cf. John 17 : 5, 24 ; see *W. N. Clarke,* Com. on Mark 1 : 11. If the passages were in the fourth gospel, and especially if they contained some such phrase as πρὸ καταβολῆς κόσμου, this explanation would have much in its favor. The absence of such limiting phrase, and the fact that the passages are in the synoptic gospels are opposed to this explanation. (*c*) as a comprehensive Historical Aorist, having the force of an English Perfect, and referring to the period of Christ's earthly existence up to the time of speaking. But against this is the absence of any adverbial phrase meaning *up to this time,* which usually accompanies an Aorist verb used in this sense. Cf. 18 and 52. (*d*) as an Aorist which has by usage come to have the meaning which is strictly appropriate to the Perfect, *I became well pleased with thee, and I am [accordingly] well pleased with thee.* Cf. 47. There are a few passages of the Septuagint that seem at first sight to favor this explanation. See Ps. 101 : 15 ; Jer. 2 : 19 ; Mal. 2 : 17. Cf. also Matt. 12 : 18 ; Luke 12 : 32. The force of this evidence is, however, greatly diminished by the fact that all these instances are capable of being explained without resort to so unusual a use of the Aorist, that both in the Septuagint and in the New Testament there is in use a regular Present form of this verb, and that the Aorist in the majority of cases clearly denotes past time. (*e*) as an Inceptive Aorist referring to some indefinite, imagined point of past time at which God is represented as becoming well pleased with Jesus. But since this point is not thought of as definitely fixed, English idiom requires a Perfect tense. Cf. 52 (p. 27), 54. It may be described, therefore, as an Inceptive Aorist equivalent to an English Perfect, and may be rendered, *I have become well pleased.* This, however, can only be a vivid way of saying, *I am well pleased.* If then this view is correct, the rendering of the English versions is a free but substantially correct paraphrase. A true Perfect would affirm the present state of pleasure and imply the past becoming pleased. The Aorist affirms the becoming pleased and leaves the present pleasure to be suggested. This explanation, therefore, differs from the preceding (*d*) in that it does not suppose the Aorist of this verb to have acquired the power of expressing an existing result, but judges the existing result to be only suggested by the affirmation of the past fact. This is rhetorical figure, on the way to become grammatical idiom, but not yet become such. Manifestly similar is the use of προσεδέξατο in Isa. 42 : 1, and of εὐδόκησεν in Matt. 12 : 18. Indeed, if Matt. 12 : 18 represents a current translation of Isa. 42 : 1, our present passages were probably affected in form by this current rendering of the Isaiah passage. Similar also are ἐκάθισαν in Matt. 23 : 2, and ἔμαθον in Phil. 4 : 11. In neither case is there any clearly established usage of the Aorist for Greek Perfect; in neither is there apparent any reference to a definite point of past time; in both the real fact intended to be suggested is the present state.

56. The Distinction between the Aorist and the Imperfect. The difference between an Historical Aorist and an Imperfect of action in progress or repeated being one not of the nature of the fact but of the speaker's conception of the fact, it is evident that the same fact may be expressed by either tense or by both. This is illustrated in Mark 12 : 41 and 44, where, with strict appropriateness in both cases, Mark writes in v. 41, πολλοὶ πλούσιοι ἔβαλλον πολλά, and in v. 44 records Jesus as stating the same fact in the words πάντες . . . ἔβαλον. The former describes the scene in progress, the latter merely states the fact.

57. From the nature of the distinction between the Imperfect and Aorist, it also results that the difference in thought represented by the choice of one form rather than the other is sometimes almost imperceptible. Cf., *e.g.*, Mark 3 : 7 and 5 : 24; Luke 2 : 18 and 4 : 22. Some verbs use one of the two tenses almost or quite to the exclusion of the other. The form ἔλεγον is used in classical Greek without emphasis on the thought of the saying as in progress or repeated, and in the New Testament the Aorist of this verb does not occur. A distinction between the Imperfect ἔλεγον and the Aorist εἶπον is scarcely to be drawn in the New Testament. Cf. *G*.MT. 56, 57, especially the following: "In all these cases the fundamental distinction of the tenses, which was inherent in the

form, remained; only it happened that either of the two distinct forms expressed the meaning which was here needed
equally well. It must not be thought, from these occasional
examples, that the Greeks of any period were not fully alive
to the distinction of the two tenses and could not use it with
skill and nicety."
This approximation of the Aorist and Imperfect, it should
be noted, occurs only in the case of the Historical Aorist (38).
The Inceptive and Resultative Aorists are clearly distinguished
in force from the Imperfect.

THE FUTURE INDICATIVE

58. The Predictive Future. The Future Indicative is
most frequently used to affirm that an action is to take
place in future time. Since it does not mark the distinction between action in progress and action conceived of
indefinitely without reference to its progress, it may be
either aoristic or progressive. *HA.* 843; *G.* 1250, 6;
*G.*MT. 63, 65; *Br.* 163.

59. THE AORISTIC FUTURE conceives of an action simply
as an event, and affirms that it will take place in future time.
It may be indefinite, inceptive, or resultative. As indefinite
it may be momentary, comprehensive, or collective. Cf. 35, 39.

1 Cor. 15 : 51, 52; πάντες οὐ κοιμηθησόμεθα, πάντες δὲ ἀλλαγησόμεθα,
ἐν ἀτόμῳ, ἐν ῥιπῇ ὀφθαλμοῦ, *we shall not all sleep* [indefinite com-
prehensive] ; or, *we shall not all fall asleep* [inceptive], *but we shall
all be changed, in a moment, in the twinkling of an eye* [indefinite
momentary].

John 14 : 26; ἐκεῖνος ὑμᾶς διδάξει πάντα καὶ ὑπομνήσει ὑμᾶς πάντα ἃ
εἶπον ὑμῖν ἐγώ, *he will teach you all things and bring to your remem-
brance all things that I said unto you* [indefinite collective].

Luke 1 : 33; καὶ βασιλεύσει ἐπὶ τὸν οἶκον Ἰακὼβ εἰς τοὺς αἰῶνας, *and he
shall reign over the house of Jacob forever* [indefinite comprehensive].

Luke 16 : 31; οὐδ' ἐάν τις ἐκ νεκρῶν ἀναστῇ πεισθήσονται, *neither will
they be persuaded if one rise from the dead* [resultative].

60. The Progressive Future affirms that an action will be in progress in future time. *HA.* 843; *G.* 1250, 6.

Phil. 1 : 18; καὶ ἐν τούτῳ χαίρω· ἀλλὰ καὶ χαρήσομαι, *and therein I rejoice, yea, and will* [*continue to*] *rejoice.* See also Rom. 6 : 2; Phil. 1 : 6; Rev. 9 : 6.

61. It may be doubted whether any of the distinctions indicated by the subdivisions of the Predictive Future are justified from the point of view of pure grammar. It is probable, rather, that the tense in all these cases makes precisely the same affirmation respecting the event, viz. *that it will take place;* and that it is the context only that conveys the distinctions referred to. These distinctions, however, are real distinctions either of fact or of thought, and such, moreover, that the writer must in most cases have had them in mind when speaking of the facts. From the exegetical point of view, therefore, the distinctions are both justified and necessary, since they represent differences of thought in the mind of the writer to be interpreted. The terms employed above are convenient terms to represent these distinctions of thought, and it is to the interpreter a matter of secondary importance whether the distinction in question is by his writer immediately connected with the tense of the verb.

62. Since the Aoristic Future is less definite respecting progress than the Progressive Future, the latter predicting the act as continuing, the former making no assertion, it is evident that any instance of the Predictive Future not clearly progressive must be accounted as aoristic. If the writer did not conceive the act or event as continuing, he left it in his own mind and for the reader undefined as respects progress, hence aoristic. Whether he left it thus undefined in his mind must of course be determined, if at all, from the context, there being no difference of form between a Progressive and an

Aoristic Future. It should be noticed that it is not enough to show that an act will be in fact continued, in order to count the verb which predicts it a Progressive Future; it must appear that the writer thought of it as continuing. Every Future form is therefore by presumption aoristic. It can be accounted progressive only on evidence that the writer thought of the act as continued.

REM. There is one exception to this principle. In verbs of effort a Progressive Future is naturally like other Progressive forms, a conative tense. An Aoristic Future of such a verb is like the Aorist, a resultative tense. Since the latter is the larger meaning, the context must give the evidence of this larger meaning, and such evidence failing, it cannot be considered established that the verb is resultative. The verb in John 12 : 32 furnishes an interesting and important illustration. Since the verb denotes effort, the Future will naturally be accounted conative if it is judged to be progressive, and resultative if it is taken as aoristic. In the latter case the meaning will be, *I will by my attraction bring all men to me.* In the former case the words will mean, *I will exert on all men an attractive influence.*

63. To decide whether a given Aoristic Future merely predicts the fact, or refers to the inception of the action, or has reference to it as a thing accomplished, must again be determined by the context or the meaning of the word. The distinction between the indefinite and the resultative senses will often be very difficult to make, and indeed the difference of thought will be but slight. Here also it results from the nature of the distinction between the indefinite use and the other two, inceptive and resultative, that any instance of the Aoristic Future not clearly inceptive or resultative must be accounted indefinite. In other words, if the writer did not define the action to his own mind as inceptive or resultative, he left it indefinite, a mere fact.

64. The distinction between momentary, comprehensive, and collective is in respect to the Future tense, as in respect to the Aorist, a distinction which primarily has reference to the facts referred to and only secondarily to the writer's conception of the facts. There may easily occur instances which will defy classification at this point. A writer may predict an event not only without at the moment thinking whether it is to be a single deed or a series of deeds, a momentary or an extended action, but even without knowing. Thus the sentence, *He will destroy his enemies*, may be uttered by one who has confidence that the person referred to will in some way destroy his enemies, without at all knowing whether he will destroy them one by one, or all at once, and whether by some long-continued process, or by one exterminating blow. In such cases the verb can only be accounted as an Aoristic Future, incapable of further classification.

65. From a different point of view from that of the above classification, the instances of the Predictive Future might be classified as (*a*) assertive, and (*b*) promissory. The distinction between the assertion that an event will take place and the promise that it shall take place is difficult to make, requiring delicate discrimination, but is often important for purposes of interpretation. It is in general not indicated in Greek, and its representation in English is complicated by the varied uses of the auxiliary verbs *shall* and *will*. In general it may be said that in principal clauses *shall* is in the first person simply assertive, *will* is promissory; in the second and third person *will* is assertive, *shall* is promissory, imperative, or solemnly predictive.

R.V. employs *shall* almost constantly in the second and third person, in most cases probably intending it as solemnly predictive.

Matt. 10 : 42 ; ἀμὴν λέγω ὑμῖν, οὐ μὴ ἀπολέσῃ τὸν μισθὸν αὐτοῦ, *verily I say unto you, he shall by no means lose his reward.*

Mark 11 : 31; ἐὰν εἴπωμεν Ἐξ οὐρανοῦ, ἐρεῖ, *if we say, From heaven, he will say.*

Luke 22 : 61; Πρὶν ἀλέκτορα φωνῆσαι σήμερον ἀπαρνήσῃ με τρίς, *before the cock crow this day, thou shalt deny me thrice.* See also Matt. 11 : 28, 29; 12 : 31; John 16 : 7, 13.

66. A Predictive Future is sometimes made emphatically negative by the use of the negative οὐ μή, Matt. 16 : 22; 26 : 35; Mark 14 : 31 (*Tisch.* Subjunctive); cf. 172.

67. The Imperative Future. The second person of the Future Indicative is often used as an Imperative. *HA.* 844; *G.* 1265.

Jas. 2 : 8; ἀγαπήσεις τὸν πλησίον σου ὡς σεαυτόν, *thou shalt love thy neighbor as thyself.*

Rem. 1. This idiom as it occurs in the New Testament shows clearly the influence of the Septuagint. It occurs most frequently in prohibitions, its negative being, as also commonly in classical Greek, not μή but οὐ. *G.*MT. 69, 70; *B.* p. 257; *WM.* pp. 396 f.; *WT.* pp. 315 f.

Rem. 2. In Matt. 15 : 6 the verb τιμήσει has the negative οὐ μή. Some interpreters take this as a Predictive Future, but the thought requires the Imperative sense, and in view of the frequent use of οὐ μή with the Future in an imperative sense in the Septuagint, and its occasional use in classical Greek, the possibility of it can hardly be denied. *WM.* p. 636 f., n. 4; *G.*MT. 297.

68. One or two probable instances of the Imperative Future in the third person occur, though perhaps no entirely certain case. Matt. 4 : 4, οὐκ ἐπ᾽ ἄρτῳ μόνῳ ζήσεται ὁ ἄνθρωπος, is probably to be so regarded, though the Hebrew of the passage quoted (Deut. 8 : 3) is apparently Gnomic rather than Imperative. On Matt. 15 : 6, see 67, Rem. 2. See also Matt. 20 : 26, 27.

69. The Gnomic Future. The Future Indicative may be used to state what will customarily happen when occasion offers.

Rom. 5:7; μόλις γὰρ ὑπὲρ δικαίου τις ἀποθανεῖται, *for scarcely for a righteous man will one die.* See also Gen. 44:15; Rom. 7:3, χρηματίσει. Observe the Gnomic Presents both before and after.

70. The Deliberative Future. The Future Indicative is sometimes used in questions of deliberation, asking not what will happen, but what can or ought to be done. Such questions may be real questions asking information, or rhetorical questions taking the place of a direct assertion. Cf. 169.

Luke 22:49; εἰ πατάξομεν ἐν μαχαίρῃ, *shall we smite with the sword?*
John 6:68; κύριε, πρὸς τίνα ἀπελευσόμεθα, *Lord, to whom shall we go?*

71. PERIPHRASTIC FORM OF THE FUTURE. A Future tense composed of a Present Participle and the Future of the verb εἰμί is found occasionally in the New Testament. The force is that of a Progressive Future, with the thought of continuance or customariness somewhat emphasized.

Luke 5:10; ἀνθρώπους ἔσῃ ζωγρῶν, *thou shalt catch men,* i.e. *shalt be a catcher of men.*
Luke 21:24; Ἰερουσαλὴμ ἔσται πατουμένη, *Jerusalem shall [continue to] be trodden under foot.*

72. Μέλλω with the Infinitive is also used with a force akin to that of the Future Indicative. It is usually employed of an action which one intends to do, or of that which is certain, destined to take place.

Matt. 2:13; μέλλει γὰρ Ἡρῴδης ζητεῖν τὸ παιδίον τοῦ ἀπολέσαι αὐτό, *for Herod will seek the young child to destroy it.*
Luke 9:44; ὁ γὰρ υἱὸς τοῦ ἀνθρώπου μέλλει παραδίδοσθαι εἰς χεῖρας τῶν ἀνθρώπων, *for the Son of man is to be delivered up into the hands of men.* See also Matt. 16:27; 20:22; Acts 5:35; 20:38; Rom. 8:13.

73. By the use of the Imperfect of μέλλω with the Infinitive it is affirmed that at a past point of time an action was about to take place or was intended or destined to occur.

John 7:39; τοῦτο δὲ εἶπεν περὶ τοῦ πνεύματος οὖ ἔμελλον λαμβάνειν οἱ πιστεύσαντες εἰς αὐτόν, *but this spake he of the Spirit which they that believed on him were to receive.* See also Luke 7:2; John 6:71.

THE PERFECT INDICATIVE

74. The Perfect of Completed Action. In its most frequent use the Perfect Indicative represents an action as standing at the time of speaking complete. The reference of the tense is thus double; it implies a past action and affirms an existing result. *HA.* 847; *G.* 1250, 3.

Acts 5:28; πεπληρώκατε τὴν Ἰερουσαλὴμ τῆς διδαχῆς ὑμῶν, *ye have filled Jerusalem with your teaching.*

Romans 5:5; ὅτι ἡ ἀγάπη τοῦ θεοῦ ἐκκέχυται ἐν ταῖς καρδίαις ἡμῶν, *because the love of God has been poured forth in our hearts.*

2 Tim. 4:7; τὸν καλὸν ἀγῶνα ἠγώνισμαι, τὸν δρόμον τετέλεκα, τὴν πίστιν τετήρηκα, *I have fought the good fight, I have finished the course, I have kept the faith.*

REM. On the use of the term *complete* as a grammatical term, see 85. On the distinction between the Perfect and the Aorist, see 86.

75. The Perfect of Existing State. The Perfect is sometimes used when the attention is directed wholly to the present resulting state, the past action of which it is the result being left out of thought. This usage occurs most frequently in a few verbs which use the Perfect in this sense only. *HA.* 849; *G.* 1263.

Matt. 27:43; πέποιθεν ἐπὶ τὸν θεόν, *he trusteth on God.*

1 Cor. 11:2; ἐπαινῶ δὲ ὑμᾶς, ὅτι πάντα μου μέμνησθε, *now I praise you that ye remember me in all things.*

Luke 24:46; οὕτως γέγραπται, *thus it is written,* i.e. *stands written.* See also Rev. 19:13.

76. There is no sharp line of distinction between the Perfect of Completed Action and the Perfect of Existing State. To the latter head are to be assigned those instances in which the past act is practically dropped from thought, and the attention turned wholly to the existing result; while under the former head are to be placed those instances in which it is evident that the writer had in mind both the past act and the present result.

77. THE INTENSIVE PERFECT. The Perfect is sometimes used in classical Greek as an emphatic or intensive Present. It is possible that under this head should be placed certain Perfects of the New Testament more commonly assigned to one of the preceding uses. Thus πέποιθα practically expresses the thought of πείθομαι intensified. Πεπίστευκα is also clearly a stronger way of saying πιστεύω. John 6 : 69 ; πεπιστεύκαμεν καὶ ἐγνώκαμεν ὅτι σὺ εἶ ὁ ἅγιος τοῦ θεοῦ, *we have believed and know that thou art the Holy One of God.* See also 2 Cor. 1 : 10. Whether this usage is in the New Testament a survival of the ancient intensive use of the Perfect, regarded by some grammarians as an original function of the tense (*Del.* IV. 94 ff., *Br.* 162), or a later development from the Perfect of completed action, affirming the present existence of the result of a past act, need not, for the purpose of the interpreter, be decided.

78. Of the Historical Perfect in the sense of a Perfect which expresses a past completed action, the result of which the speaker conceives himself to be witnessing (as in the case of the Historical Present he conceives himself to be witnessing the action itself), there is no certain New Testament instance. Possible instances are Matt. 13 : 46 ; Luke 9 : 36 ; 2 Cor. 12 : 17 ; Jas. 1 : 24. Cf. *Br.* 162. This idiom is perhaps rather rhetorical than strictly grammatical.

Κέκραγεν in John 1 : 15 is a Perfect expressing a past fact vividly conceived of as if present to the speaker. But since the Perfect of the verb had already in classical Greek come to be recognized as functionally a Present, it is from the point of view of the current usage a Historical Present rather than a Historical Perfect. Cf. *L.* and *S. s.v.*

79. The Perfect in 1 Cor. 7 : 39, δέδεται, and in 1 John 2 : 5, τετελείω- ται, is probably Gnomic, referring to a state that is wont to exist. If ἀπελήλυθεν in Jas. 1 : 24 is Gnomic, it is with nearly the force of a Gnomic Present or Aorist. *G.*MT. 154, 155.

80. THE AORISTIC PERFECT. The Perfect Indicative is sometimes used in the New Testament of a simple past fact where it is scarcely possible to suppose that the thought of existing result was in the writer's mind. See more fully under 88.

2 Cor. 2 : 13 ; οὐκ ἔσχηκα ἄνεσιν τῷ πνεύματί μου τῷ μὴ εὑρεῖν με Τίτον, *I had no relief for my spirit because I found not Titus.*
Rev. 8 : 5 ; καὶ εἴληφεν ὁ ἄγγελος τὸν λιβανωτόν, καὶ ἐγέμισεν αὐτόν, *and the angel took the censer, and filled it.* See also Matt. 25 : 6 ; 2 Cor. 1 : 9 ; 7 : 5 ; 11 : 25 ; Heb. 11 : 28 ; Rev. 7 : 14 ; 19 : 3.

81. The Perfect Indicative in indirect discourse after a verb of past time is regularly rendered into English by a Pluperfect. This involves, however, no special use of the tense, but results from the regular difference between English and Greek in the matter of indirect discourse. Cf. 353.

82. When the Perfect Indicative is used of a past event which is by reason of the context necessarily thought of as separated from the moment of speaking by an interval, it is impossible to render it into English adequately. English idiom forbids the use of the Perfect because of the interval (present in thought as well as existing in fact) between the act and the time of speaking, while the English Past tense fails to express the idea of existing result which the Greek Perfect conveys. In most of these cases R.V. has attempted to preserve the sense of the Greek at the expense of the English idiom.

Acts 7:35; τοῦτον ὁ θεὸς καὶ ἄρχοντα καὶ λυτρωτὴν ἀπέσταλκεν σὺν χειρὶ ἀγγέλου τοῦ ὀφθέντος αὐτῷ ἐν τῇ βάτῳ, *him did God send* [R.V. *hath God sent*] *to be both a ruler and a deliverer with the hand of the angel which appeared to him in the bush.* See also instances cited by *Weymouth* in *Theological Monthly*, iv. 168 f.; Rom. 16:7, *who also were* [γέγοναν, R.V. *have been*] *in Christ before me;* John 6:25, R.V. correctly, *when camest* [γέγονας] *thou here?* Heb. 7: 6, 9; 8:5.

These cases should not be confused with those treated under 80. Here the Greek tense has its normal force, though it cannot be well rendered by its usual English equivalent. There the use of the Greek tense is somewhat abnormal.

83. For the Perfect used proleptically, see 50.

84. PERIPHRASTIC FORM OF THE PERFECT. Periphrastic Perfects, formed by adding a Perfect Participle to the Present of the verb εἰμί, are frequent in the New Testament, about forty instances occurring. In function these forms more frequently denote existing state, though clear instances of the Perfect denoting completed action occur. The former use is illustrated in Luke 20:6; John 2:17; Acts 2:13; 25:10; 2 Cor. 4:3, etc.; the latter in Luke 23:15; Acts 26:26; Heb. 4:2, etc. Cf. 431.

85. It is important to observe that the term "complete" or "completed" as a grammatical term does not mean *ended*, but *accomplished*, i.e. *brought to its appropriate result, which result remains at the time denoted by the verb.* "The Perfect, although it implies the performance of the action in past time, yet states only that it stands completed at the present time."

G.MT. **44.** "Das Perf. hatte zwei altüberkommene Funktio-
nen. Einerseits hatte es intensiven, beziehentlich iterativen
Sinn. . . . Anderseits bezeichnete es die Handlung im Zustand
des Vollendet- und Fertigseins." *Br.* 162.

An action which has ceased may be expressed in Greek by
the Aorist or the Imperfect quite as well as by the Perfect,
provided only the action is thought of apart from any existing
result of it. These tenses are indeed more frequently used
of actions which are complete in the sense of having come to
an end than is the Perfect. See, *e.g.*, Gal. 4 : 8 ; τότε μὲν . . .
ἐδουλεύσατε τοῖς φύσει μὴ οὖσι θεοῖς, *at that time . . . ye were in
bondage to them which by nature are no gods;* and 2 Cor. 7, 8 ;
οὐ μεταμέλομαι· εἰ καὶ μετεμελόμην, *I do not regret it, although
I did regret [was regretting] it.* The Perfect, on the other
hand, affirms the existence of the normal result of the action,
and this even though the action itself is still in progress.
See, *e.g.*, the Perfect τετήρηκα, in 2 Tim. 4 : 7, quoted under 74.

86. Since the Aorist and the Perfect both involve reference
to a past event, the Perfect affirming the existence of the
result of the event, and the Aorist affirming the event itself,
without either affirming or denying the existence of the result,
it is evident that whenever the result of the past action does
still exist, either tense may be used, according as the writer
wishes either to affirm the result or merely the event. In
many cases the reason of the choice of one tense rather than
the other is very evident and the distinction clearly marked,
even when in accordance with the principle of 82 both tenses
must be translated by an English Past. See, *e.g.*, 1 Cor. 15:4;
ὅτι ἐτάφη, καὶ ὅτι ἐγήγερται τῇ ἡμέρᾳ τῇ τρίτῃ, *that he was buried,
and that he was raised on the third day.* The burial is simply
a past event. Of the resurrection there is an existing result,
prominently before the mind.

But there are naturally other cases in which, though each tense retains its own proper force, the two approximate very closely, and are used side by side of what seem to be quite coördinate facts. Instances of this approximation of the two tenses are especially frequent in the writings of John. See John 5 : 36, 38; 1 John 1 : 1; 4 : 9, 10; cf. also Acts 6 : 11 and 15 : 24.

87. It might be supposed that the Resultative Aorist would be especially near in force to the Perfect. The distinction is, however, clearly marked. The Resultative Aorist affirms that an action attempted in past time was accomplished, saying nothing about the present result. The Perfect, on the other hand, belongs to all classes of verbs, not merely to those that imply attempt, and affirms the existence of the result of the past action, the occurrence of which it implies.

88. It should be observed that the aoristic use of the Perfect (80) is a distinct departure from the strict and proper sense of the tense in Greek. The beginnings of this departure are to be seen in classical Greek (*G.*MT. 46), and in Greek writers of a time later than the New Testament the tendency was still further developed, until the sense of difference between the tenses was lost.

Meantime there grew up a new form of the Perfect, made as is the English Perfect, of an auxiliary denoting possession (in Greek ἔχω, as in English *have*) and a participle. This periphrastic Perfect, traces of which appear even in classical times (*G.*MT. 47), at length entirely displaced the simple Perfect for the expression of completed action, and the process by which the Perfect had become an Aorist in meaning and been succeeded in office as a Perfect tense by another form was complete. See *Jebb* in *Vincent and Dickson*, Modern Greek, pp. 326–330. In the New Testament we see the earlier stages of this process. The Perfect is still, with very few exceptions, a true Perfect, but it has begun to be an Aorist. In Latin this process was already complete so far as the assimilation of the Perfect and the Aorist was concerned; the new Perfect had not yet appeared. In modern English we see the process at a point midway between that represented by the Greek of the New Testament and that which appears in the Latin of about the same time. Modern German represents about the same stage as modern English, but a little further advanced.

It should be borne in mind that in determining whether a given Perfect form is a true Perfect in sense or not, the proper English translation is no certain criterion, since the functions of the Perfect tense in the two languages differ so widely. Cf. 52. The Perfect πεποίηκα in 2 Cor. 11 : 25 seems evidently aoristic; that it "goes quite naturally into English" (S. p. 104) does not at all show that it has the usual force of a Greek Perfect. Many Aorists even go quite naturally and correctly into English Perfects. Cf. 46. The Perfects in Luke 9 : 36; 2 Cor. 12 : 17 ; Heb. 7 : 13 (προσέσχηκεν) ; 9 : 18; 11 : 28; Rev. 3 : 3; 5 : 7 are probably also Aoristic Perfects, though it is possible that in all these cases the thought of an existing result is more or less clearly in mind and gives occasion to the use of the Perfect tense. The Perfect πέπρακεν in Matt. 13 : 46 must be either aoristic or historical, probably the former (see Sophocles, Glossary, etc., 82, 4). The evidence seems to show clearly that Matthew regularly used γέγονα in the sense of an Aorist ; some of the instances cannot, without violence, be otherwise explained, and all are naturally so explained. Mark's use of the word is possibly the same, but the evidence is not decisive. All other writers of the New Testament use the form as a true Perfect.

Still other cases should perhaps be explained as Aoristic Perfects, but for the reasons mentioned in 86 it is impossible

to decide with certainty. While there is clear evidence that
the Perfect tense was in the New Testament sometimes an
Aorist in force, yet it is to be observed that the New Testament writers had perfect command of the distinction between
the Aorist and the Perfect. The instances of the Perfect in
the sense of the Aorist are confined almost entirely to a few
forms, ἔσχηκα, εἴληφα, ἑώρακα, εἴρηκα, and γέγονα, and the use of
each of these forms in the sense of an Aorist mainly to one
or more writers whose use of it is apparently almost a personal idiosyncrasy. Thus the aoristic use of γέγονα belongs
to Matt.; of εἴληφα to John in Rev.; of ἔσχηκα to Paul; but
see also Heb. 7 : 13. The idiom is therefore confined within
narrow limits in the New Testament. Cf. Ev. Pet. 23, 31.

2 Cor. 12 : 9 and 1 John 1 : 10 are probably true Perfects of
Completed Action, the latter case being explained by v. 8.
John 1 : 18; 5 : 37; 8 : 33; and Heb. 10 : 9 also probably convey the thought of existing result, though the use of an adverb
of past time serves to give more prominence to the past action
than is usually given by a Perfect tense.

THE PLUPERFECT

89. The Pluperfect of Completed Action. The Pluperfect is used of an action which was complete at a point
of past time implied in the context. *HA.* 847; *G.* 1250, 4.

Acts 9 : 21; καὶ ὧδε εἰς τοῦτο ἐληλύθει, *and he had come hither for this
intent.*

John 9 : 22; ἤδη γὰρ συνετέθειντο οἱ Ἰουδαῖοι, *for the Jews had agreed
already.* See also Luke 8 : 2; Acts 7 : 44; 19 : 32.

90. The Pluperfect of Existing State. Verbs which
in the Perfect denote a present state, in the Pluperfect
denote a past state. *HA.* 849, c; *G.* 1263.

Luke 4 : 41; ᾔδεισαν τὸν Χριστὸν αὐτὸν εἶναι, *they knew that he was the Christ.* See also John 18 : 16, 18 ; Acts 1 : 10.

91. PERIPHRASTIC FORM OF THE PLUPERFECT. A periphrastic Pluperfect formed by adding the Perfect Participle to the Imperfect of the verb εἰμί is somewhat frequent in the New Testament. In classical Greek this was already the only form in the third person plural of liquid and mute verbs, and an occasional form elsewhere. In the New Testament these periphrastic forms are frequently, but not at all uniformly, Pluperfects of existing state; about one-third of the whole number of instances belong to the class of Pluperfects denoting completed action, referring to the past act as well as the existing result. Cf. *G*.MT. 45.

Matt. 26 : 43; ἦσαν γὰρ αὐτῶν οἱ ὀφθαλμοὶ βεβαρημένοι, *for their eyes were heavy,* lit. *weighed down.*

Luke 2 : 26; καὶ ἦν αὐτῷ κεχρηματισμένον ὑπὸ τοῦ πνεύματος τοῦ ἁγίου, *and it had been revealed to him by the Holy Spirit.*

92. The ambiguity of the English sometimes renders it impossible to distinguish in translation between a Pluperfect of Existing State and an Historical Aorist. Thus in Acts 4 : 27 and 31 we must in both cases read *were gathered,* though the verb in the former case is an Aorist and refers to an act, and in the latter a Perfect and refers to a state. Cf. also the two verbs in Luke 15 : 24.

93. The simple Future Perfect does not occur in the New Testament. Respecting Luke 19 : 40, see *B.* p. 61; and the lexicons s.v.

94. A periphrastic Future Perfect, expressing a future state, occurs in Matt. 16 : 19; 18 : 18; Luke 12 : 52; Heb. 2 : 13.

TENSES OF THE DEPENDENT MOODS

95. The tenses of the dependent moods have in general no reference to time, but characterize the action of the verb in respect to its progress only, representing it as in progress, or completed, or indefinitely, simply as an event. *HA.* 851; *G.* 1272, 1273; *G.*MT. 85.

96. The Present of the Dependent Moods is used to represent an action as in progress or as repeated. It may be altogether timeless, the action being thought of without reference to the time of its occurrence ; or its time, as past, present, or future, may be involved in the function of the mood, or may be indicated by the context.

Phil. 3 : 1 ; τὰ αὐτὰ γράφειν ὑμῖν ἐμοὶ μὲν οὐκ ὀκνηρόν, *to be writing the same things to you, to me indeed is not irksome.*

Matt. 5 : 23 ; ἐὰν οὖν προσφέρῃς τὸ δῶρόν σου ἐπὶ τὸ θυσιαστήριον, *if therefore thou shalt be offering thy gift at the altar.*

Mark 12 : 33 ; καὶ τὸ ἀγαπᾶν αὐτὸν ἐξ ὅλης καρδίας . . . περισσότερόν ἐστιν πάντων τῶν ὁλοκαυτωμάτων καὶ θυσιῶν, *and to love him with all the heart . . . is much more than all whole burnt offerings and sacrifices.*

97. PERIPHRASTIC FORM OF THE PRESENT. A periphrastic Present Infinitive, formed by adding a Present Participle to the Present Infinitive of εἰμί, and a periphrastic Present Imperative, formed by adding a Present Participle to the Present Imperative of εἰμί, occur rarely in the New Testament. Luke 9 : 18; 11 : 1; Matt. 5 : 25; Luke 19 : 17. Cf. 20, and 431.

98. The Aorist of the Dependent Moods represents the action expressed by the verb as a simple event or fact, without reference either to its progress or to the existence of its result. As in the Indicative the verb may be indefinite, inceptive or resultative (cf. 35), and when indefinite may refer to a momentary or extended action or to a series of events (cf. 39). The time of the action, if indicated at all, is shown, not by the tense, but by some fact outside of it.

An Aorist Subjunctive after ἐάν, ὅταν, ἕως etc. is sometimes properly translated by a Perfect or Future Perfect, but only because the *context* shows that the action is to precede that of the principal verb. In the great majority of cases a Present Subjunctive or a Future is the best translation. See examples under 250, 285, 303, 322.

Luke 9 : 54 ; εἴπωμεν πῦρ καταβῆναι, *shall we bid fire to come down?*

John 15 : 9 ; μείνατε ἐν τῇ ἀγάπῃ τῇ ἐμῇ, *abide ye in my love.*

Luke 17 : 4 ; καὶ ἐὰν ἑπτάκις τῆς ἡμέρας ἁμαρτήσῃ εἰς σὲ . . . ἀφήσεις αὐτῷ, *and if he sin against thee seven times in the day . . . thou shalt forgive him.*

Acts 15 : 13 ; μετὰ δὲ τὸ σιγῆσαι αὐτοὺς, ἀπεκρίθη Ἰάκωβος, *and after they had become silent, James answered.*

Acts 11 : 17 ; ἐγὼ τίς ἤμην δυνατὸς κωλῦσαι τὸν θεόν, *who was I that I could withstand God?*

REM. Compare the Presents and Aorists in the following examples :

Matt. 6 : 11 ; τὸν ἄρτον ἡμῶν τὸν ἐπιούσιον δὸς ἡμῖν σήμερον, *give us this day our daily bread.*

Luke 11 : 3 ; τὸν ἄρτον ἡμῶν τὸν ἐπιούσιον δίδου ἡμῖν τὸ καθ᾽ ἡμέραν, *give us day by day our daily bread.*

Acts 18 : 9 ; μὴ φοβοῦ, ἀλλὰ λάλει καὶ μὴ σιωπήσῃς, *be not in fear, but [continue to] speak and hold not thy peace.*

Matt. 5 : 17 ; οὐκ ἦλθον καταλῦσαι ἀλλὰ πληρῶσαι, *I came not to destroy, but to fulfil.*

John 9 : 4 ; ἡμᾶς δεῖ ἐργάζεσθαι τὰ ἔργα τοῦ πέμψαντός με ἕως ἡμέρα ἐστίν, *we must work [be doing] the works of him that sent me while it is day.*

99. The Future Optative does not occur in the New Testament.

The Future Infinitive denotes time relatively to the time of the principal verb. It is thus an exception to the general principle of the timelessness of the dependent moods.

Acts 23 : 30 ; μηνυθείσης δέ μοι ἐπιβουλῆς εἰς τὸν ἄνδρα ἔσεσθαι, and *when it was shown to me that there would be a plot against the man.*

100. The Infinitive μέλλειν with the Infinitive of another verb dependent on it has the force of a Future Infinitive of the latter verb. The dependent Infinitive is usually a Present, sometimes a Future. It is regularly a Future in the New Testament in the case of the verb εἰμί.

Acts 28 : 6 ; οἱ δὲ προσεδόκων αὐτὸν μέλλειν πίμπρασθαι ἢ καταπίπτειν ἄφνω νεκρόν, *but they expected that he would swell or fall down suddenly.* See also Acts 19 : 27 ; 27 : 10, etc.

101. The Perfect of the Dependent Moods is used of completed action. As in the Indicative, the thought may be directed both to the action and its result, or only to the result. The time of the action is indicated, as in the Present and Aorist, not by the tense but by the context or by the function of the mood.

Acts 25 : 25 ; ἐγὼ δὲ κατελαβόμην μηδὲν ἄξιον αὐτὸν θανάτου πεπραχέναι, *but I found that he had committed nothing worthy of death.*
Acts 26 : 32 ; ἀπολελύσθαι ἐδύνατο ὁ ἄνθρωπος οὗτος, *this man might have been set at liberty.*
Mark 4 : 39 ; Σιώπα, πεφίμωσο, *peace, be still.*

102. An Intensive Perfect may occur in the dependent moods as in the Indicative.

1 Tim. 6 : 17 ; τοῖς πλουσίοις ἐν τῷ νῦν αἰῶνι παράγγελλε μὴ ὑψηλοφρονεῖν μηδὲ ἠλπικέναι ἐπὶ πλούτου ἀδηλότητι, *charge them that are rich in this present world, that they be not high minded, nor have their hope set on the uncertainty of riches.*

103. PERIPHRASTIC FORM OF THE PERFECT. In the New Testament as in classical Greek, the Perfect Subjunctive Passive is formed by adding a Perfect Participle to the Present Subjunctive of the verb εἰμί. These forms are in the New Testament most commonly Perfects of Existing State. John 16 : 24 ; 17 : 19 ; 2 Cor. 1 : 9 ; etc. See also Luke 12 : 35, which furnishes an instance of a periphrastic Perfect Imperative, enjoining the maintenance of the state denoted by the Perfect Participle. Cf. 20 and 431.

104. TENSES OF THE INFINITIVE AFTER PREPOSITIONS. The general principle that the tenses of the dependent moods characterize the action of the verb only as respects progress and are properly timeless holds also respecting the Infinitive after prepositions. The Infinitive itself is properly timeless, though the time-relation is usually suggested by the meaning of the preposition or by this combined with that which the tense implies respecting the progress of the action.

105. By μετά with the Infinitive antecedence of the action denoted by the Infinitive to that denoted by the principal verb is expressed, but this meaning manifestly lies in the preposition, not in the tense of the verb. That the Aorist Infinitive is almost constantly used (the Perfect occurs once, Heb. 10 : 15) is natural, since in dating one event by another the latter is usually conceived of simply as an event without reference to its progress. See Matt. 26 : 32 ; Luke 12 : 5 ; Acts 1 : 3 ; 1 Cor. 11 : 25, etc.

106. By πρό with the Infinitive antecedence of the action of the principal verb to that of the Infinitive is expressed, and the action of the Infinitive is accordingly relatively future. But here also the time relation is expressed wholly by the preposition. The reason for the almost uniform use of the Aorist (the Present εἶναι occurs John 17 : 5) is the same as in the case of μετά. See Luke 2 : 21 ; 22 : 15 ; John 1 : 48.

107. After εἰς and πρός the Infinitive usually refers to an action which is future with respect to the principal verb. This also results from the meaning of the prepositions, which, expressing purpose or tendency, necessarily point to an action subsequent to that of the verb which the prepositional phrase limits. When πρός means *with reference to*, the time-relation is indicated only by the necessary relation of the things spoken of. See Luke 18 : 1. All three tenses of the Infinitive occur after εἰς and both Present and Aorist after πρός, the difference marked by the tense being not of time but of progress. See Rom. 12 : 2 ; Phil. 1 : 23 ; Heb. 11 : 3 ; Matt. 6 : 1 ; Mark 13 : 22. Cf. 409–414.

108. After διά the three Infinitives distinguish the action as respects the writer's conception of its progress, as continued, completed, or indefinite. Time relations are secondary and suggested. The Aorist Infinitive occurs only in Matt. 24 : 12, where τὸ πληθυνθῆναι τὴν ἀνομίαν apparently refers to the multiplication of iniquity as a fact of that time without exclusive reference to its preceding the action of the principal verb. The Present Infinitive refers to action in progress usually shown by the context to be contemporaneous with the action of the principal verb. See Matt. 13 : 5, 6 ; Acts 12 : 20 ; Heb. 10 : 2 ; Jas. 4 : 2. The Perfect Infinitive has its usual force, denoting an action standing complete. The time of the state of completeness appears from the context ; it is usually that of the principal verb. See Acts 8 : 11 ; 18 : 2 ; 27 : 9 ; but cf. Mark 5 : 4, where δεδέσθαι denotes an action whose result was existing, not at the time of speaking, but at an earlier time. Cf. 408.

109. After ἐν we naturally expect to find only the Present Infinitive, the preposition by its meaning suggesting an action thought of as in progress ; and this is indeed the more common usage. Luke, however, who uses ἐν with the Infinitive far more frequently than all the other New Testament writers, has ἐν with the Aorist Infinitive nine times, and the same construction occurs in Hebrews twice, and in 1 Corinthians once. Since the Aorist Infinitive conceives of an action simply as an event without thought of its continuance, it is natural to take ἐν with it in the same sense which the preposition bears with nouns which denote an event rather than a continued action or state (cf. 98), viz. as marking the *time at which* the action expressed by the principal verb takes place. The preposition in this sense does not seem necessarily to denote exact coincidence, but in no case expresses antecedence. In 1 Cor. 11 : 21 and Heb. 3 : 12 the action of the Infinitive cannot be antecedent to that of the principal verb ; see also Gen. 19 : 16. In Luke 9 : 34 such a relation is very difficult, and in Luke 14 : 1 improbable in view of the Imperfect tense following. In Luke 2 : 27 ; 11 : 37 ; 19 : 15 ; 24 : 30 ; Acts 11 : 15, the action denoted by the Infinitive, strictly speaking, precedes the action of the principal verb, yet may be thought of by the writer as marking more or less exactly the time at which the action of the verb takes place. As respects the relation of the action to that of the principal verb, the Aorist Infinitive after ἐν may be compared to the Aorist Indicative after ὅτε, which simply marks in general the time of the event denoted by the principal verb, leaving it to the context to indicate the precise nature of the chronological relation. See Matt. 12 : 3 ; 21 : 34 ; 27 : 31 ; John 19 : 6, 30. Similarly indefinite is the use of the English preposition *on* with verbal nouns, as, *e.g.*, *On the completion of his twenty-first year he becomes of legal age; On the arrival of the train the procession will be formed.* Luke 3 : 21 cannot in view of the Aorist tense be rendered, *while all the people were being baptized*, nor in view of the preposition ἐν, *after all the people had been baptized*, but must be understood as affirming that the baptism of Jesus occurred at the time (in general) of the baptism of all the people. Luke 9 : 36 can only mean, *when the voice came*, a meaning entirely appropriate to the context. Cf. 415.

110. The Tenses of the Dependent Moods in Indirect Discourse. The Optative and Infinitive in indirect discourse preserve the conception of the action as respects progress which belonged to the direct discourse. The Present Optative and Infinitive represent tense forms which in the direct discourse denoted action in progress. Similarly the Aorist of these moods represents forms which expressed action indefinitely, and the Perfect stands for forms denoting completed action. The Future represents a Future Indicative of the direct discourse. In the majority of cases each tense of the Optative or Infinitive in indirect discourse stands for the same tense of the Indicative or Subjunctive of the direct form. Yet it is doubtful whether, strictly speaking, the dependent moods in indirect discourse express time-relations. The correspondence of tenses probably rather results from the necessity of preserving the original conception of the action as respects its progress, and the time-relation is conveyed by the context rather than by the tense of the verb.

Rem. Cf. Br. 161. "Der opt. und inf. aor. von vergangenen Handlungen als Vertreter des ind. aor. in der or. obl. entbehrten ebenso wie opt. und inf. praes. (§ 158) des Ausdrucks der Zeitbeziehung, die nur aus der

Natur der in der Rede in Verbindung gebrachten Verbalbegriffe oder aus der ganzen in Rede stehenden Situation erkannt .wurde." Cf. *G*.MT. 85, *contra*.

111. The Present Optative in indirect discourse in the New Testament usually represents the Present Indicative of the direct form. Luke 1: 29; 3: 15; Acts 17: 11; etc. In Acts 25 : 16, it stands for a Present Subjunctive of the direct form. The Optative with ἄν is taken unchanged from the direct discourse. Luke 1: 62; 6: 11; etc. The Aorist Optative occurs in indirect discourse only in Acts 25 : 16, where it represents a Subjunctive of the direct form referring to the future. Neither the Perfect Optative nor the Future Optative occurs in the New Testament.

112. The Present Infinitive in indirect discourse in the New Testament stands for the Present Indicative of the direct form. Matt. 22 : 23; Luke 11 : 18; 20 : 41; Acts 4 : 32; 1 Cor. 7 : 36; 1 John 2 : 9. Similarly the Perfect Infinitive represents the Perfect Indicative of the direct discourse. Luke 22 : 34; John 12 : 29; Acts 14 : 19; 2 Tim. 2 : 18. The Present Infinitive as the representative of the Imperfect, and the Perfect Infinitive as the representative of the Pluperfect (*G*.MT. 119, 123) apparently do not occur in the New Testament. The Future Infinitive is, as stated above (99), an exception to the general rule of the timelessness of the dependent moods. It represents a Future Indicative of the direct form. John 21 : 25; Acts 23 : 30; Heb. 3 : 18.

113. The Aorist Infinitive occurs in the New Testament, as in classical Greek, as a regular construction after verbs signifying *to hope, to promise, to swear, to command*, etc. In this case the action denoted by the Aorist Infinitive is, by the nature of the case, future with reference to that of the principal verb, but this time-relation is not expressed by the tense. The Aorist Infinitive is here as elsewhere timeless. These instances, though closely akin in force to those of indirect discourse, are not usually included under that head. Cf. *G.MT.* 684.

114. The Aorist Infinitive referring to what is future with reference to the principal verb also occurs in a few instances after verbs of assertion. These must be accounted cases in which the Aorist Infinitive in indirect discourse is timeless.

Luke 24:46; ὅτι οὕτως γέγραπται παθεῖν τὸν χριστὸν καὶ ἀναστῆναι ἐκ νεκρῶν τῇ τρίτῃ ἡμέρᾳ, *thus it is written, that the Christ should suffer, and rise again from the dead the third day.* See also Luke 2:26; Acts 3:18. Cf. Hom. Od. 2. 171, φημὶ τελευτηθῆναι ἅπαντα, the accomplishment being still future (*Carter* in *Cl. Rev.* Feb. 1891, p. 5). Plat. Euthyd. 278, C. ἐφάτην ἐπιδείξασθαι τὴν προτρεπτικὴν σοφίαν, *they said that they would give a sample of the hortatory wisdom.* Protag. 316, C. τοῦτο δὲ οἴεταί οἱ μάλιστα γενέσθαι, εἰ σοὶ ξυγγένοιτο, *and he supposes that he would be most likely to attain this if he should associate with you;* and other examples in *Riddell*, Digest of Platonic Idioms, § 81; also in *G.MT.* 127.

There is apparently no instance in the New Testament of the Aorist Infinitive in indirect discourse representing the Aorist Indicative of the direct form. Cf. 390.

TENSES OF THE PARTICIPLE

115. The participle is a verbal adjective, sharing in part the characteristics of both the verb and the adjective; it describes its subject as a doer of the action denoted by the verb. For the proper understanding of a participle three things must be observed:

(a) The grammatical agreement.
(b) The use of the tense.
(c) The modal significance, or logical force.

116. In grammatical agreement, a participle follows the rule for adjectives, agreeing with its noun or pronoun in gender, number, and case.

117. The logical force of the participle, usually the most important consideration from the point of view of interpretation, will be treated at a later point. See 419 ff. The matter now under consideration is the significance of the tense of a participle.

118. The tenses of the participle, like those of the other dependent moods, do not, in general, in themselves denote time. To this general rule the Future Participle is the leading exception, its functions being such as necessarily to express time-relations. The fundamental distinguishing mark of each of the other tenses is the same for the participle as for the dependent moods in general. The Present denotes action in progress; the Aorist, action conceived of indefinitely; the Perfect, completed action. These distinctions, however, impose certain limitations upon the classes of events which may be expressed by the participle of each tense, and thus indirectly and to a limited extent, the tense of the participle is an indication of the time-relation of the event denoted by it. Since for purposes of interpretation it is often needful to define the time-relation of an event expressed by the participle, it becomes expedient to treat the tenses of the participle apart from those of the dependent moods in general.

THE PRESENT PARTICIPLE

119. The Present Participle of Simultaneous Action. The Present Participle most frequently denotes an action in progress, simultaneous with the action of the principal verb. *HA.* 856; *G.* 1288.

Mark 16 : 20 ; ἐκεῖνοι δὲ ἐξελθόντες ἐκήρυξαν πανταχοῦ, τοῦ κυρίου συνεργοῦντος, *and they went forth and preached everywhere, the Lord working with them.*

Acts 10 : 44 ; ἔτι λαλοῦντος τοῦ Πέτρου τὰ ῥήματα ταῦτα ἐπέπεσε τὸ πνεῦμα τὸ ἅγιον ἐπὶ πάντας τοὺς ἀκούοντας τὸν λόγον, *while Peter was yet speaking these words, the Holy Ghost fell on all them which heard the word.*

REM. The action of the verb and that of the participle may be of the same extent (Mark 16 : 20), but are not necessarily so. Oftener the action of the verb falls within the period covered by the participle (Acts 10 : 44).

Even a subsequent action is occasionally expressed by a Present Participle, which in this case stands after the verb. Cf. 145.

Acts 19 : 9 ; ἀφώρισεν τοὺς μαθητὰς, καθ' ἡμέραν διαλεγόμενος ἐν τῇ σχολῇ Τυράννου, *he separated the disciples, reasoning daily in the school of Tyrannus.* See also Acts 17 : 13 ; 18 : 23.

120. The Present Participle of Identical Action. The Present Participle not infrequently denotes the same action which is expressed by the verb of the clause in which it stands.

John 6 : 6 ; τοῦτο δὲ ἔλεγεν πειράζων αὐτόν, *and this he said trying him.* See also Matt. 27 : 41 ; John 21 : 19 ; Acts 9 : 22 ; Gal. 3 : 23.

121. The verb and the participle of identical action, though denoting the same action, usually describe it from a different point of view. The relation between the different points of view varies greatly. It may be the relation of fact to method, as in Acts 9 : 22 ; 15 : 24, 29 ; of outward form to inner significance or quality, as in Luke 22 : 65 ; or of act to purpose or result, as in Matt. 16 : 1 ; John 6 : 6.

122. A Present Participle of Identical Action, since it denotes action in progress, most naturally accompanies a verb denoting action in progress. Sometimes, however, a Present Participle accompanies an Aorist verb denoting the same action; regularly so in the phrase ἀπεκρίνατο (ἀπεκρίθη) λέγων; see Mark 15:9; Luke 3:16; John 1:26; etc.

Acts 15:24; ἐτάραξαν ὑμᾶς λόγοις ἀνασκευάζοντες τὰς ψυχὰς ὑμῶν, *they have troubled you with words, subverting your souls.* See also Acts 1:3; 22:4; Gen. 43:6.

Similarly a Present Participle representing the action as in progress, may accompany an Aoristic Future, which conceives of it simply as an event. Acts 15:29; 1 Macc. 12:22.

123. The General Present Participle. The Present Participle is also used without reference to time or progress, simply defining its subject as belonging to a certain class, *i.e.* the class of those who do the action denoted by the verb. The participle in this case becomes a simple adjective or noun and is, like any other adjective or noun, timeless and indefinite. *B.* pp. 296 f.; *WM.* p. 444; *WT.* p. 353.

Acts 10:22; Κορνήλιος ἑκατοντάρχης, ἀνὴρ δίκαιος καὶ φοβούμενος τὸν θεόν, *Cornelius a centurion, a righteous and God-fearing man.*
Mark 5:16; πῶς ἐγένετο τῷ δαιμονιζομένῳ, *what had happened to the demoniac.*
Gal. 6:6; κοινωνείτω δὲ ὁ κατηχούμενος τὸν λόγον τῷ κατηχοῦντι ἐν πᾶσιν ἀγαθοῖς, *but let him that is taught in the word communicate to him that teacheth in all good things.*

124. A class may consist of those who habitually or constantly do a given act, or of those who once do the act the single doing of which is the mark of the class. The former case is illustrated in Matt. 5:6; the latter in Rev. 14:13.

Matt. 5:6; μακάριοι οἱ πεινῶντες καὶ διψῶντες τὴν δικαιοσύνην, *blessed are they that hunger and thirst after righteousness.*
Rev. 14:13; μακάριοι οἱ νεκροὶ οἱ ἐν κυρίῳ ἀποθνήσκοντες, *blessed are the dead which die in the Lord.* See also Matt. 7:13.

In the first class of cases the Present Participle only can be used; in the second class either an Aorist (as in Matt. 23 : 20; 26 : 52; John 16 : 2, *et al.*) or a Present may occur, and that, either in the plural designating the class as such, or in the singular designating an individual of the class.

Thus παντὶ ἀνθρώπῳ περιτεμνομένῳ (Gal. 5 : 3; cf. 6 : 13) does not mean, *to every man that is wont to be circumcised,* but, *to every man that is circumcised,* i.e. *that receives circumcision* (R.V., correctly though not literally). So also in Heb. 5 : 1 λαμβανόμενος does not mean, *one that is wont to be taken,* but, *that is taken. Being once taken* is the mark of the class here referred to, as *being once circumcised* is the mark of the class referred to in Gal. 5 : 3. The customariness applies not to the action of the individual member of the class, but to that of the class as a whole; as in Heb. 5 : 1, the Present Indicative καθίσταται may be rendered, *is wont to be appointed,* not in the sense, *each one is wont to be [repeatedly] appointed,* but, *it is wont to happen to each that he is appointed.* Cf. 125. In Luke 16 : 18 πᾶς ὁ ἀπολύων means not, *every one that is wont to divorce,* still less, *every one that has divorced,* but, *every one that divorces.*

125. Through the ambiguity of the English Passive form, such Present Participles as those just referred to (124) are easily taken by the English interpreter as equivalent to Perfect Participles, but always to the greater or less distortion of the meaning of the passage.[1]

Thus in Gal. 5 : 3 (see 124) περιτεμνομένῳ is not equivalent to a Perfect, *every circumcised man.* The apostle is not speaking of circumcision as an accomplished fact, but of becoming circumcised. Similarly Heb. 5 : 1 refers not to *one that has been taken* (German: *ist genommen worden*), but *that is taken* (German: *wird genommen*). In Heb. 5 : 4 καλούμενος is *one that is* (not, *has been*) *called.* In Luke 13 : 23, εἰ ὀλίγοι οἱ

[1] This ambiguity of the English may be illustrated by the form *is written.* In the sentence, *It is written in your law,* etc., *is written* is a Perfect of Existing State, and is expressed by the Greek Perfect γέγραπται. The German would be *ist geschrieben.* In the sentence, *The name of each scholar is written in the register as he enters the school,* the same form is a Present of customary action, and would be expressed in Greek by γράφεται, and in German by *wird geschrieben.*

σωζόμενοι, the participle is undoubtedly a General Present, the inquiry being neither on the one hand as to the number of *those that are* already *saved* (Perfect of Existing State) or *that have been saved* (Perfect of Completed Action) nor, on the other, with reference to *those that are being saved* (Progressive Present of Simultaneous Action), but with reference to *those that are* [i.e. *become*] *saved.* Cf. Luther's version, *meinst du, dass wenige selig werden?* and Weizsäcker's, *sind es wenige, die gerettet werden?*

The same participle in Acts 2 : 47 ; 1 Cor. 1 : 18 ; 2 Cor. 2 : 15, may be understood in the same way, and be rendered, *we that are* (in the sense *we that become*) *saved,* or may be taken as in R.V. as a Progressive Present of Simultaneous Action.   It cannot mean *the saved* in the sense of *those that have been saved.*   The statement of Dr. *T. W. Chambers* in *J.B.L.* June 1886, p. 40, that "the passive participle of the present tense in Greek is often, if not generally, used to express a completed action," is wholly incorrect, and derives all its verisimilitude from the ambiguity of the English Passive forms.

126. A General Present Participle sometimes occurs in the singular when the person to whom it refers constitutes the class designated.   This limitation of the phrase to an individual is accomplished, however, not by the participle, but by its limitations.   John 13 : 11, τὸν παραδιδόντα αὐτόν, probably means simply *his betrayer.*   The participle παραδιδούς alone designates any one belonging to the class of betrayers.   It is the addition of the article and an object that restricts the participle to one person.

127. The Present Participle for the Imperfect.   The Present Participle is also sometimes used as an Imperfect to denote a continued action antecedent to that of the principal verb.   *HA.* 856, a ; *G.* 1289 ; *G.*MT. 140.

Matt. 2 : 20 ; τεθνήκασιν γὰρ οἱ ζητοῦντες τὴν ψυχὴν τοῦ παιδίου, *for they are dead that were seeking the young child's life.*   See also John 12 : 17 ; Acts 4 : 34 (cf. v. 37) ; 10 : 7 ; Gal. 1 : 23.

128. The following uses of the Present Participle are closely analogous to the uses of the Present Indicative already described under similar names.   They are of somewhat infrequent occurrence in the New Testament.

129. (*a*) THE CONATIVE PRESENT.

Matt. 23 : 13 (*WH. et al.*, 14); οὐδὲ τοὺς εἰσερχομένους ἀφίετε εἰσελθεῖν, *neither suffer ye them that are entering in to enter.* See also Acts 28 : 23.

130. (*b*) THE PRESENT FOR THE FUTURE, the action denoted being thought of as future with reference to the time of the principal verb.

Acts 21 : 3; ἐκεῖσε γὰρ τὸ πλοῖον ἦν ἀποφορτιζόμενον τὸν γόμον, *for there the ship was to unlade her burden.*

131. (*c*) THE PRESENT OF PAST ACTION STILL IN PROGRESS, the action denoted beginning before the action of the principal verb and continuing in progress at the time denoted by the latter.

Acts 9 : 33; εὗρεν δὲ ἐκεῖ ἄνθρωπόν τινα ὀνόματι Αἰνέαν ἐξ ἐτῶν ὀκτὼ κατακείμενον ἐπὶ κραβάττου, *and there he found a certain man named Æneas, who had been lying on a bed eight years.* See also Matt. 9 : 20; Mark 5 : 25; Luke 8 : 43; John 5 : 5; Acts 24 : 10.

THE AORIST PARTICIPLE

132. The general statement made under 118, that the tenses of the participle do not in general in themselves denote time, applies also to the Aorist Participle. It is very important for the right interpretation of the Aorist Participle that it be borne in mind that the proper and leading function of the tense is not to express time, but to mark the fact that the action of the verb is conceived of indefinitely, as a simple event. The assumption that the Aorist Participle properly denotes past time, from the point of view either of the speaker or of the principal verb, leads to constant misinterpretation of the form. The action denoted by the Aorist Participle may be past, present, or future with reference to the speaker, and antecedent to, coincident with, or subsequent to, the action of the principal verb. The Aorist Participle, like the participles of the other tenses, may be most simply thought of as a noun or adjective, the designation of one who performs the action denoted by the verb, and like any other noun or adjective timeless. The distinction of the Aorist Participle is not that it expresses a different time-relation from that expressed by the Present or Perfect, but that it conceives of the action denoted by it, not as in progress (Present), nor as an existing result (Perfect), but as a simple fact. Such an adjective or noun will not ordinarily be used if contemporaneousness with the action of the principal verb is distinctly in mind, since contemporaneousness suggests action in progress, and action in progress is expressed, not by the Aorist, but by the Present tense. Nor will it be used when the mind distinctly contemplates the existence of the result of the action, it being the function, not of the Aorist, but of the Perfect, to express existing result. Nor, again, will the Aorist noun be used if the writer desires distinctly to indicate that the doer of the action will perform it in time subsequent to that of the principal verb, the Aorist being incapable in itself of suggesting subsequence or futurity. But, when these cases have been excluded, there remains a considerable variety of relations to which the Aorist is applicable, the common mark of them all being that the action denoted by the participle is thought of simply as an event. Among these various relations the case of action antecedent to that of the principal verb furnishes the largest number of instances. It is thus, numerically considered, the leading use of the Aorist Participle, and this fact has even to some extent reacted on the meaning of the tense, so that there is associated with the tense as a secondary, acquired, and wholly subordinate characteristic a certain suggestion of antecedence.

Yet this use is no more than the other uses a primary function of the tense, nor did it ever displace the others, or force them into a position of subordination or abnormality. The instances in which the action denoted by the participle is not antecedent to the action of the principal verb are as normal as that in which it is so, and were evidently so recognized alike in classical and in New Testament Greek. The Aorist Participle of Antecedent Action does not *denote* antecedence; it is used of antecedent action, where antecedence is implied, not by the Aorist tense as a tense of past time, but in some other way. The same principle holds respecting all the uses of this tense. The following section (133) is accordingly a definition of the constant function of the Aorist Participle, while 134, 139, and 142 enumerate the classes of events with reference to which it may be used.

REM. Compare the following statements of modern grammarians:

"Since the participle, like the other non-augmented forms of the aorist, has nothing whatever to do with the denotation of past time, and since time previous to a point in past time is not the less a kind of past time, we do not here understand at once how the participle became used in this sense. But the enigma is solved when we examine the nature of the aorist and participle. The latter, an adjective in origin, fixes one action in relation to another. The action which is denoted by the finite verb is the principal one. When the secondary action continues side by side with the principal action, it must stand [παρατατικῶς] in the participle of the present; if, again, referred to the future, the proper sign of the future is needed ; and similarly, the perfect participle serves to express an action regarded as complete in reference to the principal action. If, however, it is intended to denote the secondary action without any reference to continuousness and completion and futurity, but merely as a point or moment, the aorist participle alone remains for this purpose. We indeed, by a sort of necessity, regard a point which is fixed in reference to another action as prior to it, but, strictly speaking, this notion of priority in past time is not signified by the aorist participle." — *Curtius*, Elucidations of the Student's Greek Grammar, pp. 216 f.

62   THE TENSES

" An und für sich bezeichnet das aoristische Particip ebenso wenig als irgend eine andere aoristische Form ausser dem Indicativ, der in seinem Augment ein deutliches Merkmal der Vergangenheit hat, etwas Vergangenes. Das Particip des kürzesten und von uns genauer betrachteten Aorists, dessen Stamm eben nur die Verbalgrundform selbst ist, ist also nur Particip an und für sich, das heisst es bezeichnet eine Handlung, mit der noch kein Satz als abgeschlossen gedacht werden soll; im Uebrigen liegt sein Characteristisches für uns nur darin, dass es als aoristisches Particip nicht wie das präsentische Particip auch die Bedeutung der Dauer in sich enthält, sondern etwas bezeichnet, bei dem die Zeitdauer, die es in Anspruch genommen, nicht weiter in Frage kommen, oder das überhaupt nur als ganz kurze Zeit dauernd bezeichnet werden soll."
— *Leo Meyer*, Griechische Aoriste, pp. 124, 125.

" In sätzen wie ἐπειδὴ εἶπεν, ἀπῄει; εἰπὼν ταῦτα ἀπῄει; ἐάν τι φάγωσιν, ἀναστήσονται (Xen. An. IV. 5, 8) erschien die syntaktisch untergeordnete aoristische Handlung gegenüber dem anderen Vorgang darum als vergangen, weil die beiden Handlungen sachlich verschieden waren. Das Bedeutungsmoment der ungeteilten Vollständigkeit und Abgeschlossenheit der Handlung liess die Vorstellung, dass die Haupthandlung in den Verlauf der Nebenhandlung hineinfalle und neben ihr hergehe (Gleichzeitigkeit), nicht zu. Die Vorstellung der Vergangenheit in Bezug auf das Hauptverbum war also nicht durch die Aoristform an sich, sondern durch die besondere Natur der beiden Verbalbegriffe, die zu einander in Beziehung gesetzt wurden, gegeben. Man erkennt diesen Sachverhalt am besten durch Vergleichung mit Sätzen wie *E* 98, καὶ βάλ' ἐπαΐσσοντα τυχὼν κατὰ δεξιὸν ὦμον, Herod. 5, 24, εὖ ἐποίησας ἀπικόμενος, Xen. An. I. 3, 17, βουλοίμην δ' ἂν ἄκοντος ἀπιὼν Κύρου λαθεῖν αὐτὸν ἀπελθών, Thuk. 6, 4, ἔτεσι δὲ ἐγγύτατα ὀκτὼ καὶ ἑκατὸν μετὰ τὴν σφετέραν οἴκισιν Γελῷοι 'Ακράγαντα ᾤκισαν, τὴν μὲν πόλιν ἀπὸ τοῦ 'Ακράγοντος ποταμοῦ ὀνομάσαντες, οἰκιστὰς δὲ ποιήσαντες 'Αριστόνουν καὶ Πυστίλον, νόμιμα δὲ τὰ Γελῴων δόντες, wo die Vorstellung einer Zeitverschiedenheit darum nicht entstehen konnte, weil es sich um ein und denselben Vorgang handelte und das Partizip oder die Partizipien nur eine, beziehungsweise mehrere besondere Seiten der Handlung des regierenden Verbums zum Ausdruck brachten." —
Br. 161.

133. The Aorist Participle is used of an action conceived of as a simple event.

It may be used with reference to an action or event in its entirety (indefinite), or with reference to the inception of a state (inceptive), or with reference to the accomplishment of an attempt (resultative). When indefinite it may be used of momentary or extended actions or of a series of events. Cf. 35, and 39, and see examples below.

134. The Aorist Participle of Antecedent Action. The Aorist Participle is most frequently used of an action antecedent in time to the action of the principal verb.

Matt. 4 : 2 ; καὶ νηστεύσας ἡμέρας τεσσεράκοντα καὶ νύκτας τεσσεράκοντα ὕστερον ἐπείνασεν, *and having fasted forty days and forty nights, he afterward hungered.*

Mark 1 : 31 ; ἤγειρεν αὐτὴν κρατήσας τῆς χειρός, *and taking her by the hand he raised her up.*

John 5 : 13 ; ὁ δὲ ἰαθεὶς οὐκ ᾔδει τίς ἐστιν, *but he that had been healed wist not who it was.*

Acts 14 : 19 ; καὶ πείσαντες τοὺς ὄχλους καὶ λιθάσαντες τὸν Παῦλον, ἔσυρον ἔξω τῆς πόλεως, *and having persuaded the multitudes they stoned Paul, and dragged him out of the city.*

Acts 27 : 13 ; δόξαντες τῆς προθέσεως κεκρατηκέναι ἄραντες ἆσσον παρελέγοντο τὴν Κρήτην, *supposing that they had obtained their purpose, they weighed anchor, and sailed along Crete.*

Rom. 5 : 1 ; δικαιωθέντες οὖν ἐκ πίστεως εἰρήνην ἔχωμεν πρὸς τὸν θεόν, *having therefore been justified by faith, let us have peace with God.*

1 Cor. 1 : 4 ; εὐχαριστῶ τῷ θεῷ . . . ἐπὶ τῇ χάριτι τοῦ θεοῦ τῇ δοθείσῃ ὑμῖν, *I thank God . . . for the grace of God which was given you.*

Col. 1 : 3, 4 ; εὐχαριστοῦμεν τῷ θεῷ . . . ἀκούσαντες τὴν πίστιν ὑμῶν, *we give thanks to God . . . having heard of your faith.*

2 Tim. 4 : 11 ; Μάρκον ἀναλαβὼν ἄγε μετὰ σεαυτοῦ, *take Mark and bring him with thee.*

135. The Aorist Participle of Antecedent Action is frequently used attributively as the equivalent of a relative clause ; in this case it usually has the article, and its position is determined by the same considerations which govern the position of any other noun or adjective in similar construction. See John 5 : 13 ; 1 Cor. 1 : 4, above.

136. It is still more frequently used adverbially and is equivalent to an adverbial clause or coördinate verb with *and;* in this case the article does not occur, and the participle usually precedes the verb, but sometimes follows it. See Rom. 5 : 1 ; and Col. 1 : 3, 4 (134).

137. In some instances of the Aorist Participle of Antecedent Action, it is the inception of the action only which precedes the action of the principal verb. And this occurs not only in verbs of state (cf. 35, and see Mark 5 : 33; Acts 23 : 1), but also in verbs of action, which in the Indicative are not inceptive. Acts 27 : 13 (134); 13 : 27; 2 Tim. 4 : 10.

138. The Aorist Participle of Antecedent Action is by no means always best translated into English by the so-called Perfect Participle. The English Present Participle is very frequently placed before a verb to express an antecedent action, and that, too, without implying that the action is thought of as in progress. It is accordingly in many cases the best translation of an Aorist Participle. See Mark 1 : 31 (134); also Mark 5 : 36; Acts 13 : 16, R.V. Frequently also the Aorist Participle of the Greek is best reproduced in English by a finite verb with *and.* See Acts 14 : 19; 27 : 13; 2 Tim. 4 : 11 (134); also Luke 21 : 1; Acts 21 : 1; Acts 10 : 23, R.V.

139. The Aorist Participle of Identical Action. The Aorist Participle agreeing with the subject of a verb not infrequently denotes the same action that is expressed by the verb. *HA.* 856, b; *G.* 1290; *G.*MT. 150.

Matt. 27 : 4; ἥμαρτον παραδοὺς αἷμα δίκαιον, *I sinned in that I betrayed innocent blood.*

Acts 10 : 33; σύ τε καλῶς ἐποίησας παραγενόμενος, *and thou hast well done that thou hast come.* See also Matt. 19 : 27 (and the numerous instances of the phrase ἀποκριθεὶς εἶπεν); Acts 27 : 3; 1 Cor. 15 : 18; Eph. 1 : 9; Heb. 7 : 27; Gen. 43 : 5.

140. The verb and the participle of identical action, though denoting the same action, usually describe it from a different point of view. Respecting this difference in point of view, see 121.

141. An Aorist Participle of Identical Action most frequently accompanies an Aorist verb, both verb and participle thus describing the action indefinitely as a simple event. It occurs also with the Future, with which as an aoristic tense it is entirely appropriate (Luke 9:25; 3 John 6), with the Present and Imperfect (Mark 8:29; Acts 7:26), and with the Perfect (Acts 13:33; 1 Sam. 12:19).

142. The Aorist Participle used attributively as the equivalent of a relative clause sometimes refers to an action subsequent to that of the principal verb, though antecedent to the time of the speaker. Instances occur both in classical Greek (see *G.MT.* 152; *Carter* and *Humphreys* in *Cl. Rev.* Feb. 1891) and in the New Testament.

Acts 1:16; ἣν προεῖπε τὸ πνεῦμα τὸ ἅγιον διὰ στόματος Δαυεὶδ περὶ Ἰούδα τοῦ γενομένου ὁδηγοῦ τοῖς συλλαβοῦσιν Ἰησοῦν, *which the Holy Spirit spake before by the mouth of David concerning Judas who became guide to them that took Jesus.* See also Matt. 10:4; 11:21; John 11:2; Col. 1:8.

143. It should be clearly observed that the participle in these cases does not by its tense denote either antecedence to the time of speaking or subsequence to that of the principal verb. The participle is properly timeless, and the time-relations are learned from the context or outside sources.

144. Whether the Aorist Participle used adverbially, as the equivalent of an adverbial or coördinate clause, ever refers to an action subsequent to that of the principal verb is more difficult to determine. No certain instance has been observed in classical Greek, though several possible ones occur. See

Dem. XIX. (F.L.) 255 (423) cited by *Carter*, and Thuc. II.
49. 2, cited by *Humphreys*, in *Cl. Rev.* Feb. 1891. See also
Hom. Il. E. 369; N. 35, and Pindar, Pyth. IV. 189.

145. The New Testament furnishes one almost indubitable
instance of an Aorist Participle so used if we accept the best
attested text.

Acts 25 : 13, Ἀγρίππας ὁ βασιλεὺς καὶ Βερνίκη κατήντησαν εἰς Καισα-
ρίαν ἀσπασάμενοι τὸν Φῆστον, *Agrippa the King and Bernice arrived
at Cæsarea and saluted Festus.*

The doubt concerning the text rests not on the insufficiency
of the documentary evidence, but on the rarity of this use of
the participle. Cf. *Hort* in *WH.* II. App. p. 100. "The
authority for -άμενοι is absolutely overwhelming, and as a
matter of transmission -όμενοι can only be a correction. Yet
it is difficult to remain satisfied that there is no prior corrup-
tion of some kind." With this case should also be compared
Acts 16 : 23; 22 : 24; 23 : 35; 24 : 23, where the participle,
which is without the article and follows the verb, is most
naturally interpreted as referring to an action subsequent in
thought and fact to that of the verb which it follows, and
equivalent to καί with a coördinate verb. These instances are
perhaps due to Aramaic influence. See *Ka.* § 76. d; and cf.
Dan. 2 : 26, 27; 3 : 13, 24, 26, 27, etc.

In Rom. 4 : 19, καὶ μὴ ἀσθενήσας τῇ πίστει κατενόησεν τὸ ἑαυτοῦ σῶμα
[ἤδη] νενεκρωμένον, the participle ἀσθενήσας, though preceding the verb, is
naturally interpreted as referring to a (conceived) result of the action
denoted by κατενόησεν. It is in that case an inceptive Aorist Participle
denoting a subsequent action. Its position is doubtless due to the
emphasis laid upon it. In Heb. 9 : 12 the symmetry of the figure is best
preserved if εὑράμενος is thought of as referring to an action subsequent to
that of εἰσῆλθεν. But it is possible that εἰσῆλθεν is used to describe the
whole highpriestly act, including both the entrance into the holy place and
the subsequent offering of the blood, and that εὑράμενος is thus a participle
of identical action. In either case it shóuld be translated not *having*

obtained as in R.V., but *obtaining* or *and obtained*. In Phil. 2 : 7 γενόμενος is related to λαβών as a participle of identical action ; the relation of λαβών to ἐκένωσεν is less certain. It may denote the same action as ἐκένωσεν viewed from the opposite point of view (identical action), or may be thought of as an additional fact (subsequent action) to ἐκένωσεν. In Rom. 4 : 21 the participles δούς and πληροφορηθείς may be understood as together defining ἐνεδυναμώθη τῇ πίστει, though δούς is strictly subsequent to ἐνεδυναμώθη. Somewhat similar is 1 Pet. 3 : 18, where ζωοποιηθείς is clearly subsequent to ἀπέθανεν [or ἔπαθεν], but is probably to be taken together with θανατωθείς as defining the whole of the preceding clause Χριστὸς ἅπαξ περὶ ἁμαρτιῶν ἀπέθανεν, δίκαιος ὑπὲρ ἀδίκων, ἵνα ὑμᾶς προσαγάγῃ τῷ θεῷ.

146. The Aorist Participle used as an integral part of the object of a verb of perception represents the action which it denotes as a simple event without defining its time. The action may be one which is directly perceived and hence coincident in time with that of the principal verb, or it may be one which is ascertained or learned, and hence antecedent to the action of the principal verb. In the latter case it takes the place of a clause of indirect discourse having its verb in the Aorist Indicative.

Acts 9 : 12 ; καὶ εἶδεν ἄνδρα . . . Ἀνανίαν ὀνόματι εἰσελθόντα καὶ ἐπιθέντα αὐτῷ χεῖρας, *and he has seen a man named Ananias come in and lay hands upon him.* See also Luke 10 : 18 ; Acts 10 : 3 ; 11 : 3 ; 26 : 13 ; 2 Pet. 1 : 18.

Luke 4 : 23 ; ὅσα ἠκούσαμεν γενόμενα, *whatever things we have heard to have been done.*

147. The Aorist Participle with λανθάνω denotes the same time as the principal verb. It occurs but once in the New Testament (Heb. 13 : 2), the similar construction with φθάνω and τυγχάνω, not at all. *HA.* 856, b ; *G.* 1290.

148. The categories named above, Aorist Participle of Antecedent Action, of Identical Action, etc., which, it must be remembered, represent, not diverse functions of the tense, but only classes of cases for which the Aorist Participle may be used, do not include absolutely all the instances. There are, for example, cases in which the time-relation of the action of the participle to that of the verb is left undefined. John 16 : 2, ὁ ἀποκτείνας [ὑμᾶς] δόξῃ λατρείαν προσφέρειν τῷ θεῷ, means, *every slayer of you will think*, etc. Whether he will have such thought before he shall slay, when he slays, or after he shall have slain, is not at all defined. Cf. Gen. 4 : 15.

149. Very rarely also the Aorist Participle used adverbially refers to an action evidently in a general way coincident in time with the action of the verb, yet not identical with it.

Heb. 2 : 10; ἔπρεπεν γὰρ αὐτῷ, δι' ὃν τὰ πάντα καὶ δι' οὗ τὰ πάντα, πολλοὺς υἱοὺς εἰς δόξαν ἀγαγόντα τὸν ἀρχηγὸν τῆς σωτηρίας αὐτῶν διὰ παθημάτων τελειῶσαι, *for it became him, for whom are all things, and through whom are all things, in bringing many sons unto glory, to make the author of their salvation perfect through sufferings.* The participle ἀγαγόντα is neither antecedent nor subsequent to τελειῶσαι, nor yet strictly identical with it. Nearly the same thought might be expressed in English by *when he brought* or *in bringing*, and in Greek by ὅτε ἤγαγεν or ἐν τῷ ἀγαγεῖν (cf. 109).

The choice of the Aorist Participle rather than the Present in such cases is due to the fact that the action is thought of, not as in progress, but as a simple event or fact. Concerning a similar use of the Aorist Participle in Homer, see *Leo Meyer*, Griechische Aoriste, p. 125; *T. D. Seymour* in *T.A.P.A.*, 1881, pp. 89, 94. The rarity of these instances is due not to any abnormality in such a use of the tense, but to the fact that an action, temporally coincident with another and subordinate to it (and not simply the same action viewed from a different point of view), is naturally thought of as in progress, and hence is expressed by a Present Participle. Cf. exx. under 119.

150. As an aid to interpretation it may be observed that the Aorist Participle with the article may sometimes be used instead of a relative clause with the Aorist Indicative, sometimes instead of such a clause with the verb in the Aorist Subjunctive.[1] But it should not be supposed that from the point of view of the Greek language these were two distinct functions of the Aorist Participle. The phrase ὃς ἔλαβε referred in Greek to past time, ὃς ἂν λάβῃ to present or future time. It is not probable that in the mind of a Greek ὁ λαβών was the precise equivalent of both of these, standing alternately for the one or the other, so that when he wrote ὁ λαβών he sometimes thought ὃς ἔλαβε, sometimes ὃς ἂν λάβῃ. The fact is doubtless rather that the Aorist Participle was always, strictly speaking, timeless, and that ὁ λαβών meant simply *the receiver*, the act of receiving being thought of as a simple fact without reference to progress. Thus for ὁ λαβών in Matt. 25 : 16 ὃς ἔλαβε might have stood, and it may be translated, *he that received;* while for ὁ ὀμόσας in Matt. 23 : 20 ὃς ἂν ὀμόσῃ might have stood, and it may be translated, *whoever sweareth;* and for ὁ ὑπομείνας in Matt. 24 : 13 ὃς ἂν ὑπομείνῃ might have stood, and it may be translated, *whoever shall endure.* Cf. Luke 12 : 8-10. But these differences are due not to a difference in the force of the tense in the three cases. In each case a translation by a timeless verbal noun — *receiver, swearer, endurer* — would correctly (though from the point of view of English rather awkwardly) represent the thought of the Greek. As respects the time-relation of the action of the participle to that of the principal verb ὁ λαβών and ὁ ὑπομείνας are participles of antecedent action, ὁ ὀμόσας is a participle of identical action. But these distinctions, again, as stated above, are made, not to mark different functions of the Greek tense, but to aid in a fuller interpretation of the facts of the case.

151. Some scholars have endeavored to explain all participles with the article as equivalent to the relative pronoun with the corresponding tense of the Indicative. It is true that such participial phrases may often be resolved in this way and the sense essentially preserved. But that this is not a general principle will be evident from a comparison of the function of the tense in the Indicative and in the participle.

(*a*) All the tenses of the Indicative express time-relations from the point of view, not of the principal verb, but of the speaker. This principle holds in a relative clause as well as in a principal sentence. An Aorist verb standing in a relative clause may indeed refer to an action antecedent to the time of the principal verb, but this antecedence is not expressed by the tense of the verb. All that the Aorist tense does in respect to

[1] *W. G. Ballantine*, Attributive Aorist Participles in Protasis, in *Bib. Sac.* Apr. 1889.

time is to place the action in past time ; its relation in that past time to the action of the principal verb must be learned from some other source. The corresponding thing is true of the Present tense, which in a relative clause denotes time not contemporaneous with the action of the principal verb, but present from the point of view of the speaker. See, *e.g.*, Matt. 11 : 4 ; 13 : 17.

(*b*) The participle, on the other hand, is in itself timeless, and gains whatever suggestion of time-relation it conveys from its relation to the rest of the sentence. It is not affirmed that the Aorist Participle denotes time relative to that of the principal verb, but that its time-relations are not independent, like those of the Indicative, but dependent.

It is thus apparent that the whole attitude, so to speak, of the participle toward time-relations is different from that of the Indicative, and no formula of equivalence between them can be constructed. *A timeless noun or adjective cannot by any fixed rule be translated into a time-expressing verb.*

Somewhat less of error is introduced if the rule is made to read that the participle may be translated into English by a relative clause using that tense of the English Indicative which corresponds to the tense of the Greek participle. Relative clauses in English frequently use the tenses apparently to denote time relative to that of the principal verb. Thus in the sentence, *When I am in London I will come to see you*, the present tense, *am*, really denotes time future with reference to the speaker, time present relative to that of the principal verb. Similarly in the sentence, *They that have done good shall come forth to the resurrection of life* — *have done* is past, not with reference to the time of speaking, but to that of the principal verb. But such uses of tenses in English are merely permissible, not uniform. *Shall have done* would be more exact in the last sentence. Moreover, the rule as thus stated is false in principle, and not uniformly applicable in fact. It would require, *e.g.*, that a Present Participle, standing in connection with an Aorist verb, should be rendered by an English Present, instead of by an English Past as it should usually be. See John 2 : 16 ; Acts 10 : 35.

THE FUTURE PARTICIPLE

152. The Future Participle represents an action as future from the point of view of the principal verb. *HA.* 856 ; *G.* 1288.

Acts. 24 : 11 ; οὐ πλείους εἰσίν μοι ἡμέραι δώδεκα ἀφ' ἧς ἀνέβην προσκυνήσων εἰς Ἰερουσαλήμ, *it is not more than twelve days since I went
up to worship at Jerusalem.*

1 Cor. 15 : 37 ; οὐ τὸ σῶμα τὸ γενησόμενον σπείρεις, *thou sowest not the
body that shall be.*

Rem. The Future Participle is of later origin than the participles of
the other tenses, and is a clearly marked exception to the general timelessness of the participle. While its function was probably not primarily
temporal, the relations which it expressed necessarily suggested subsequence to the action of the principal verb, and hence gave to the tense a
temporal force. *Del.* iv. pp. 97 ff. ; *Br.* 163.

153. The Present Participle μέλλων followed by an Infinitive of another verb is used as a periphrasis for a Future
Participle of the latter verb, but with a somewhat different
range of use. To express that which is to take place, either
form may be used. But μέλλων is not used to express the
purpose of an action, and is used, as the Future Participle is
not, to express intention without designating the intended
action as the purpose of another act. See John 12 : 4 (cf. John
6 : 64); Acts 18 : 14; 20 : 3, 7.

THE PERFECT PARTICIPLE

154. The Perfect Participle is used of completed action. Like the Perfect Indicative it may have reference
to the past action and the resulting state or only to the
resulting state. The time of the resulting state is usually
that of the principal verb. *HA.* 856 ; *G.* 1288.

Acts 10 : 17 ; οἱ ἄνδρες οἱ ἀπεσταλμένοι . . . ἐπέστησαν ἐπὶ τὸν πυλῶνα,
the men who had been sent . . . stood before the gate.

Rom. 15 : 14 ; πεπληρωμένοι πάσης τῆς γνώσεως, *filled with all knowledge.*

Luke 8 : 46 ; ἔγνων δύναμιν ἐξεληλυθυῖαν ἀπ' ἐμοῦ, *I perceived that power
had gone forth from me.*

155. The Perfect Participle stands in two passages of the New Testament as the predicate of the participle ὤν. The effect is of a Perfect Participle clearly marked as one of existing state. See Eph. 4 : 18 ; Col. 1 : 21.

156. The Perfect Participle is occasionally used as a Pluperfect to denote a state existing antecedent to the time of the principal verb. The action of which it is the result is, of course, still earlier.

John 11 : 44 ; ἐξῆλθεν ὁ τεθνηκὼς δεδεμένος τοὺς πόδας καὶ τὰς χεῖρας κειρίαις, *he that was* [or *had been*] *dead came forth bound hand and foot with grave-clothes.* See also Mark 5 : 15, ἐσχηκότα, noting the Present Participle in the same verse and the Aorist Participle in v. 18; also 1 Cor. 2 : 7, ἀποκεκρυμμένην, comparing v. 10.

THE MOODS

MOODS IN PRINCIPAL CLAUSES

THE INDICATIVE MOOD

157. The Indicative is primarily the mood of the unqualified assertion or simple question of fact. *HA.* 865;
G. 1317.

John 1 : 1; *ἐν ἀρχῇ ἦν ὁ λόγος, in the beginning was the Word.*
Mark 4 : 7; *καὶ καρπὸν οὐκ ἔδωκεν, and it yielded no fruit.*
Matt. 2 : 2; *ποῦ ἐστιν ὁ τεχθεὶς βασιλεὺς τῶν Ἰουδαίων, where is he
that is born King of the Jews?*
John 1 : 38; *τί ζητεῖτε, what are ye seeking?*

158. The Indicative has substantially the same assertive
force in many principal clauses containing qualified assertions.
The action is conceived of as a fact, though the assertion of
the fact is qualified.

John 13 : 8; *ἐὰν μὴ νίψω σε, οὐκ ἔχεις μέρος μετ᾽ ἐμοῦ, if I wash thee not,
thou hast no part with me.*

159. (a) When qualified by particles such as *ἄν, εἴθε,* etc.,
the Indicative expresses various shades of desirability, improb-
ability, etc. Respecting these secondary uses of the Indicative
in principal clauses, see 26, 27, 248.

(b) Respecting the uses of the Future Indicative in other
than a purely assertive sense, see 67, 69, 70.

73

(c) Respecting the uses of the Indicative in subordinate clauses, see 185–360, *passim*.

REM. The uses of the Indicative described in 157 and 158 are substantially the same in English and in Greek and occasion no special difficulty to the English interpreter of Greek. The uses referred to in 159 exhibit more difference between Greek and English, and each particular usage requires separate consideration.

THE SUBJUNCTIVE MOOD

The uses of the Subjunctive in principal clauses are as follows:

160. The Hortatory Subjunctive. The Subjunctive is used in the first person plural in exhortations, the speaker thus exhorting others to join him in the doing of an action. *HA.* 866, 1; *G.* 1344; *B.* p. 209; *WM.* p. 355; *G.*MT. 255, 256.

Heb. 12 : 1; δι' ὑπομονῆς τρέχωμεν τὸν προκείμενον ἡμῖν ἀγῶνα, *let us run with patience the race that is set before us.*

1 John 4 : 7; ἀγαπητοί, ἀγαπῶμεν ἀλλήλους, *beloved, let us love one another.*

161. Occasionally the first person singular is used with ἄφες or δεῦρο prefixed, the exhortation in that case becoming a request of the speaker to the person addressed to permit him to do something.

Matt. 7 : 4; ἄφες ἐκβάλω τὸ κάρφος ἐκ τοῦ ὀφθαλμοῦ σου, *let me cast out the mote out of thine eye.* See also Luke 6 : 42; Acts 7 : 34.

The sense of ἄφες in Matt. 27 : 49 and of ἄφετε in Mark 15 : 36 is doubtful (see R.V. *ad loc.* and *Th.*, ἀφίημι, 2, E.).

In Matt. 21 : 38 (Mark 12 : 7) δεῦτε is prefixed to a hortatory first person plural without affecting the meaning of the Subjunctive.

In none of these cases is a conjunction to be supplied before the Subjunctive. Cf. the use of ἄγε, φέρε, etc., in classical Greek. *G*.MT. 257; *B*. p. 210; *WM*. p. 356.

162. The Prohibitory Subjunctive. The Aorist Subjunctive is used in the second person with μή to express a prohibition or a negative entreaty. *HA*. 866, 2; *G*. 1346; *G*.MT. 259.

Matt. 6 : 34; μὴ οὖν μεριμνήσητε εἰς τὴν αὔριον, *be not therefore anxious for the morrow.*

Heb. 3 : 8; μὴ σκληρύνητε τὰς καρδίας ὑμῶν, *harden not your hearts.*

Matt. 6 : 13; καὶ μὴ εἰσενέγκῃς ἡμᾶς εἰς πειρασμόν, *and bring us not into temptation.*

163. Prohibitions are expressed either by the Aorist Subjunctive or by the Present Imperative, the only exceptions being a few instances of the third person Aorist Imperative with μή. The difference between an Aorist Subjunctive with μή and a Present Imperative with μή is in the conception of the action as respects its progress. *HA*. 874. Thus

164. (*a*) The Aorist Subjunctive forbids the action as a simple event with reference to the action as a whole or to its inception, and is most frequently used when the action has not been begun.

Acts 18 : 9; λάλει καὶ μὴ σιωπήσῃς, *speak and hold not thy peace.*

Rev. 7 : 3; μὴ ἀδικήσητε τὴν γῆν, *hurt not the earth.*

165. (*b*) The Present Imperative (180–184) forbids the continuance of the action, most frequently when it is already in progress; in this case, it is a demand to desist from the action.

Mark 6 : 50; ἐγώ εἰμι, μὴ φοβεῖσθε, *it is I, be not afraid.*

John 5 : 14; μηκέτι ἁμάρτανε, *sin no more.*

When the action is not yet begun, it enjoins continued abstinence from it.

Mark 13 : 21 ; καὶ τότε ἐάν τις ὑμῖν εἴπῃ ˚Ἴδε ὧδε ὁ χριστός ˚Ἴδε ἐκεῖ, μὴ πιστεύετε, *and then if any man shall say unto you, Lo, here is the Christ; or, Lo, there; believe it not.* Cf. Matt. 24 : 23.

166. The Prohibitory Subjunctive occurs rarely in the third person. 1 Cor. 16 : 11 ; 2 Thess. 2 : 3.

167. The strong negative, οὐ μή, occurs rarely in prohibitions with the Aorist Subjunctive.

Matt. 13 : 14 and Acts 28 : 26, from Septuagint, Isa. 6 : 9, are probably to be understood as prohibitory (as in the Hebrew of the passage in Isa.), rather than emphatically predictive, as in R.V. Cf. Gen. 3 : 1, οὐ μὴ φάγητε, which is clearly prohibitory. *G.*MT. 297. Cf. 162.

In Matt. 21 : 19, on the other hand, the emphatic predictive sense, *there shall be no fruit from thee henceforward forever*, is more probable, being more consistent with general usage and entirely appropriate to the context. The imperative rendering of the R.V. makes the passage doubly exceptional, the Imperative Subjunctive being rare in the third person, and οὐ μή being unusual in prohibitions.

168. **The Deliberative Subjunctive.** The Subjunctive is used in deliberative questions and in rhetorical questions having reference to the future. *HA.* 866, 3 ; *G.* 1358.

Luke 3 : 10 ; τί οὖν ποιήσωμεν, *what then shall we do?*
Luke 11 : 5 ; τίς ἐξ ὑμῶν ἕξει φίλον . . . καὶ εἴπῃ αὐτῷ, *which of you shall have a friend . . . and shall say to him?*

169. Questions may be classified as questions of fact and questions of deliberation. In the question of fact the speaker asks what is (*or* was *or* will be). In the question of deliberation, the speaker asks what he is to do, or what is to be done ; it concerns not fact but possibility, desirability, or necessity. But questions may be classified also as interrogative or real questions, and rhetorical questions. The former makes a real inquiry (for information or advice) ; the latter is a rhetorical substitute for an assertion, often equivalent to a negative answer to itself, or, if the question is negative, to a positive answer.

Since both questions of fact and questions of deliberation may be either interrogative or rhetorical, it results that there are four classes of questions that require to be distinguished for purposes of interpretation.

(a) *The interrogative question of fact.*

Matt. 16 : 13; τίνα λέγουσιν οἱ ἄνθρωποι εἶναι τὸν υἱὸν τοῦ ἀνθρώπου, *who do men say that the Son of man is?* See also Mark 16 : 3; John 7 : 45; Acts 17 : 18.

(b) *The rhetorical question of fact.*

1 Cor. 9 : 1; οὐκ εἰμὶ ἀπόστολος, *am I not an apostle?*

Luke 23 : 31; ὅτι εἰ ἐν ὑγρῷ ξύλῳ ταῦτα ποιοῦσιν, ἐν τῷ ξηρῷ τί γένηται, *for if they do these things in a green tree, what will be done in the dry?* See also Luke 11 : 5; 16 : 11.

(c) *The interrogative deliberative question.*

Mark 12 : 14; δῶμεν, ἢ μὴ δῶμεν, *shall we give, or shall we not give?* See also Matt. 6 : 31; 18 : 21; Luke 22 : 49.

(d) *The rhetorical deliberative question.*

Rom. 10 : 14; πῶς οὖν ἐπικαλέσωνται εἰς ὃν οὐκ ἐπίστευσαν; πῶς δὲ πιστεύσωσιν οὗ οὐκ ἤκουσαν; . . . πῶς δὲ κηρύξωσιν ἐὰν μὴ ἀποσταλῶσιν, *how then shall they call on him in whom they have not believed? how shall they believe in him whom they have not heard? . . . how shall they preach except they be sent?* See also Matt. 26 : 54; Luke 14 : 34; John 6 : 68.

Interrogative questions of fact, and rhetorical questions of fact having reference to the present or past, employ the tenses and moods as they are used in simple declarative sentences. Rhetorical questions of fact having reference to the future, and all deliberative questions, use either the Subjunctive or the Future Indicative.

170. The verb of a deliberative question is most frequently in the first person; but occasionally in the second or third. Matt. 23 : 33; Rom. 10 : 14. The verb of a rhetorical question may be of any person.

171. The Deliberative Subjunctive is sometimes preceded by θέλεις, θέλετε, or βούλεσθε. No conjunction is to be supplied in these cases. The verb θέλειν is sometimes followed by a clause introduced by ἵνα, but ἵνα never occurs when the verb θέλειν is in the second person, and the following verb in the first person, *i.e.* when the relations of the verbs are such as to make a Deliberative Subjunctive probable.

Luke 22 : 9; ποῦ θέλεις ἑτοιμάσωμεν, *where wilt thou that we make ready?* See also Matt. 26 : 17; 27 : 17, 21; Mark 10 : 36, 51; 14 : 12; 15 : 9; Luke 9 : 54; 18 : 41; 1 Cor. 4 : 21 (N.B.), and cf. (ἵνα) Matt. 7 : 12; Mark 6 : 25; Luke 6 : 31; 1 Cor. 14 : 5.

172. The Subjunctive in Negative Assertions. The Aorist Subjunctive is used with οὐ μή in the sense of an emphatic Future Indicative. *HA.* 1032; *G.* 1360.

Heb. 13 : 5; οὐ μή σε ἀνῶ οὐδ' οὐ μή σε ἐγκαταλίπω, *I will in no wise fail thee, neither will I in any wise forsake thee.* See also Matt. 5 : 18; Mark 13 : 30; Luke 9 : 27, *et freq.* Cf. *Gild.* in *A.J.P.* III. 202 f.

REM. In Luke 18 : 7 and Rev. 15 : 4 the Subjunctive with οὐ μή is used in a rhetorical question. The Subjunctive may be explained as occasioned by the emphatic negative or by the rhetorical nature of the question.

173. This emphatically predictive Subjunctive is of frequent occurrence in Hellenistic Greek. The Present Subjunctive is sometimes used with οὐ μή in classical Greek, but no instance occurs in the New Testament. Concerning the rare use of the Future with οὐ μή see 66 ; cf. *Gild.* u.s.

THE OPTATIVE MOOD

174. The Optative Mood is much less frequent in the New Testament, and in Hellenistic writers generally, than in classical Greek. Cf. *Harmon*, The Optative Mood in Hellenistic Greek, in *J.B.L.* Dec. 1886.

It is mainly confined to four uses, two of which are in principal clauses.

175. The Optative of Wishing. The Optative is used without ἄν to express a wish. *HA.* 870 ; *G.* 1507.

1 Pet. 1 : 2 ; χάρις ὑμῖν καὶ εἰρήνη πληθυνθείη, *grace to you and peace be multiplied.*

2 Thess. 3 : 16 ; αὐτὸς δὲ ὁ κύριος τῆς εἰρήνης δῴη ὑμῖν τὴν εἰρήνην, *now the Lord of peace himself give you peace.*

176. The Optative of Wishing occurs thirty-five times in the New Testament: Mark 11 : 14 ; Luke 1 : 38 ; 20 : 16 ; Acts 8 : 20 ; Rom. 3 : 4 ; 3 : 6 ; 3 : 31 ; 6 : 2, 15 ; 7 : 7, 13 ; 9 : 14 ; 11 : 1, 11 ; 15 : 5, 13 ; 1 Cor. 6 : 15 ; Gal. 2 : 17 ; 3 : 21 ; 6 : 14 ; 1 Thess. 3 : 11, 12 ; 5 : 23 ; 2 Thess. 2 : 17 ; 3 : 5, 16 ; 2 Tim. 1 : 16, 18 ; Philem. 20 ; Heb. 13 : 21 ; 1 Pet. 1 : 2 ; 2 Pet. 1 : 2 ; always, except Philem. 20, in the third person singular. It most frequently expresses a prayer. Mark 11 : 14 and Acts 8 : 20 are peculiar in being imprecations of evil.

177. The phrase μὴ γένοιτο is an Optative of Wishing which strongly deprecates something suggested by a previous question or assertion. Fourteen of the fifteen New Testament instances are in Paul's writings, and in twelve of these it expresses the apostle's abhorrence of an inference which he fears may be (falsely) drawn from his argument. Cf. *Mey.* on Rom. 3 : 4, and *Ltft.* on Gal. 2 : 17. On Gal. 6 : 14 cf. 1 Macc. 9 : 10.

178. The Potential Optative. The Optative with ἄν is used to express what would happen on the fulfilment of some supposed condition. It is thus an apodosis correlative to a protasis expressed or implied. It is usually to be translated by the English Potential. *HA.* 872; *G.* 1327 ff.

Acts 8 : 31; πῶς γὰρ ἂν δυναίμην ἐὰν μή τις ὁδηγήσει με, *how should I be able unless some one shall guide me?*
Acts 17 : 18; τί ἂν θέλοι ὁ σπερμολόγος οὗτος λέγειν, *what would this babbler wish to say?*

179. The Optative with ἄν occurs in the New Testament only in Luke's writings: Luke *1 : 62; *6 : 11; *9 : 46; [*15 : 26; 18 : 36]; Acts *5 : 24; †8 : 31; *10 : 17; †17 : 18; [26 : 29]. Of these instances the six marked with * are in indirect questions; the two marked with † are in direct questions; those in brackets are of doubtful text; others still more doubtful might be added. In only one instance (Acts 8 : 31) is the condition expressed.

THE IMPERATIVE MOOD

180. **The Imperative Mood** is used in commands and exhortations. *HA.* 873; *G.* 1342.

Matt. 5 : 42; τῷ αἰτοῦντί σε δός, *give to him that asketh thee.*
1 Thess. 5 : 19; τὸ πνεῦμα μὴ σβέννυτε, *quench not the spirit.*

Rem. Respecting other methods of expressing a command, see 67, 160–167, 364.

181. The Imperative Mood is also used in entreaties and petitions.

Mark 9 : 22; ἀλλ᾽ εἴ τι δύνῃ, βοήθησον ἡμῖν σπλαγχνισθεὶς ἐφ᾽ ἡμᾶς, *but if thou canst do anything, have compassion on us and help us.*
Luke 17 : 5; καὶ εἶπαν οἱ ἀπόστολοι τῷ κυρίῳ Πρόσθες ἡμῖν πίστιν, *and the apostles said to the Lord, Increase our faith.*
John 17 : 11; πάτερ ἅγιε, τήρησον αὐτοὺς ἐν τῷ ὀνόματί σου, *holy Father, keep them in thy name.*

182. The Imperative Mood is also used to express consent, or merely to propose an hypothesis.

Matt. 8:31, 32; οἱ δὲ δαίμονες παρεκάλουν αὐτόν λέγοντες Εἰ ἐκβάλλεις ἡμᾶς, ἀπόστειλον ἡμᾶς εἰς τὴν ἀγέλην τῶν χοίρων. καὶ εἶπεν αὐτοῖς Ὑπάγετε, *and the demons besought him saying, If thou cast us out, send us away into the herd of swine. And he said unto them, Go.*

John 2:19; ἀπεκρίθη Ἰησοῦς καὶ εἶπεν αὐτοῖς Λύσατε τὸν ναὸν τοῦτον καὶ [ἐν] τρισὶν ἡμέραις ἐγερῶ αὐτόν, *Jesus answered and said unto them, Destroy this temple, and in three days I will raise it up.*

1 Cor. 7:36; καὶ (εἰ) οὕτως ὀφείλει γίνεσθαι, ὁ θέλει ποιείτω· οὐχ ἁμαρτάνει· γαμείτωσαν, *and if need so require, let him do what he will; he sinneth not; let them marry.*

183. An Imperative suggesting a hypothesis may or may not retain its imperative or hortatory force.

Luke 6:37; μὴ κρίνετε, καὶ οὐ μὴ κριθῆτε, *judge not, and ye shall not be judged.* Cf. John 2:19, above.

184. Any tense of the Imperative may be used in positive commands, the distinction of force being that of the tenses of the dependent moods in general. Cf. 95 ff. In prohibitions, on the other hand, the use of the Imperative is confined almost entirely to the Present tense. A few instances only of the Aorist occur. Cf. 163.

FINITE MOODS IN SUBORDINATE CLAUSES

185. Many subordinate clauses employ the moods and tenses with the same force that they have in principal clauses. Others, however, give to the mood or tense a force different from that which they usually have in principal clauses. Hence arises the necessity for special treatment of the moods and tenses in subordinate clauses. Principal clauses also require discussion in so far as their mood or tense affects or is affected by the subordinate clauses which limit them.

186. Clauses considered as elements of the sentence may be classified as follows:

I. SUBSTANTIVE

> (1) As subject or predicate nominative (211–214, 357–360).
> (2) As object in indirect discourse (334–356).
> (3) As object after verbs of exhorting, etc. (200–204).
> (4) As object after verbs of striving, etc. (205–210).
> (5) As object after verbs of fear and danger (224–227).

II. ADJECTIVE

> (1) Appositive (211, 213).
> (2) Relative (289–333, in part).
> (3) Definitive (215, 216, in part).

III. ADVERBIAL, denoting

> (1) Time (289–316, in part; 321–333).
> (2) Place (289–316, in part).
> (3) Condition (238–277, 296–315).
> (4) Concession (278–288).
> (5) Cause (228–233, 294).
> (6) Purpose ([188–196], 197–199, 317).
> (7) Indirect object, etc. (215, 217, in part; 318, 319).
> (8) Result (218, 219, 234–237).
> (9) Manner (217, 289–316, in part).
> (10) Comparison, expressing equality or inequality (289–316, in part).

REM. Conditional relative clauses introduced by relative pronouns, and relative clauses denoting cause and purpose introduced in the same way, partake at the same time of the nature of adjective and of adverbial clauses.

187. The arrangement of the matter in the following sections (188–347) is not based upon a logical classification of clauses, such as is indicated in the preceding section, but in part on genetic relationships, and in part on considerations of practical convenience. The following is the general order of treatment:

> Moods in clauses introduced by final particles . .   188–227.
> Moods in clauses of cause   . . . .   228–233.
> Moods in clauses of result . . . .   234–237.

MOODS IN CLAUSES INTRODUCED BY FINAL PARTICLES

188. CLASSIFICATION. Under the general head of clauses introduced by final particles are included in New Testament Greek:

(1) Pure final clauses.

(2) Object clauses after verbs of *exhorting,* etc.

(3) Object clauses after verbs of *striving,* etc.

(4) Object clauses after verbs of *fearing.*

(5) Subject, predicate, and appositive clauses.

(6) Complementary and epexegetic clauses.

(7) Clauses of conceived result.

189. General Usage. The relations expressed by the clauses enumerated in 188 are in classical Greek expressed in various ways, but, in the New Testament, these differences have, by a process of assimilation, to a considerable extent disappeared. Clauses modeled after final clauses take the place of Infinitives in various relations; the Optative disappears from this class of clauses; the distinction between the Subjunctive and the Future Indicative is partially ignored. It results that the seven classes of clauses named above conform in general to one rule, viz.:

Clauses introduced by a final particle usually employ the Subjunctive after both primary and secondary tenses, less frequently the Future Indicative.

REM. Concerning the Present Indicative after ἵνα, see 198, Rem.

190. Final Particles. The New Testament employs as final particles ἵνα, ὅπως, and μή.

REM. The usage of the final particles in classical Greek is elaborately discussed by *Weber* in *Schanz*, Beiträge zur historischen Syntax der griechischen Sprache, Hefte IV., V., and by *Gild.* (on the basis of Weber's work) in *A.J.P.* IV. 416 ff., VI. 53 ff.

191. NEW TESTAMENT USE OF ἵνα. ῞Ινα occurs very frequently in the New Testament, and with a greater variety of usage than in classical Greek. Not only does it assume in part the functions which in classical Greek belonged to the other final particles, but clauses introduced by it encroach largely upon the function of the Infinitive. This extension of the use of ἵνα is one of the notable characteristics of the Greek of the New Testament and of all later Greek. ῞Ινα occurs in the New Testament in

(1) Pure final clauses.
(2) Object clauses after verbs of *exhorting*, etc.
(3) Object clauses after verbs of *striving*, etc.
(4) Subject, predicate, and appositive clauses.
(5) Complementary and epexegetic clauses.
(6) Clauses of conceived result.

Of these clauses, the first class is the only one that regularly employs ἵνα in classical Greek. Cf. *G*.MT. 311.

192. NEW TESTAMENT USE OF ὅπως. ῞Οπως occurs in the New Testament, as in classical Greek, in

(1) Pure final clauses.

(2) Object clauses after verbs of *exhorting,* etc.

(3) Object clauses after verbs of *striving,* etc.   Cf. *G*.MT.
313.

193. New Testament Use of μή.   Μή is used in the New
Testament, as in classical Greek, in

(1) Pure final clauses.

(2) Object clauses after verbs of *striving,* etc.

(3) Object clauses after verbs of *fearing.*   Cf. *G*.MT.
307–310, 339, 352.

194. Ὡς, which occurs as a final particle in classical prose,
appears in a final clause in the New Testament in only one
passage and that of doubtful text, Acts 20 : 24.   Ὄφρα, which
was used as a final particle in epic and lyric poetry, does not
occur in the New Testament.   Cf. *G*.MT. 312, 314.

195. In classical Greek, final clauses and object clauses after verbs
of *striving,* etc., frequently have ὅπως ἄν or ὡς ἄν.   *G*.MT. 328; *Meist.*
p. 212.   According to *Gild.* ἄν gives to the clause, except in the formal
language of inscriptions, a relative or conditional force, ὅπως ἄν being
equivalent to ἤν πως.   *A.J.P.* IV. pp. 422, 425; VI. pp. 53–73; *L. and S.*
ὅπως.   In the New Testament ὅπως ἄν occurs four times (ὅπως alone forty-
nine times), always in a final clause proper.   In Luke 2 : 35 ; Acts 3 : 19 ;
15 : 17 the contingent color may perhaps be detected ; but in Rom. 3 : 4,
quoted from the Septuagint, it is impossible to discover it.

196. Ὅπως after verbs of *fearing,* which is found occasionally in
classical Greek, does not occur in the New Testament.

197. Pure Final Clauses.   A pure final clause is one
whose office is to express the purpose of the action stated
in the predicate which it limits.

In classical Greek, final clauses take the Subjunctive

after primary tenses; after secondary tenses either the
Optative or the Subjunctive. *HA.* 881; *G.* 1365.

In the New Testament, the Optative does not occur.
The Subjunctive is regularly used after primary and secondary tenses alike.

Matt. 7:1; μὴ κρίνετε, ἵνα μὴ κριθῆτε, *judge not, that ye be not judged.*

Rom. 1:11; ἐπιποθῶ γὰρ ἰδεῖν ὑμᾶς, ἵνα τι μεταδῶ χάρισμα ὑμῖν πνευ-
ματικόν, *for I long to see you, that I may impart unto you some spiritual
gift.*

Rom. 9:17; εἰς αὐτὸ τοῦτο ἐξήγειρά σε ὅπως ἐνδείξωμαι ἐν σοὶ τὴν
δύναμίν μου, *for this very purpose did I raise thee up that I might
show in thee my power.*

Acts 28:27; καὶ τοὺς ὀφθαλμοὺς αὐτῶν ἐκκάμμυσαν· μή ποτε ἴδωσιν
τοῖς ὀφθαλμοῖς, *and their eyes they have closed ; lest haply they should
perceive with their eyes.*

198. Pure final clauses occasionally take the Future Indicative in the New Testament as in classical Greek. *HA.* 881, c;
G. 1366; *B.* pp. 234 f.; *WM.* pp. 360 f.; *WT.* pp. 289 f.

Luke 20:10; ἀπέστειλεν πρὸς τοὺς γεωργοὺς δοῦλον, ἵνα . . . δώσουσιν,
he sent to the husbandmen a servant, that they might give. See also 199.

Rem. Some MSS. give a Present Indicative after ἵνα in John 5:20;
Gal. 6:12; **Tit.** 2:4; **Rev.** 12:6; 13:17. In 1 John 5:20 γινώσκομεν is
probably pregnant in force, "that we may know, and whereby we do
know." Ζηλοῦτε in Gal. 4:17, and φυσιοῦσθε in 1 Cor. 4:6 are regarded
by *Hort* (*WH.* II. App. p. 167), *Schmiedel* (*WS.* p. 52), and *Blass*
(Grammatik, p. 207), as Subjunctives. On John 17:3 see 213, Rem.

199. The Future Indicative occurs in pure final clauses in classical
Greek chiefly after ὅπως, rarely after μή, ὡς, and ὄφρα, never after ἵνα.
*G.*MT. 324 ; *Weber*, u.s.; *Gild.* u.s. The New Testament instances are
chiefly after ἵνα ; a few instances occur after μή (μήποτε) and one after ὅπως.
The manuscripts show not a few variations between Subjunctive and Future
Indicative, and both forms are sometimes found together, after the same
conjunction. The following passages contain the Future, or both Future
and Subjunctive : Matt. 7:6 ; 13:15 ; Mark 14:2 ; Luke 14:10 ; 20:10 ;
John 7:3 ; 17:2 ; Acts 21:24 ; 28:27 ; Rom. 3:4 ; Gal. 2:4 ; 1 Pet. 3:1.

200. Object Clauses after Verbs of Exhorting, etc.
In classical Greek, verbs of *exhorting, commanding, entreating*, and *persuading* are sometimes followed by an object clause instead of the more usual Infinitive. Such a clause usually employs ὅπως and the Future Indicative, sometimes the Subjunctive. *G.* 1373; *G.MT.* 355.

In the New Testament, object clauses after such verbs are frequent; they use both ἵνα and ὅπως; and employ the Subjunctive to the exclusion of the Future Indicative.

Mark 5 : 18; παρεκάλει αὐτὸν ὁ δαιμονισθεὶς ἵνα μετ᾽ αὐτοῦ ᾖ, *he who had been possessed with a demon besought him that he might be with him.*
Luke 10 : 2; δεήθητε οὖν τοῦ κυρίου τοῦ θερισμοῦ ὅπως ἐργάτας ἐκβάλῃ εἰς τὸν θερισμὸν αὐτοῦ, *pray ye therefore the Lord of the harvest that he send forth laborers into his harvest.* See also Matt. 4 : 3; 14 : 36; 16 : 20; Acts 23 : 15; 1 Cor. 1 : 10; 2 Cor. 8 : 6; Mark 13 : 18 (cf. Matt. 24 : 20); Luke 22 : 46 (cf. v. 40).

REM. In Eph. 1 : 17 δώῃ (Subjunctive) should be read rather than δῴη (Optative). Cf. 225, Rem. 2.

201. The use of ἵνα in an object clause after a verb of exhorting is almost unknown in classical Greek. *G.*MT. 357. In the New Testament ἵνα occurs much more frequently than ὅπως in such clauses.

202. The regular construction in classical Greek after verbs of *exhorting*, etc., is the Infinitive. This is also in the New Testament the most frequent construction, occurring nearly twice as often as the ἵνα and ὅπως clauses. Κελεύω and the compounds of τάσσω take only the Infinitive. Ἐντέλλομαι employs both constructions.

203. Under the head of verbs of *exhorting*, etc., is to be included the verb θέλω when used with reference to a command or request addressed to another. It is frequently followed by an object clause introduced by ἵνα. Here also belongs the verb εἶπον, used in the sense of *command;* also such phrases as κάμπτω τὰ γόνατα (Eph. 3 : 14), and μνείαν ποιοῦμαι ἐπὶ τῶν προσευχῶν (Eph. 1 : 16 ; Philem. 4 ; cf. Col. 4 : 12), which are paraphrases for προσεύχομαι.

204. In many cases a clause or Infinitive after a verb of *commanding* or *entreating* may be regarded as a command indirectly quoted. It is then a species of indirect discourse, though not usually included under that head. Cf. 337, and *G*.MT. 684. Matt. 16 : 20 ; Mark 9 : 9 ; 13 : 34.

205. Object Clauses after Verbs of Striving, etc. In classical Greek, verbs signifying *to strive for, to take care, to plan, to effect,* are followed by ὅπως with the Future Indicative, less frequently the Subjunctive, after both primary and secondary tenses. *HA.* 885 ; *G.* 1372.

In the New Testament, the Subjunctive occurs more frequently than the Future Indicative, and ἵνα more frequently than ὅπως.

John 12 : 10 ; ἐβουλεύσαντο δὲ οἱ ἀρχιερεῖς ἵνα καὶ τὸν Λάζαρον ἀποκτείνωσιν, *but the chief priests took counsel to put Lazarus also to death.*
Rev. 3 : 9 ; ἰδοὺ ποιήσω αὐτοὺς ἵνα ἥξουσιν καὶ προσκυνήσουσιν ἐνώπιον τῶν ποδῶν σου, καὶ γνῶσιν ὅτι ἐγὼ ἠγάπησά σε, *behold, I will make them to come and worship before thy feet, and to know that I have loved thee.* See also 1 Cor. 16 : 10 ; Col. 4 : 16, 17 ; Rev. 13 : 12, 16.

206. When the object clause after a verb meaning *to care for, to take heed,* is negative, classical Greek sometimes uses μή (instead of ὅπως μή) with the Subjunctive, or less frequently with the Future Indicative. *G.* 1375 ; *G.*MT. 354. This is the common New Testament usage. See Matt. 24 : 4 ; Acts 13 : 40 ; 1 Cor. 8 : 9 ; 10 : 12 ; Gal. 6 : 1 ; Col. 2 : 8 ; 1 Thess. 5 : 15 ; Heb. 3 : 12.

Ὅπως μή with the Future in classical Greek, and ἵνα μή with the Subjunctive in New Testament Greek, also occur. John 11 : 37 ; 2 John 8.

207. ῞Οπως occurs in the New Testament in such clauses (205) only in Matt. 12 : 14 ; 22 : 15 ; Mark 3 : 6, and in all these cases after a phrase meaning *to plan*. The clause thus closely approximates an indirect deliberative question. Cf. Mark 11 : 18. See *Th. ὅπως*, II. 2.

208. The Optative sometimes occurs in classical Greek after a secondary tense of verbs of *striving*, etc., but is not found in the New Testament.

209. It is sometimes difficult to say with certainty whether μή with the Subjunctive after ὅρα or ὁρᾶτε is an objective clause or an independent Prohibitory Subjunctive. In classical Greek the dependent construction was already fully developed (cf. *G.MT.* 354, 307) ; and though in the New Testament ὅρα is sometimes prefixed to the Imperative (Matt. 9 : 30 ; 24 : 6), showing that the paratactic construction is still possible, μή with the Subjunctive in such passages as Matt. 18 : 10 ; 1 Thess. 5 : 15 is best regarded as constituting an object clause.

Μή with the Subjunctive after βλέπω is also probably to be regarded as dependent. It is true that βλέπω does not take an objective clause in classical Greek, that in the New Testament only the Imperative of this verb is followed by a clause defining the action to be done or avoided, and that in a few instances the second verb is an Aorist Subjunctive in the second person with μή, and might therefore be regarded as a Prohibitory Subjunctive (Luke 21 : 8 ; Gal. 5 : 15 ; Heb. 12 : 25). Yet in a larger number of cases the verb is in the third person (Matt. 24 : 4 ; Mark 13 : 5 ; Acts 13 : 40 ; 1 Cor. 8 : 9, etc.), and in at least one instance is introduced by ἵνα (1 Cor. 16 : 10). This indicates that we have not a coördinate imperative expression, but a dependent clause. In Col. 4 : 17 βλέπε, and in 2 John 8 βλέπετε, is followed by ἵνα with the Subjunctive ; the clause in such case being probably objective, but possibly pure final. In Heb. 3 : 12 the Future Indicative with μή is evidently an objective clause.

REM. Concerning Luke 11 : 35, see *B.* p. 243 ; *WM.* p. 374, foot-note, and p. 631 ; *WT.* p. 503 ; *Th. μή*, III. 2 ; R.V. *ad loc.*

210. Verbs of *striving*, etc., may also take the Infinitive as object. With Matt. 26 : 4, and John 11 : 53, cf. Acts 9 : 23 ; with Rev. 13 : 12 cf. 13 : 13.

The verbs ζητέω and ἀφίημι, which are usually followed by

an Infinitive, are each followed in one instance by ἵνα with the Subjunctive. See Mark 11 : 16; 1 Cor. 14 : 12; cf. also 1 Cor. 4 : 2.

211. Subject, Predicate, and Appositive Clauses introduced by ἵνα. Clauses introduced by ἵνα are frequently used in the New Testament as subject, predicate, or appositive, with a force closely akin to that of an Infinitive. The verb is usually in the Subjunctive, less frequently in the Future Indicative.

These clauses may be further classified as follows :

212. (*a*) Subject of the passive of verbs of *exhorting, striving*, etc., which in the active take such a clause as object, and of other verbs of somewhat similar force.   Cf. 200, 205.

1 Cor. 4 : 2 ; ζητεῖται ἐν τοῖς οἰκονόμοις ἵνα πιστός τις εὑρεθῇ, *it is required in stewards that a man be found faithful.*

Rev. 9 : 4 ; καὶ ἐρρέθη αὐταῖς ἵνα μὴ ἀδικήσουσιν τὸν χόρτον τῆς γῆς, *and it was said unto them that they should not hurt the grass of the earth.*   See also Mark 9 : 12 (γέγραπται implies command or will); Rev. 9 : 5.

213. (*b*) Subject, Predicate, or Appositive with nouns of various significance, especially such as are cognate with the verbs which take such a clause as object, and with pronouns, the clause constituting a definition of the content of the noun or pronoun.

John 4 : 34 ; ἐμὸν βρῶμά ἐστιν ἵνα ποιήσω τὸ θέλημα τοῦ πέμψαντός με καὶ τελειώσω τὸ ἔργον αὐτοῦ, *my meat is to do the will of him that sent me and to accomplish his work.*

John 15 : 12 ; αὕτη ἐστὶν ἡ ἐντολὴ ἡ ἐμή, ἵνα ἀγαπᾶτε ἀλλήλους, *this is my commandment, that ye love one another.*   See also Luke 1 : 43; John 6 : 29, 39, 40 ; 15 : 8, 13; 18 : 39; 1 Cor. 9 : 18; 1 John 3 : 1; 2 John 6 ; 3 John 4.

REM. The Present Indicative occurs in MSS. of John 17:3 and is adopted by *Tisch.* and *Treg.* (*text*).

214. (*c*) SUBJECT of phrases signifying *it is profitable, it is sufficient,* etc.

Matt. 10:25; ἀρκετὸν τῷ μαθητῇ ἵνα γένηται ὡς ὁ διδάσκαλος αὐτοῦ, *it is enough for the disciple that he be as his master.* See also Matt. 5:29, 30; 18:6; Luke 17:2; John 11:50; 16:7; 1 Cor. 4:3.

215. Complementary and Epexegetic Clauses introduced by ἵνα. Clauses introduced by ἵνα are used in the New Testament to express a complementary or epexegetic limitation, with a force closely akin to that of an Infinitive. The verb of the clause is usually in the Subjunctive, sometimes in the Future Indicative.

These clauses may be classified as follows:

216. (*a*) Complementary limitation of nouns and adjectives signifying *authority, power, fitness, need, set time,* etc.

Mark 11:28; ἢ τίς σοι ἔδωκεν τὴν ἐξουσίαν ταύτην ἵνα ταῦτα ποιῇς, *or who gave thee this authority to do these things?*
John 12:23; ἐλήλυθεν ἡ ὥρα ἵνα δοξασθῇ ὁ υἱὸς τοῦ ἀνθρώπου, *the hour is come that the Son of man should be glorified.* See also Matt. 8:8; Luke 7:6; John 1:27; 2:25; 16:2, 32; 1 John 2:27; Rev. 21:23.

217. (*b*) Complementary or epexegetic limitation of verbs of various significance; the clause defines the content, ground, or method of the action denoted by the verb, or constitutes an indirect object of the verb.

John 8:56; Ἀβραὰμ ὁ πατὴρ ὑμῶν ἠγαλλιάσατο ἵνα ἴδῃ τὴν ἡμέραν τὴν ἐμήν, *your father Abraham rejoiced to see my day.*

Phil. 2 : 2 ; πληρώσατέ μου τὴν χαρὰν ἵνα τὸ αὐτὸ φρονῆτε, *fulfil ye
my joy, that ye be of the same mind.* (See an Infinitive similarly
used in Acts 15 : 10.) See also John 9 : 22; Gal. 2 : 9 ; in both
these latter passages the ἵνα clause defines the content of the agreement mentioned in the preceding portion of the sentence. See also
John 5 : 7. Cf. Martyr. Polyc. 10. 1.

218. Clauses of Conceived Result introduced by ἵνα.
Clauses introduced by ἵνα are used in the New Testament
to express the conceived result of an action.

John 9 : 2 ; τίς ἥμαρτεν, οὗτος ἢ οἱ γονεῖς αὐτοῦ, ἵνα τυφλὸς γεννηθῇ,
who did sin, this man or his parents, that he should be born blind ?
1 Thess. 5 : 4 ; ὑμεῖς δέ, ἀδελφοί, οὐκ ἐστὲ ἐν σκότει, ἵνα ἡ ἡμέρα
ὑμᾶς ὡς κλέπτας καταλάβῃ, *but ye, brethren, are not in darkness, that
that day should overtake you as thieves.* See also 1 John 1 : 9 (cf.
Heb. 6 : 10 — Infinitive in similar construction) ; 2 Cor. 1 : 17 ; Rev.
9 : 20 (cf. Matt. 21 : 32); 14 : 13; 22 : 14.

219. The relation of thought between the fact expressed in
the principal clause and that expressed in the clause of conceived result introduced by ἵνα is that of cause and effect, but
it is recognized by the speaker that this relation is one of
theory or inference rather than of observed fact. In some
cases the effect is actual and observed, the cause is inferred.
So, *e.g.*, John 9 : 2. In other cases the cause is observed, the
effect is inferred. So, *e.g.*, 1 Thess. 5 : 4. In all the cases the
action of the principal clause is regarded as the necessary condition of that of the subordinate clause, the action of the subordinate clause as the result which is to be expected to follow
from that of the principal clause.

It is worthy of notice that in English the form of expression which ordinarily expresses pure purpose most distinctly
may also be used to express this relation of conceived result.
We say, *He must have suffered very severe losses in order to be
so reduced in circumstances.* Such forms of expression are

probably the product of false analogy, arising from imitation of a construction which really expresses purpose. Thus in the sentence, *He labored diligently in order to accumulate property,* the subordinate clause expresses pure purpose. In the sentence, *He must have labored diligently in order to accumulate such a property,* the sentence may be so conceived that the subordinate clause would express purpose, but it would usually mean rather that if he accumulated such a property he must have labored diligently; that is, the property is conceived of as a result the existence of which proves diligent labor. This becomes still more evident if we say, *He must have labored diligently to have accumulated such a property.* But when we say, *He must have suffered severe losses to have become so reduced in circumstances,* it is evident that the idea of purpose has entirely disappeared, and only that of inferred result remains. Actual result observed to be the effect of observed causes is not, however, thus expressed except by a rhetorical figure. With these illustrations from the English, compare the following from the Greek. Jas. 1 : 4; ἡ δὲ ὑπομονὴ ἔργον τέλειον ἐχέτω, ἵνα ἦτε τέλειοι καὶ ὁλόκληροι, *and let patience have its perfect work, that ye may be perfect and entire.* Heb. 10 : 36; ὑπομονῆς γὰρ ἔχετε χρείαν ἵνα τὸ θέλημα τοῦ θεοῦ ποιήσαντες κομίσησθε τὴν ἐπαγγελίαν, *for ye have need of patience, that, having done the will of God, ye may receive the promise.* In the first sentence the ἵνα clause expresses the purpose of ἐχέτω. In the second, though the purpose of ὑπομονή is contained in the clause ἵνα . . . ἐπαγγελίαν, yet the function of this clause in the sentence is not telic. Its office is not to express the purpose of the principal clause, but to set forth a result (conceived, not actual) of which the possession of ὑπομονή is the necessary condition. In John 9 : 2 the idiom is developed a step further, for in this case the ἵνα clause in no sense expresses the purpose of the action of the principal clause, but a fact conceived to be the result of a cause concerning which the principal clause makes inquiry.

This use of ἵνα with the Subjunctive is closely akin in force to the normal force of ὥστε with the Infinitive. Cf. 370, c, and especially *G*.MT. 582–584.

220. Some of the instances under 215–217 might be considered as expressing conceived result, but the idiom has developed beyond the point of conceived result, the clause becoming a mere complementary limitation. The possible course of development may perhaps be suggested by examining the following illustrations: John 17 : 2 ; Mark 11 : 28 ; Luke 7 : 6 ; 1 John 2 : 27. In the first case the clause probably expresses pure purpose. In the last the idea of purpose has altogether disappeared.

221. In all these constructions, 211–218, which are distinct departures from classical usage, being later invasions of the ἵνα clause upon the domain occupied in classical Greek by the Infinitive, the Infinitive remains also in use in the New Testament, being indeed in most of these constructions more frequent than the ἵνα clause.

222. There is no certain, scarcely a probable, instance in the New Testament of a clause introduced by ἵνα denoting actual result conceived of as such.

Luke 9 : 45 probably expresses pure purpose (cf. Matt. 11 : 25 ; *WM*. p. 574 ; *WT*. p. 459). Gal. 5 : 17 is also best explained as expressing the purpose of the hostility of the flesh and the Spirit, viewed, so far as the ἵνα clause is concerned, as a hostility of the flesh to the Spirit. So, apparently, R.V. Rev. 13 : 13 is the most probable instance of ἵνα denoting actual result ; ἵνα . . . ποιῇ is probably equivalent to ὥστε ποιεῖν, and is epexegetic of μεγάλα. It would be best translated, *so as even to make.*

Respecting ἵνα πληρωθῇ, Matt. 1 : 22 and frequently in the first gospel, there is no room for doubt. The writer of the first gospel never uses ἵνα to express result, either actual or conceived ; and that he by this phrase at least intends to express purpose is made especially clear by his employment of ὅπως (which is never ecbatic) interchangeably with ἵνα. With 1 : 22 ; 2 : 15 ; 4 : 14 ; 12 : 17 ; 21 : 4 ; 26 : 56, cf. 2 : 23 ; 8 : 17 ; 13 : 35.

223. Concerning the post-classical usage of ἵνα in general see *Jebb* in *Vincent and Dickson*, Modern Greek, pp. 319–321. Concerning whether ἵνα in the New Testament is always in the strict sense telic, and whether it is ever ecbatic (two distinct questions not always clearly distinguished), see *Meyer* on Matt. 1 : 22 : "῝Ινα ist niemals ἐκβατικόν, *so dass*, sondern immer τελικόν, *damit*," — the first half of which is true, the second half far from true. *Fritzsche* on Matt. pp. 836 ff.; *WT.* pp. 457–462 ; *WM.* pp. 573–578 ; *B.* pp. 235–240 : " And although it [ἵνα] never stands in the strict ecbatic sense (for ὥστε with the finite verb), it has nevertheless here reached the very boundary line where the difference between the two relations (the telic and the ecbatic) disappears, and it is nearer to the ecbatic sense than to its original final sense. Necessary as the demand is, that in a systematic inquiry into the use of the particle, even within a comparatively restricted field, we should always make its original telic force, which is the only force it has in earlier Greek writers, our point of departure, and trace out thence the transitions to its diverse shades of meaning ; the interests of exegesis would gain very little, if in every individual passage of the N.T. even (the language of which has already departed so far from original classic Greek usage) we should still take pains, at the cost of the simple and natural sense, and by a recourse to artificial means, always to introduce the telic force," p. 239. *Hunzinger,* " Die in der klassischen Gräcität nicht gebräuchliche finale Bedeutung der Partikel ἵνα im neutestamentlichen Sprachgebrauch," in *Zeitschrift für Kirchliche Wissenschaft,* 1883, pp. 632–643 — a valuable article which elaborately disproves its own conclusion — " dass ἵνα im N.T. in allen Fällen final verstanden werden kann," unless a very broad and loose sense be given to the term *final.*

224. Object Clauses after Verbs of Fear and Danger.

In classical Greek, clauses after verbs of *fear* and *danger* employ μή with the Subjunctive after primary tenses ; the Optative, more rarely the Subjunctive, after secondary tenses. *HA.* 887 ; *G.* 1378.

In the New Testament the Subjunctive only is used.

2 Cor. 12 : 20 ; φοβοῦμαι γὰρ μή πως ἐλθὼν οὐχ οἵους θέλω εὕρω ὑμᾶς, *for I fear, lest by any means, when I come, I shall find you not such as I would.* See also Acts 23 : 10; 27 : 29; 2 Cor. 11 : 3; Heb. 4 : 1.

REM. 1. Acts 5 : 26 may be understood as in R.V., τὸν λαόν denoting the persons feared, and μὴ λιθασθῶσιν the thing feared (cf. the familiar

96 THE MOODS

idiom with οἶδα illustrated in Mark 1 : 24 ; see also Gal. 4 : 11), so that the
meaning would be expressed in English by translating, *for they were
afraid that they should be stoned by the people;* or ἐφοβοῦντο . . . λαόν may
be taken as parenthetical, and μὴ λιθασθῶσιν made to limit ἦγεν αὐτούς,
οὐ μετὰ βίας; so *Tisch.* and *WH.*

REM. 2. Some MSS. and editors read a Future Indicative in 2 Cor.
12 : 21.

225. The verb of *fearing* is sometimes unexpressed, the idea
of fear being suggested by the context; so, it may be, in Acts
5 : 39, and Matt. 25 : 9.

REM. 1. 2 Tim. 2 : 25, μή ποτε δώῃ αὐτοῖς ὁ θεὸς μετάνοιαν is probably
best explained in the same way. For the gentleness and meekness in
dealing with those that oppose themselves, which he has enjoined, the
apostle adds the argument, [*fearing*] *lest God may perchance grant them
repentance*, i.e. *lest on the assumption that they are past repentance you
be found dealing in harshness with those to whom God will yet grant
repentance.*

REM. 2. Δώῃ (Subjunctive) is to be preferred to δώῃ (Optative) in
this passage as in Eph. 1 : 17. See the evidence in *WS.* p. 120 that this
form occurs as a Subjunctive not only in the Old Ionic language, but in
inscriptions of the second century B.C. Cf. *WH.* II. App. p. 168.

226. It is evident tnat object clauses after verbs of *fear* are closely
akin to negative object clauses after verbs signifying *to care for*. *G.*MT.
354. Some of the instances cited under 206 might not inappropriately be
placed under 224. On the probable common origin of both, and their
development from the original parataxis, see *G.*MT. 307, 352.

227. When thè object of apprehension is conceived of as
already present or past, *i.e.* as a thing already decided, although the issue is at the time of speaking unknown, the Indicative is used both in classical and New Testament Greek.
HA. 888; *G.* 1380.

Gal. 4 : 11; φοβοῦμαι ὑμᾶς μή πως εἰκῇ κεκοπίακα εἰς ὑμᾶς, *I am afraid
I have perhaps bestowed labor upon you in vain.* See also Gal. 2 : 2;
1 Thess. 3 : 5; Gen. 43 : 11.

MOODS IN CLAUSES OF CAUSE

228. A causal clause is one which gives either the cause or the reason of the fact stated in the principal clause. Causal clauses are introduced by ὅτι, διότι, ἐπεί, ἐπειδή, ἐπειδήπερ, ἐφ' ᾧ, etc. *HA*. 925; *G*. 1505.

229. Moods and Tenses in Causal Clauses. The moods and tenses are used in causal clauses with the same force as in principal clauses.

John 14 : 19 ; ὅτι ἐγὼ ζῶ καὶ ὑμεῖς ζήσετε, *because I live, ye shall live also*. 1 Cor. 14 : 12 ; ἐπεὶ ζηλωταί ἐστε πνευμάτων, πρὸς τὴν οἰκοδομὴν τῆς ἐκκλησίας ζητεῖτε ἵνα περισσεύητε, *since ye are zealous of spiritual gifts, seek that ye may abound unto the edifying of the church*. See also Luke 1 : 1 ; Acts 15 : 24 ; Rom. 5 : 12.

230. From the significance of a causal clause it naturally results that its verb is usually an Indicative affirming a fact. Any form, however, which expresses or implies either qualified or unqualified assertion may stand after a causal conjunction. Thus we find, *e.g.*, a rhetorical question, or an apodosis of a conditional sentence. In the latter case the protasis may be omitted. In the following instances all three of these phenomena coincide ; the causal clause is an apodosis, its protasis is omitted, it is expressed in the form of a rhetorical question.

1 Cor. 15 : 29 ; ἐπεὶ τί ποιήσουσιν οἱ βαπτιζόμενοι ὑπὲρ τῶν νεκρῶν, *else what shall they do which are baptized for the dead?* i.e., *since* [*if the dead are not raised*] *they that are baptized for the dead are baptized to no purpose.*
Heb. 10 : 2 ; ἐπεὶ οὐκ ἂν ἐπαύσαντο προσφερόμεναι, *else would they not have ceased to be offered?* i.e., *since* [*if what was said above were not true*] *they would have ceased to be offered.* Cf. also Acts 5 : 38.

231. From the nature of the causal clause as making an assertion, it results that it is easily disjoined from the clause which states the fact of which it gives the cause or reason, and becomes an independent sentence.

Matt. 6 : 5 ; καὶ ὅταν προσεύχησθε, οὐκ ἔσεσθε ὡς οἱ ὑποκριταί· ὅτι φιλοῦσιν ἐν ταῖς συναγωγαῖς καὶ ἐν ταῖς γωνίαις τῶν πλατειῶν ἑστῶτες προσεύχεσθαι, *and when ye pray, ye shall not be as the hypocrites: because they love to stand and pray in the synagogues and in the corners of the streets* (cf. 6 : 16, where in a closely similar sentence, γάρ is used instead of ὅτι). See also Luke 11 : 32; 1 Cor. 1 : 22, and cf. v. 21, where the same conjunction ἐπειδή introduces a subordinate clause.

232. The distinction between a subordinate causal clause and an independent sentence affirming a cause or reason is usually one of the degree of emphasis on the causal relation between the two facts. When the chief thing asserted is the existence of the causal relation, as happens, *e.g.*, when one fact or the other is already present as a fact before the mind, the causal clause is manifestly subordinate. When the emphasis is upon the separate assertions as assertions, rather than on the *relation* of the facts asserted, the causal clause easily becomes an independent sentence. Thus in Rev. 3 : 16, *because thou art lukewarm, and neither hot nor cold, I will spew thee out of my mouth*, the causal clause is subordinate. So also in John 16 : 3, *and these things they will do, because they have not known the Father nor me*, where the words *these things* refer to an assertion already made, and the intent of the sentence is to state *why* they will do these things. See also John 20 : 29. On the other hand, in Matt. 6 : 5 ; Luke 11 : 32 ; 1 Cor. 1 : 22 (see 231) ; and in 1 Cor. 15 : 29 ; Heb. 10 : 2 (see 230), the casual clause is evidently independent, and the particles ὅτι, ἐπεί, ἐπειδή have substantially the force of γάρ.

233. Causal relations may also be expressed by a relative clause (294), by an Infinitive with the article governed by διά (408), and by a participle (439).

MOODS IN CLAUSES OF RESULT

234. A consecutive clause is one which expresses the result, actual or potential, of the action stated in the principal clause or a preceding sentence.

In the New Testament consecutive clauses are introduced by ὥστε. *HA.* 927; *G.* 1449.

235. A consecutive clause commonly takes either the Indicative or the Infinitive. The Indicative properly expresses the actual result produced by the action previously mentioned, the Infinitive the result which the action of the principal verb tends or is calculated to produce. Since, however, an actual result may always be conceived of as that which the cause in question is calculated or adapted to produce, the Infinitive may be used when the result is obviously actual. Thus if senselessness tends to credulity, one may say οὕτως ἀνόητοί ἐστε ὥστε τὸ ἀδύνατον πιστεύετε or οὕτως ἀνόητοί ἐστε ὥστε τὸ ἀδύνατον πιστεύειν, with little difference of meaning, though strictly the latter represents believing the impossible simply as the measure of the folly, while the former represents it as the actual result of such folly. *G.MT.* 582, 583; *HA.* 927; *G.* 1450, 1451.

The use of the Infinitive is the older idiom. Attic writers show on the whole a tendency to an increased use of the Indicative, Aristophanes and Xenophon, *e.g.*, using it more frequently than the Infinitive. See *Gild. A.J.P.* vii. 161–175 ; xiv. 240–242. But in the New Testament the Infinitive greatly predominates, occurring fifty times as against twenty-one instances of the Indicative, but one of which is in a clause clearly subordinate.

On ὥστε introducing a principal clause see 237. On different conceptions of result, and the use of the Infinitive to express result, see 369–371.

236. The Indicative with ὥστε **expresses actual result.**

John 3 : 16 ; οὕτως γὰρ ἠγάπησεν ὁ θεὸς τὸν κόσμον ὥστε τὸν υἱὸν τὸν μονογενῆ ἔδωκεν, *for God so loved the world that he gave his only begotten Son.*

Rᴇᴍ. With John 3 : 16, which is the only clear instance in the New Testament of ὥστε with the Indicative so closely joined to what precedes as to constitute a subordinate clause, is usually reckoned also Gal. 2 : 13.

237. The clause introduced by ὥστε is sometimes so disjoined from the antecedent sentence expressing the causal fact that it becomes an independent sentence. In such cases ὥστε has the meaning *therefore,* or *accordingly,* and the verb introduced by it may be in any form capable of standing in a principal clause. *HA.* 927, a ; *G.* 1454.

Mark 2 : 28; ὥστε κύριός ἐστιν ὁ υἱὸς τοῦ ἀνθρώπου καὶ τοῦ σαββάτου, *so that the Son of man is lord even of the sabbath.*
1 Cor. 5 : 8; ὥστε ἑορτάζωμεν, *wherefore let us keep the feast.*
1 Thess. 4 : 18; ὥστε παρακαλεῖτε ἀλλήλους ἐν τοῖς λόγοις τούτοις, *wherefore comfort one another with these words.*

MOODS IN CONDITIONAL SENTENCES

238. A conditional sentence consists of a subordinate clause which states a supposition, and a principal clause which states a conclusion conditioned on the fulfilment of the supposition stated in the subordinate clause. The conditional clause is called the protasis. The principal clause is called the apodosis.

239. Suppositions are either particular or general. When the protasis supposes a certain definite event and the apodosis conditions its assertion on the occurrence of this event, the supposition is particular. When the protasis supposes any occurrence of an act of a certain class, and the apodosis states what is or was wont to take place in any instance of an act of the class supposed in the protasis, the supposition is general.

Thus in the sentence, *If he believes this act to be wrong, he will not do it,* the supposition is particular. But in the sentence, *If [in any instance] he believes an act to be wrong, he does not [is not wont to] do it,* the supposition is general. In the sentence, *If he has read this book, he will be able to tell what it contains*, the supposition is particular. But in the sentence, *If he read a book, he could always tell what it contained*, the supposition is general.

240. It should be noted that the occurrence of an indefinite pronoun in the protasis does not necessarily make the supposition general. If the writer, though using an indefinite term, refers to a particular instance, and in the apodosis states what happened, is happening, or will happen in this case, the supposition is particular. If, on the other hand, the supposition refers to any instance of the class of cases described, and the apodosis states what is or was *wont* to happen in any such instance, the supposition is general. Thus, in the sentence, *If any one has eaten any of the food, he is by this time dead*, the supposition is particular. In the sentence, *If any one* [*in any instance*] *ate any of the food,* [*it was wont to happen that*] *he died*, the supposition is general. In 2 Cor. 2 : 5, *but if any one hath caused sorrow, he hath caused sorrow not to me, but . . . to you all*, the supposition refers to a specific case, and is particular. Even the mental selection of one of many possible instances suffices to make a supposition particular. So in 1 Cor. 3 : 12, it is probable that we ought to read, *if any man is building*, and in 3 : 17, *if any man is destroying*, and take the clauses as referring to what was then, hypothetically, going on rather than to what might at any time occur. On the other hand, in John 11 : 9, *if a man walk in the day, he stumbleth not*, the supposition refers to any instance of walking in the day, and is general.

Concerning a protasis which refers to the truth of a general principle as such, see 243.

241. Of the six classes of conditional sentences which are found in classical Greek, five occur in the New Testament, not however without occasional variations of form.

Rem. 1. The classification of conditional sentences here followed is substantially that of Professor Goodwin. The numbering of the Present General Suppositions and Past General Suppositions as fifth and sixth classes respectively, instead of including them as subdivisions under the first class, is adopted to facilitate reference.

Rem. 2. It should be observed that the titles of the several classes of conditional sentences describe the suppositions not from the point of view of fact, but from that of the representation of the case to the speaker's own mind or to that of his hearer. Cf., *e.g.*, Luke 7 : 39 ; John 18 : 30.

242. A. Simple Present or Past Particular Supposition. The protasis *simply states* a supposition which refers to a particular case in the present or past, implying nothing as to its fulfilment.

The protasis is expressed by εἰ with a present or past tense of the Indicative; any form of the finite verb may stand in the apodosis. *HA.* 893; *G.* 1390.

John 15 : 20; εἰ ἐμὲ ἐδίωξαν, καὶ ὑμᾶς διώξουσιν, *if they have persecuted me, they will also persecute you.*

Gal. 5 : 18; εἰ δὲ πνεύματι ἄγεσθε, οὐκ ἐστὲ ὑπὸ νόμον, *but if ye are led by the Spirit, ye are not under the law.* See also Matt. 4 : 3; Luke 16 : 11; Acts 5 : 39; Rom. 4 : 2; 8 : 10; Gal. 2 : 17; Rev. 20 : 15.

REM. Concerning the use of the negatives μή and οὐ in the protasis of conditional sentences of this class, see 469, 470.

243. When a supposition refers to the truth of a general principle as such, and the apodosis conditions its assertion on the truth of this principle, not on the occurrence of any instance of a supposed class of events, the supposition is particular. It is expressed in Greek by εἰ with the Indicative, and the sentence belongs to the first class.

Matt. 19 : 10; εἰ οὕτως ἐστὶν ἡ αἰτία τοῦ ἀνθρώπου μετὰ τῆς γυναικός, οὐ συμφέρει γαμῆσαι, *if the case of the man is so with his wife, it is not expedient to marry.* See also Matt. 6 : 30; Gal. 2 : 21; cf. Plat. Prot. 340, C. In Rom. 4 : 14; 8 : 17; 11 : 6, the verb is omitted. The use of εἰ and the nature of the sentence, however, easily suggest what form of the verb would be required if it were expressed.

244. Conditional clauses of the first class are frequently used when the condition is fulfilled, and the use of the hypothetical form suggests no doubt of the fact. This fact of fulfilment lies, however, not in the conditional sentence, but in the context. John 3 : 12; 7 : 23; Rom. 5 : 10.

245. On the other hand, conditional clauses of the first class may be used of what is regarded by the speaker as an unfulfilled condition. But this also is not expressed or implied by the form of the sentence, which is in itself wholly colorless, suggesting nothing as to the fulfilment of the condition. Luke 23 : 35, 37 ; John 18 : 23 ; Rom. 4 : 2 ; Gal. 5 : 11.

246. Even a Future Indicative may stand in the protasis of a conditional sentence of the first class when reference is had to a present necessity or intention, or when the writer desires to state not what will take place on the fulfilment of a future possibility, but merely to affirm a necessary logical consequence of a future event. 1 Cor. 9 : 11. Cf. *G*.MT. 407.

247. In a few instances ἐάν is used with the Present Indicative in the protasis of a conditional sentence, apparently to express a simple present supposition. 1 Thess. 3 : 8; 1 John 5 : 15.

248. B. Supposition contrary to Fact. The protasis states a supposition which refers to the present or past, implying that it is not or was not fulfilled.

The protasis is expressed by εἰ with a past tense of the Indicative ; the apodosis by a past tense of the Indicative with ἄν. *HA.* 895; *G.* 1397.

The Imperfect denotes continued action; the Aorist a simple fact; the Pluperfect completed action. The time is implied in the context, not expressed by the verb.

John 11 : 21 ; Κύριε, εἰ ἦς ὧδε οὐκ ἂν ἀπέθανεν ὁ ἀδελφός μου, *Lord, if thou hadst been here, my brother would not have died.*
Gal. 1 : 10 ; εἰ ἔτι ἀνθρώποις ἤρεσκον, Χριστοῦ δοῦλος οὐκ ἂν ἤμην, *if I were still pleasing men, I should not be a servant of Christ.* See also John 14 : 28; Acts 18 : 14; Heb. 4 : 8; 11 : 15.

249. Ἄν is sometimes omitted from the apodosis. Cf. 30.
B. pp. 216 f., 225 f.; *WM.* pp. 382 f.; *WT.* pp. 305 f.; cf. *G.*MT.
pp. 415 ff., esp. 422, 423.

John 9 : 33 ; εἰ μὴ ἦν οὗτος παρὰ θεοῦ, οὐκ ἠδύνατο ποιεῖν οὐδέν, *if this
man were not from God, he could do nothing.* See also Matt. 26 : 24;
John 15 : 22; 19 : 11; 1 Cor. 5 : 10; Gal. 4 : 15; Heb. 9 : 26.

250. C. **Future Supposition with More Probability.**
The protasis states a supposition which refers to the
future, suggesting some probability of its fulfilment.

The protasis is usually expressed by ἐάν (or ἄν) with
the Subjunctive; the apodosis by the Future Indicative or
by some other form referring to future time. *HA.* 898;
G. 1403.

Matt. 9 : 21; ἐὰν μόνον ἅψωμαι τοῦ ἱματίου αὐτοῦ σωθήσομαι, *if I shall
but touch his garments, I shall be made whole.*
John 12 : 26; ἐάν τις ἐμοὶ διακονῇ τιμήσει αὐτὸν ὁ πατήρ, *if any man
serve me, him will the Father honor.*
John 14 : 15; ἐὰν ἀγαπᾶτέ με, τὰς ἐντολὰς τὰς ἐμὰς τηρήσετε, *if ye love
me, ye will keep my commandments.* See also Matt. 5 : 20; 1 Cor.
4 : 19; Gal. 5 : 2; Jas. 2 : 15, 16.

251. In addition to ἐάν with the Subjunctive, which is the
usual form both in classical and New Testament Greek, the
following forms of protasis also occur occasionally in the New
Testament to express a future supposition with more probability:

252. (a) Εἰ with the Subjunctive.

Luke 9 : 13; οὐκ εἰσὶν ἡμῖν πλεῖον ἢ ἄρτοι πέντε καὶ ἰχθύες δύο, εἰ μήτι
πορευθέντες ἡμεῖς ἀγοράσωμεν εἰς πάντα τὸν λαὸν τοῦτον βρώματα,
*we have no more than five loaves and two fishes; unless we are to go
and buy food for all this people.* See also 1 Cor. 14 : 5; 1 Thess.
5 : 10; Judg. 11 : 9.

253. This usage also occurs in Homer and the tragic poets, but is very rare in Attic prose. It is found in the Septuagint and becomes very common in later Hellenistic and Byzantine writers. *G.*MT. 453, 454 ; *Clapp* in *T.A.P.A.* 1887, p. 49 ; 1891, pp. 88 f.; *WT.* pp. 294 f. ; *WM.* pp. 368, 374, f.n.

For the few New Testament instances there is possibly in each case a special reason. Thus in Luke 9 : 13 there is probably a mixture of a conditional clause and a deliberative question : *unless indeed — are we to go?* i.e., *unless indeed we are to go.* In 1 Cor. 14 : 5 and 1 Thess. 5 : 10 a preference for the more common εἰ μή and εἴτε . . . εἴτε over the somewhat unusual ἐὰν μή and ἐάντε . . . ἐάντε may have led to the use of the former in spite of the fact that the meaning called for a Subjunctive. 1 Thess. 5 : 10 can hardly be explained as attraction (*B.* and *W.*), since the nature of the thought itself calls for a Subjunctive. On Phil. 3 : 11, 12, cf. 276. It is doubtful, however, whether the discovery of any difference in force between εἰ with the Subjunctive and ἐάν with the Subjunctive in these latter passages is not an over-refinement.

254. (*b*) Εἰ or ἐάν with the Future Indicative.

2 Tim. 2 : 12 ; εἰ ἀρνησόμεθα, κἀκεῖνος ἀρνήσεται ἡμᾶς, *if we shall deny him, he also will deny us.*

Acts 8 : 31 ; ἐὰν μή τις ὁδηγήσει με, *unless some one shall guide me.* See also Luke 19 : 40.

255. Εἰ with the Future Indicative occurs as a protasis of a condition of the third form not infrequently in classical writers, especially in tragedy. *G.*MT. 447. Of the New Testament instances of εἰ followed by a Future (about twenty in number), one, 2 Tim. 2 : 12, illustrates the *minatory* or *monitory* force attributed to such clauses by *Gild.*, *T.A.P.A.* 1876, pp. 9 ff. ; *A.J.P.* XIII. pp. 123 ff. Concerning the other instances, see 246, 254, 272, 276, 340.

256. (*c*) Εἰ with the Present Indicative. The protasis is then apparently of the first class (242). The instances which belong here are distinguished by evident reference of the protasis to the future.

Matt. 8 : 31 ; εἰ ἐκβάλλεις ἡμᾶς, ἀπόστειλον ἡμᾶς εἰς τὴν ἀγέλην τῶν χοίρων, *if thou cast us out, send us away into the herd of swine.* See also 1 Cor. 10 : 27 (cf. v. 28) ; 2 John 10 ; Gen. 4 : 14 ; 20 : 7 ; 44 : 26 ; and as possible instances Matt. 5 : 29, 30 ; 18 : 8, 9 ; Luke 14 : 26 ; 2 Tim. 2 : 12.

257. There is no distinction in form either in Greek or in English between a particular and a general supposition referring to the future. The distinction in thought is of course the same as in the case of present or past suppositions (239). Thus in Matt. 9 : 21, *if I shall but touch his garment, I shall be made whole*, the supposition evidently refers to a specific case, and is particular. But in John 16 : 23, *if ye shall ask anything of the Father, he will give it you in my name*, the supposition is evidently general. A large number of the future suppositions in the New Testament are apparently general. It is almost always possible, however, to suppose that a particular imagined instance is mentally selected as the illustration of the class. Cf. 240, 261.

258. When a conditional clause which as originally uttered or thought was of the first or third class and expressed by εἰ with the Indicative or ἐάν with the Subjunctive is so incorporated into a sentence as to be made dependent on a verb of past time, it may be changed to εἰ with the Optative. This principle applies even when the apodosis on which the protasis depends is not itself strictly in indirect discourse. Cf. 334–347, esp. 342, 347. See *G*.MT. 457, 694 ff.

Acts. 20 : 16 ; ἔσπευδεν γὰρ εἰ δυνατὸν εἴη αὐτῷ τὴν ἡμέραν τῆς πεντη-κοστῆς γενέσθαι εἰς Ἱεροσόλυμα, *for he was hastening, if it were possible for him, to be at Jerusalem the day of Pentecost*. In this sentence εἰ δυνατὸν εἴη represents the protasis of the sentence ἐὰν δυνατὸν ᾖ γενησόμεθα which expressed the original thought of Paul, to which the writer here refers. The same explanation applies to Acts 24 : 19, and to 27 : 39 (unless εἰ δύναιντο is an indirect question); also to Acts 17 : 27 and 27 : 12, but on these cases see also 276.

259. D. Future Supposition with Less Probability. The protasis states a supposition which refers to the future, suggesting less probability of its fulfilment than is suggested by ἐάν with the Subjunctive.

The protasis is expressed by εἰ with the Optative ; the apodosis by the Optative with ἄν. *HA*. 900 ; *G*. 1408.

There is no perfect example of this form in the New Testament. Protases occur in 1 Cor. and 1 Pet., but never with a regular and fully expressed apodosis. Apodoses occur in Luke and Acts, but never with a regular protasis.

1 Pet. 3 : 17; κρεῖττον γὰρ ἀγαθοποιοῦντας, εἰ θέλοι τὸ θέλημα τοῦ θεοῦ, πάσχειν ἢ κακοποιοῦντας, *for it is better, if the will of God should so will, that ye suffer for well doing than for evil doing.* See also 1 Cor. 14 : 10; 15 : 37; 1 Pet. 3 : 14.

260. E. Present General Supposition. The supposition refers to any occurrence of an act of a certain class in the (general) present, and the apodosis states what is wont to take place in any instance of an act of the class referred to in the protasis.

The protasis is expressed by ἐάν with the Subjunctive, the apodosis by the Present Indicative. *HA.* 894, 1; *G.* 1393, 1.

John 11 : 9; ἐάν τις περιπατῇ ἐν τῇ ἡμέρᾳ, οὐ προσκόπτει, *if a man walk in the day, he stumbleth not.*

2 Tim. 2 : 5; ἐὰν δὲ καὶ ἀθλῇ τις, οὐ στεφανοῦται ἐὰν μὴ νομίμως ἀθλήσῃ, *and if also a man contend in the games, he is not crowned, unless he contend lawfully.* See also Mark 3 : 24; John 7 : 51; 12 : 24; 1 Cor. 7 : 39, 40.

261. Εἰ with the Present Indicative not infrequently occurs in clauses which apparently express a present general supposition. *G.*MT. 467. Yet in most New Testament passages of this kind, it is possible that a particular imagined instance in the present or future is before the mind as an illustration of the general class of cases. Cf. 242, 256. It is scarcely possible to decide in each case whether the supposition was conceived of as general or particular.

Luke 14 : 26 ; εἴ τις ἔρχεται πρός με καὶ οὐ μισεῖ . . . τὴν ψυχὴν
ἑαυτοῦ, οὐ δύναται εἶναί μου μαθητής, *if any man cometh unto me, and
hateth not . . . his own life, he cannot be my disciple.* Cf. John 8 : 51 ;
12 : 26 ; where in protases of apparently similar force ἐάν with the
Subjunctive occurs, and the apodosis refers to the future.

Rom. 8 : 25 ; εἰ δὲ ὃ οὐ βλέπομεν ἐλπίζομεν, δι᾽ ὑπομονῆς ἀπεκδεχόμεθα,
*but if we hope for that which we see not, then do we with patience wait
for it.* See also Jas. 1 : 26.

262. The third and fifth classes of conditional sentences are very
similar not only in form, but also in meaning. When the subject or other
leading term of the protasis is an indefinite or generic word, the third
class differs from the fifth only in that a sentence of the third class tells
what will happen in a particular instance or in any instance of the fulfilment of the supposition, while a sentence of the fifth class tells what
is wont to happen in any such case. Cf., *e.g.*, Mark 3 : 24 with 25 ; also
the two sentences of Rom. 7 : 3.

263. It should be observed that a Present Indicative in the principal
clause after a protasis consisting of ἐάν with the Subjunctive does not
always indicate that the sentence is of the fifth class. If the fact stated
in the apodosis is already true at the time of speaking, or if the issue
involved has already been determined, though not necessarily known, the
Present Indicative is frequently used after a protasis referring to future
time. The thought would be expressed more fully but less forcibly by
supplying some such phrase as *it will appear that* or *it will still be true
that.* In other instances the true apodosis is omitted, that which stands
in its place being a reason for the unexpressed apodosis. In still other
cases the Present is merely the familiar Present for Future (15).

John 8 : 31 ; ἐὰν ὑμεῖς μείνητε ἐν τῷ λόγῳ τῷ ἐμῷ, ἀληθῶς μαθηταί μού
ἐστε, *if ye shall abide in my word, [ye will show that] ye are truly
my disciples.* Observe the Future in the next clause.

1 John 1 : 9 ; ἐὰν ὁμολογῶμεν τὰς ἁμαρτίας ἡμῶν, πιστός ἐστιν καὶ
δίκαιος ἵνα ἀφῇ ἡμῖν τὰς ἁμαρτίας, *if we shall confess our sins, [he
will forgive us, for] he is faithful and righteous to forgive us our sins.*
See also Mark 1 : 40 ; John 19 : 12 ; Acts 26 : 5.

264. The difference in force between the fifth class of suppositions and
the class described under 243 should be clearly marked. There the issue
raised by the protasis is as to the truth or falsity of the principle as a gen-

eral principle, while the apodosis affirms some other general or particular statement to be true if the general principle is true. Here the protasis raises no question of the truth or falsity of the general principle, but suggests as an hypothesis, that a general statement is in any single case realized, and the apodosis states what is wont to take place when the supposition of the protasis is thus realized. Thus in Matt. 19 : 10 (243) the disciples say that *if the principle* stated by Jesus *is true, it follows as a general principle that it is not expedient to marry.* On the other hand, ἐὰν οὕτως ἔχῃ, οὐ συμφέρει γαμῆσαι would mean, *If in any instance the case supposed is realized, then it is wont to happen that it is not expedient to marry.* Cf. examples under 260.

265. F. Past General Supposition. The supposition refers to any past occurrence of an act of a certain class, and the apodosis states what was wont to take place in any instance of an act of the class referred to in the protasis.

The protasis is expressed by εἰ with the Optative, the apodosis by the Imperfect Indicative. *HA.* 894, 2; *G.* 1393, 2.

There is apparently no instance of this form in the New Testament.

266. Peculiarities of Conditional Sentences. Nearly all the peculiar variations of conditional sentences mentioned in the classical grammars are illustrated in the New Testament. See *HA.* 901–907 ; *G.* 1413–1424.

267. (*a*) A protasis of one form is sometimes joined with an apodosis of another form.

Acts 8 : 31 ; πῶς γὰρ ἂν δυναίμην ἐὰν μή τις ὁδηγήσει με, *how can I, unless some one shall guide me ?*

268. (*b*) An apodosis may be accompanied by more than one protasis ; these protases may be of different form, each retaining its own proper force.

John 13 : 17 ; εἰ ταῦτα οἴδατε, μακάριοί ἐστε ἐὰν ποιῆτε αὐτά, *if ye know these things, blessed are ye if ye do them.* See also 1 Cor. 9 : 11.

269. (c) The place of the protasis with εἰ or ἐάν is sometimes supplied by a participle, an Imperative, or other form of expression suggesting a supposition.

Matt. 26 : 15 ; Τί θέλετέ μοι δοῦναι κἀγὼ ὑμῖν παραδώσω αὐτόν, *what are ye willing to give me, and I will deliver him unto you.*

Mark 11 : 24 ; πάντα ὅσα προσεύχεσθε καὶ αἰτεῖσθε, πιστεύετε ὅτι ἐλάβετε, καὶ ἔσται ὑμῖν, *all things whatsoever ye pray and ask for, believe that ye have received them, and ye shall have them.* See also Matt. 7 : 10 ; Mark 1 : 17 ; and exx. under 436.

Rem. In Jas. 1 : 5, αἰτείτω is the apodosis of εἰ δέ τις ὑμῶν λείπεται σοφίας, and at the same time fills the place of protasis to δοθήσεται. See also Matt. 19 : 21.

270. (d) The protasis is sometimes omitted.   Luke 1 : 62 ; Acts 17 : 18.

271. (e) The apodosis is sometimes omitted.

Luke 13 : 9 ; κἂν μὲν ποιήσῃ καρπὸν εἰς τὸ μέλλον — εἰ δὲ μήγε, ἐκκόψεις αὐτήν, *and if it bear fruit thenceforth, — but if not, thou shalt cut it down.* See also Luke 19 : 42 ; Acts 23 : 9.

272. Εἰ with the Future Indicative is used by Hebraism without an apodosis, with the force of an emphatic negative assertion or oath.   Cf. *Hr.* 48, 9, a.

Mark 8 : 12 ; ἀμὴν λέγω, εἰ δοθήσεται τῇ γενεᾷ ταύτῃ σημεῖον, *verily I say unto you, there shall no sign be given unto this generation.* See also Heb. 3 : 11 ; 4 : 3, 5. On Heb. 6 : 14 see *Th.* εἰ, iii. 11.

273. (f) The verb of the protasis or apodosis may be omitted.

Rom. 4 : 14 ; εἰ γὰρ οἱ ἐκ νόμου κληρονόμοι, κεκένωται ἡ πίστις καὶ κατήργηται ἡ ἐπαγγελία, *for if they which are of the law are heirs, faith is made void, and the promise is made of none effect.* See also Rom. 8 : 17; 11 : 16; 1 Cor. 7 : 5, 8; 12 : 19; 1 Pet. 3 : 14. In 2 Cor. 11 : 16 κἄν stands for καὶ ἐὰν δέξησθε.

274. (*g*) Εἰ μή without a dependent verb occurs very frequently in the sense of *except*. It may be followed by any form of expression which could have stood as subject or as limitation of the principal predicate. The origin of this usage was of course in a conditional clause the verb of which was omitted because it was identical with the verb of the apodosis. Both in classical and New Testament Greek the ellipsis is unconscious, and the limitation is not strictly conditional, but exceptive. Like the English *except* it states not a condition on fulfilment of which the apodosis is true or its action takes place, but a limitation of the principal statement. It is, however, never in the New Testament purely adversative. Cf. *Ltft.* on Gal. 1 : 7, 19.

275. (*h*) Εἰ δὲ μή and εἰ δὲ μήγε are used elliptically in the sense of *otherwise*, i.e. *if so*, or *if not*, to introduce an alternative statement or command. Having become fixed phrases, they are used even when the preceding sentence is negative; also when the nature of the condition would naturally call for ἐάν rather than εἰ. Matt. 9 : 17; Luke 10 : 6; 13 : 9; Rev. 2 : 5. *G*.MT. 478; *B*. p. 393.

276. (*i*) An omitted apodosis is sometimes virtually contained in the protasis, and the latter expresses a possibility which is an object of hope or desire, and hence has nearly the force of a final clause. In some instances it approaches the force of an indirect question. *G*.MT. 486–493. In classical Greek such protases are introduced by εἰ or ἐάν. In the New Testament they occur with εἰ only, and take the Subjunctive, Optative, or Future Indicative.

Phil. 3 : 12; διώκω δὲ εἰ καὶ καταλάβω, *but I press on, if so be that I may apprehend.*

Acts 27 : 12; οἱ πλείονες ἔθεντο βουλὴν ἀναχθῆναι ἐκεῖθεν, εἴ πως δύναιντο καταντήσαντες εἰς Φοίνικα παραχειμάσαι, *the more part advised to put to sea from thence, if by any means they could reach Phœnix, and winter there.* See also Mark 11 : 13; Acts 8 : 22; 17 : 27; Rom. 1 : 10; 11 : 14; Phil. 3 : 11.

277. (*j*) After expressions of *wonder*, etc., a clause introduced by εἰ has nearly the force of a clause introduced by ὅτι. Mark 15 : 44; Acts 26 : 8; cf. 1 John 3 : 13.

MOODS IN CONCESSIVE SENTENCES

278. A concessive clause is a protasis that states a supposition the fulfilment of which is thought of or represented as unfavorable to the fulfilment of the apodosis.

The force of a concessive sentence is thus very different from that of a conditional sentence. The latter represents the fulfilment of the apodosis as conditioned on the fulfilment of the protasis; the former represents the apodosis as fulfilled in spite of the fulfilment of the protasis. Yet there are cases in which by the weakening of the characteristic force of each construction, or by the complexity of the elements expressed by the protasis, the two usages approach so near to each other as to make distinction between them difficult.

In Gal. 1 : 8, *e.g.*, the fulfilment of the element of the protasis expressed in παρ' ὃ εὐηγγελισάμεθα is favorable to the fulfilment of the apodosis ἀνάθεμα ἔστω, and the clause is so far forth conditional. But the element expressed in ἡμεῖς ἢ ἄγγελος ἐξ οὐρανοῦ, which is emphasized by the καί, is unfavorable to the fulfilment of the apodosis, and the clause is so far forth concessive. It might be resolved into two clauses, thus,

*If any one shall preach unto you any gospel other than that we
preached unto you [let him be anathema] ; yea, though we or an
angel from heaven so preach, let him be anathema.*

279. A concessive clause is commonly introduced by εἰ (ἐάν)
καί or καὶ εἰ (ἐάν). But a clause introduced by εἰ or ἐάν alone
may also be in thought concessive, though the concessive
element is not emphasized in the form. Matt. 26 : 33 (cf. Mark
14 : 29) ; Mark 14 : 31 (cf. Matt. 26 : 35).

280. Εἰ (ἐάν) καί concessive in the New Testament generally
introduces a supposition conceived of as actually fulfilled or
likely to be fulfilled. See examples under **284, 285**. Yet,
in concessive as well as in conditional clauses (cf. **282**),
καί may belong not to the whole clause but to the word next
after it, having an intensive force, and suggesting that the
supposition is in some sense or respect an extreme one, *e.g.*,
especially improbable or especially unfavorable to the fulfilment of the apodosis. So probably Mark 14 : 29.

281. Καὶ εἰ (ἐάν) concessive occurs somewhat rarely in the
New Testament. See Matt. 26 : 35; John 8 : 16; 1 Cor. 8 : 5;
Gal. 1 : 8; 1 Pet. 3 : 1 (but cf. *WH.*). The force of the καί is
apparently intensive, representing the supposition as actually
or from a rhetorical point of view an extreme case, improbable
in itself, or specially unfavorable to the fulfilment of the
apodosis.

REM. *Paley*, Greek Particles, p. 31, thus distinguishes the force of εἰ
καί and καὶ εἰ, "generally with this difference, that εἰ καί implies an admitted fact 'even though,' καὶ εἰ a somewhat improbable supposition;
'even if.'" See other statements and references in *Th.* εἰ III. 7 ; and
especially *J.* 861. It should be observed that a concessive supposition
may be probable or improbable ; it is not this or that that makes it concessive, but the fact that its fulfilment is unfavorable to the fulfilment of
the apodosis.

282. Carefully to be distinguished from the cases of καὶ εἰ (ἐάν) and εἰ (ἐάν) καί concessive are those in which εἰ (ἐάν) is conditional and καί means *and* (Matt. 11 : 14 ; Luke 6 : 32, 33, 34 ; John 8 : 55, etc.), or *also* (Luke 11 : 18 ; 2 Cor. 11 : 15), or is simply intensive, emphasizing the following word and suggesting a supposition in some sense extreme (1 Cor. 4 : 7 ; 7 : 11). Such a supposition is not necessarily unfavorable to the fulfilment of the apodosis, and hence may be conditional however extreme. Cf. 280.

283. Moods and Tenses in Concessive Clauses. In their use of moods and tenses concessive clauses follow in general the rules for conditional clauses. The variety of usage is in the New Testament, however, much less in the case of concessive clauses than of conditional clauses.

284. Concessive clauses of the class corresponding to the first class of conditional sentences are most frequent in the New Testament. The event referred to in the concessive clause is in general not contingent, but conceived of as actual.

2 Cor. 7 : 8 ; ὅτι εἰ καὶ ἐλύπησα ὑμᾶς ἐν τῇ ἐπιστολῇ, οὐ μεταμέλομαι, *for, though I made you sorry with my epistle, I do not regret it.* See also Luke 18 : 4 ; 2 Cor. 4 : 16 ; 7 : 12 ; 11 : 6 ; 12 : 11 ; Phil. 2 : 17 ; Col. 2 : 5 ; Heb. 6 : 9.

285. Concessive clauses referring to the future occur in two forms.

(*a*) They take εἰ καί or εἰ, and a Future Indicative referring to what is regarded as certain or likely to occur. In logical force this construction is closely akin to that discussed under 246.

Luke 11 : 8 ; εἰ καὶ οὐ δώσει αὐτῷ ἀναστὰς διὰ τὸ εἶναι φίλον αὐτοῦ, διά γε τὴν ἀναιδίαν αὐτοῦ ἐγερθεὶς δώσει αὐτῷ ὅσων χρῄζει, *though he will not rise and give him because he is his friend, yet because of his importunity he will arise and give him as many as he needeth.* See also Matt. 26 : 33 ; Mark 14 : 29.

(b) They take ἐὰν καί, καὶ ἐάν, or ἐάν, with the Subjunctive referring to a future possibility, or what is rhetorically conceived to be possible. Καὶ ἐάν introduces an extreme case, usually one which is represented as highly improbable.

Gal. 6 : 1; ἐὰν καὶ προλημφθῇ ἄνθρωπος ἔν τινι παραπτώματι, ὑμεῖς οἱ πνευματικοὶ καταρτίζετε τὸν τοιοῦτον ἐν πνεύματι πραΰτητος,.even if a man be overtaken in any trespass, ye which are spiritual, restore such a one in a spirit of meekness.

Gal. 1 : 8; ἀλλὰ καὶ ἐὰν ἡμεῖς ἢ ἄγγελος ἐξ οὐρανοῦ εὐαγγελίσηται [ὑμῖν] παρ᾽ ὃ εὐηγγελισάμεθα ὑμῖν, ἀνάθεμα ἔστω, but even if we, or an angel from heaven, preach unto you any gospel other than that which we preached unto you, let him be anathema. See also Luke 22 : 67, 68; John 8 : 16; 10 : 38; Rom. 9 : 27.

REM. The apodosis after a concessive protasis referring to the future, sometimes has a Present Indicative, affirming what is true and will still be true though the supposition of the protasis be fulfilled. See John 8 : 14; 1 Cor. 9 : 16. Cf. 263.

286. The New Testament furnishes no clear instance of a concessive clause corresponding to the fourth class of conditional clauses. In 1 Pet. 3 : 14, εἰ καὶ πάσχοιτε διὰ δικαιοσύνην, μακάριοι, the use of καὶ before πάσχοιτε suggests that the writer has in mind that suffering is apparently opposed to blessedness. Yet it is probable that he intends to affirm that blessedness comes, not in spite of, but through, suffering for righteousness' sake. (On the thought cf. Matt. 5 : 10 f.) Thus the protasis suggests, even intentionally, a concession, but is, strictly speaking, a true causal conditional clause. Cf. 282.

287. The New Testament instances of concessive clauses corresponding to the fifth class of conditional clauses are few, and the concessive force is not strongly marked. See 2 Tim. 2 : 5 (first clause) under 260; 2 Tim. 2 : 13.

288. Concessive clauses in English are introduced by *though, although,* and *even if,* occasionally by *if* alone. *Even if* introduces an improbable supposition or one especially unfavorable to the fulfilment of the apodosis. *Though* and

although with the Indicative usually imply an admitted fact.
With the Subjunctive and Potential, with the Present Indicative in the sense of a Future, and with a Past tense of the
Indicative in conditions contrary to fact, *though* and *although*
have substantially the same force as *even if*. *Even if* thus
corresponds in force very nearly to καὶ εἰ; *though* and *although*
to εἰ καί.

MOODS IN RELATIVE CLAUSES

289. Relative Clauses are introduced by relative pronouns
and by relative adverbs of time, place, and manner.

They may be divided into two classes :

I. Definite Relative Clauses, *i.e.* clauses which refer to a
definite and actual event or fact. The antecedent may be expressed or understood. If not in itself definite, it is made so
by the definiteness of the relative clause.

II. Indefinite or Conditional Relative Clauses, *i.e.* clauses
which refer not to a definite and actual event, but to a supposed event or instance, and hence imply a condition. The
antecedent may be expressed or understood; if expressed, it is
usually some indefinite or generic word.

290. It should be observed that the distinction between the definite
and the indefinite relative clause cannot be drawn simply by reference
to the relative pronoun employed, or to the word which stands as the
antecedent of the relative. A definite relative clause may be introduced
by an indefinite relative pronoun or may have an indefinite pronoun as
its antecedent. On the other hand, an indefinite relative clause may
have as its antecedent a definite term, *e.g.*, a demonstrative pronoun, and
may be introduced by the simple relative. A clause and its antecedent
are made definite by the reference of the clause to a definite and actual
event ; they are made indefinite by the reference of the clause to a supposed event or instance. Thus if one say, *He received whatever profit
was made,* meaning, *In a certain transaction, or in certain transactions,
profit was made, and he received it,* the relative clause is definite, because

it refers to an actual event or series of events. But if one use the same words meaning, *If any profit was made, he received it*, the relative clause is indefinite, because it implies a condition, referring to an event — the making of profit — which is only supposed. In John 1 : 12, *but as many as received him, to them gave he the right to become children of God*, we are doubtless to understand the relative clause as definite, not because of the expressed antecedent, *them*, but because the clause refers to a certain class who actually received him. In Rom. 8 : 24, on the other hand, *who hopeth for that which he seeth ?* the relative clause apparently does not refer to a definite thing seen and an actual act of seeing, but is equivalent to a conditional clause, *if he seeth anything.* In Mark 3 : 11, *whensoever they beheld him, they fell down before him*, the form of the Greek sentence shows that the meaning is, *If at any time they saw him, they were wont to fall down before him.* That is, while the class of events is actual, the relative clause presents the successive instances distributively as suppositions. These examples serve to show how slight may be the difference at times between a definite and an indefinite relative clause, and that it must often be a matter of choice for the writer whether he will refer to an event as actual, or present it as a supposition.

291. Relative clauses denoting purpose, and relative clauses introduced by ἕως and other words meaning *until*, show special peculiarities of usage and require separate discussion. For purposes of treatment therefore we must recognize four classes of relative clauses.

I. Definite relative clauses, excluding those which express purpose, and those introduced by words meaning *until*.

II. Indefinite or Conditional relative clauses, excluding those which express purpose, and those introduced by words meaning *until*.

III. Relative clauses expressing purpose.

IV. Relative clauses introduced by words meaning *until*.

I. Definite Relative Clauses

292. Under the head of definite relative clauses are included not only adjective clauses introduced by relative pronouns, ὅς, ὅστις, οἷος, ὅσος, but all clauses of time, place, manner, and comparison, such clauses being introduced by relative words, either pronouns, or adverbs, ὅτε, ὡς (expressing either time or manner), ὅπου, ὥσπερ, etc.

293. Moods in Definite Relative Clauses. Definite relative clauses in general (excluding III. and IV. above) show no special uses of mood and tense, but employ the verb as it is used in principal clauses. *HA.* 909; *G.* 1427.

John 6 : 63 ; τὰ ῥήματα ἃ ἐγὼ λελάληκα ὑμῖν πνεῦμά ἐστιν καὶ ζωή ἐστιν, *the words that I have spoken unto you are spirit, and are life.*

John 12 : 36 ; ὡς τὸ φῶς ἔχετε, πιστεύετε εἰς τὸ φῶς, *while ye have the light, believe on the light.*

Gal. 4 : 4 ; ὅτε δὲ ἦλθεν τὸ πλήρωμα τοῦ χρόνου, ἐξαπέστειλεν ὁ θεὸς τὸν υἱὸν αὐτοῦ, *but when the fulness of the time came, God sent forth his son.*

Jas. 2 : 26 ; ὥσπερ τὸ σῶμα χωρὶς πνεύματος νεκρόν ἐστιν, οὕτως καὶ ἡ πίστις χωρὶς ἔργων νεκρά ἐστιν, *as the body apart from the spirit is dead, even so faith apart from works is dead.*

Rev. 3 : 11 ; κράτει ὃ ἔχεις, *hold fast that which thou hast.*

Rev. 21 : 16 ; καὶ τὸ μῆκος αὐτῆς ὅσον τὸ πλάτος, *and the length thereof is as great as the breadth.* Cf. Heb. 10 : 25. See also Matt. 26 : 19 ; Col. 2 : 6.

294. A definite relative clause may imply a relation of cause, result, or concession, without affecting the mood or tense of the verb. *HA.* 910; *G.* 1445.

Rom. 6 : 2 ; οἵτινες ἀπεθάνομεν τῇ ἁμαρτίᾳ, πῶς ἔτι ζήσομεν ἐν αὐτῇ, *we who died to sin, how shall we any longer live therein?*

Jas. 4 : 13, 14 ; ἄγε νῦν οἱ λέγοντες Σήμερον ἢ αὔριον πορευσόμεθα εἰς τήνδε τὴν πόλιν καὶ ποιήσομεν ἐκεῖ ἐνιαυτὸν καὶ ἐμπορευσόμεθα καὶ κερδήσομεν · οἵτινες οὐκ ἐπίστασθε τῆς αὔριον ποία ἡ ζωὴ ὑμῶν, *go to now, ye that say, To-day or to-morrow we will go into this city, and spend a year there and trade and get gain; whereas* [i.e. *although*] *ye know not of what sort your life will be on the morrow.*

295. All relative clauses whether adjective or adverbial may be distinguished as either restrictive or explanatory. A restrictive clause defines its antecedent, indicating what person, thing, place, or manner is signified. An explanatory clause adds a description to what is already known or sufficiently defined. The former *identifies*, the latter *describes*.

Restrictive clauses: John 15 : 20; μνημονεύετε τοῦ λόγου οὗ ἐγὼ εἶπον ὑμῖν, *remember the word that I said unto you.*

Matt. 28 : 6; δεῦτε ἴδετε τὸν τόπον ὅπου ἔκειτο, *come, see the place where he lay.*

Mark 2 : 20; ἐλεύσονται δὲ ἡμέραι ὅταν ἀπαρθῇ ἀπ᾽ αὐτῶν ὁ νυμφίος, *but days will come when the bridegroom shall be taken away from them.*

Explanatory clauses: Luke 4 : 16; καὶ ἦλθεν εἰς Ναζαρά, οὗ ἦν τεθραμμένος, *and he came to Nazareth, where he had been brought up.*

Eph. 6 : 17; τὴν μάχαιραν τοῦ πνεύματος, ὅ ἐστιν ῥῆμα θεοῦ, *the sword of the Spirit, which is the word of God.*

II. Conditional Relative Sentences

296. An indefinite relative clause, since it refers to a supposed event or instance, implies a condition, and is therefore called a conditional relative clause. *HA.* 912; *G.* 1428.

Mark 10 : 43; ὃς ἂν θέλῃ μέγας γενέσθαι ἐν ὑμῖν, ἔσται ὑμῶν διάκονος, *whosoever would become great among you, shall be your minister.* Cf. Mark 9 : 35; εἴ τις θέλει πρῶτος εἶναι ἔσται πάντων ἔσχατος καὶ πάντων διάκονος. It is evident that the relative clause in the former passage is as really conditional as the conditional clause in the latter.

297. Since a conditional relative clause implies a supposition, conditional relative sentences may be classified according to the nature of the implied supposition, as other conditional sentences are classified according to the expressed supposition.

298. The implied supposition may be particular or general. When the relative clause refers to a particular supposed event or instance, and the principal clause conditions its assertion on the occurrence of this event, the implied supposition is particular. When the relative clause refers to any occurrence of an act of a certain class, and the principal clause states what is or was wont to take place in any instance of an act of the class supposed, the implied supposition is general.

Thus in the sentence, *The act which he believes to be wrong he will not do*, if reference is had to a particular occasion, or to one made particular in thought, so that the sentence means, *If on that occasion, or a certain occasion, he believes an act to be wrong, he will not do it*, the implied supposition is particular. But in the sentence, *Whatever act he [in any instance] believes to be wrong, he does not [is not wont to] do*, the implied supposition is general. Cf. 239.

299. The distinction between the relative clause implying a particular supposition and the relative clause implying a general supposition is not marked either in Greek or in English by any uniform difference in the pronouns employed either in the relative clause or in the antecedent clause. The terms particular and general apply not to the relative or its antecedent, but to the implied supposition. Thus if one say, *He received whatever profit was made*, meaning, *If [in a certain transaction] any profit was made, he received it*, the relative clause implies a particular condition. But if one use the same words, meaning, *If [in any transaction] any profit was made, [it was wont to happen that] he received it*, the implied condition is general. So also in John 1 : 33, *upon whomsoever thou shalt see the Spirit descending, and abiding upon him, the same is he that baptizeth with the Holy Spirit*, we have not a general principle applying to any one of many cases, but a supposition and an assertion referring to a particular case. But in 1 John 3 : 22, *whatsoever we ask, we receive of him*, the supposition refers to any instance of asking, and is general.

Whether the implied supposition is particular or general can usually be most clearly discerned from the nature of the principal clause. If this states what is true in a particular case, or expresses a command with reference to a particular case, the implied supposition is particular. If it states a general principle, or expresses a general injunction which applies in any instance of the event described in the relative clause, the implied supposition is usually general. Cf. 240.

300. Of the six classes of conditional relative sentences found in classical Greek, but four occur in the New Testament, and these with considerable deviation from classical usage. They are designated here according to the kind of condition implied in the relative clause.

301. A. Simple Present or Past Particular Supposition. The relative clause states a particular supposition which refers to the present or past. It has a present or past tense of the Indicative. The principal clause may have any form of the verb. *HA.* 914, A; *G.* 1430.

Rom. 2 : 12 ; ὅσοι γὰρ ἀνόμως ἥμαρτον, ἀνόμως καὶ ἀπολοῦνται· καὶ ὅσοι ἐν νόμῳ ἥμαρτον, διὰ νόμου κριθήσονται, *for as many as have sinned without law shall also perish without law : and as many as have sinned under law shall be judged by law.*

Phil. 4 : 8 ; τὸ λοιπόν, ἀδελφοί, ὅσα ἐστὶν ἀληθῆ, ὅσα σεμνά, ὅσα δίκαια, ὅσα ἁγνά, ὅσα προσφιλῆ, ὅσα εὔφημα, εἴ τις ἀρετὴ καὶ εἴ τις ἔπαινος, ταῦτα λογίζεσθε. See also 2 Cor. 2 : 10.

Rem. Respecting the use of the negatives μή and οὐ in relative clauses of this class, see 469, 470.

302. B. Supposition contrary to Fact. The relative clause states a supposition which refers to the present or past implying that it is not, or was not, fulfilled. It has a past tense of the Indicative. The principal clause has a past tense of the Indicative with ἄν. *HA.* 915; *G.* 1433. No instance occurs in the New Testament.

303. C. Future Supposition with More Probability. The relative clause states a supposition which refers to the future, suggesting some probability of its fulfilment. It has the Subjunctive with ἄν. The principal clause may have any form referring to future time. *HA.* 916; *G.* 1434.

Matt. 5 : 19; ὃς δ' ἂν ποιήσῃ καὶ διδάξῃ, οὗτος μέγας κληθήσεται ἐν τῇ βασιλείᾳ τῶν οὐρανῶν, *but whosoever shall do and teach them, he shall be called great in the kingdom of heaven.*

Mark 13 : 11; καὶ ὅταν ἄγωσιν ὑμᾶς παραδιδόντες, μὴ προμεριμνᾶτε τί λαλήσητε, ἀλλ' ὃ ἐὰν δοθῇ ὑμῖν ἐν ἐκείνῃ τῇ ὥρᾳ τοῦτο λαλεῖτε, οὐ γάρ ἐστε ὑμεῖς οἱ λαλοῦντες ἀλλὰ τὸ πνεῦμα τὸ ἅγιον, *and when they lead you to judgment, and deliver you up, be not anxious beforehand what ye shall speak: but whatsoever shall be given you in that hour, that speak ye: for it is not ye that speak, but the Holy Ghost.* See also Luke 13 : 25; Rev. 11 : 7; instances are very frequent in the New Testament.

304. In the New Testament ἐάν not infrequently stands in a conditional relative clause instead of the simple ἄν. Matt. 7 : 12; Mark 3 : 28; Luke 9 : 57; Acts 2 : 21, *et al.* See *WH.* ii. App. p. 173.

305. The Subjunctive with ἄν in a relative clause is in the New Testament usually retained in indirect discourse, or in a sentence having the effect of indirect discourse, even after a past tense. Matt. 14 : 7; Rev. 12 : 4. Cf. 251. On Acts 25 : 16 see 333, 344, Rem. 1.

306. In addition to the relative clause having the Subjunctive with ἄν (303), which is the regular form both in classical and New Testament Greek, the following forms of the relative clause also require mention as occurring in the New Testament to express a future supposition with more probability:

307. (*a*) The Subjunctive without ἄν. This is very unusual in classical Greek in relative clauses referring to the future. In the New Testament also it is rare. Jas. 2 : 10 probably belongs here; Matt. 10 : 33 also, if (with *Treg.* and *WH. text*) we read ὅστις δὲ ἀρνήσηταί με . . . ἀρνήσομαι.

308. (*b*) The Future Indicative with or without ἄν.

Matt. 5 : 41; ὅστις σε ἀγγαρεύσει μίλιον ἕν, ὕπαγε μετ' αὐτοῦ δύο, *who-soever shall compel thee to go one mile, go with him two.* See also Matt. 10 : 32 (cf. v. 33); 18 : 4 (cf. v. 5); 23 : 12; Mark 8 : 35; Luke 12 : 8, 10; 17 : 31; Acts 7 : 7; Rev. 4 : 9. Cf. *WH.* ii. App. p. 172.

309. (*c*) The Present Indicative with or without ἄν.

Mark 11 : 25; ὅταν στήκετε προσευχόμενοι, ἀφίετε, *whensoever ye stand praying, forgive.* See also Matt. 5 : 39; Luke 12 : 34; John 12 : 26; 14 : 3.

310. There is no distinction in form either in Greek or in English between a relative clause implying a particular supposition, and a relative clause implying a general supposition, when the supposition refers to the future. The difference in thought is the same as that which distinguishes particular and general suppositions referring to the present or past. Cf. 298, 299. In Matt. 26 : 48, *whomsoever I shall kiss, that is he*, the supposition is particular, referring to a specific occasion and event. So also in 1 Cor. 16 : 3. But in Luke 9 : 4, *into whatsoever house ye enter, there abide, and thence depart*, the supposition is general, referring to any one of a class of acts. A large part of the conditional relative clauses referring to the future found in the New Testament are apparently general. See, *e.g.*, Matt. 5 : 19; 10 : 14; 16 : 25; Mark 11 : 23; Luke 8 : 18, etc. Yet in many cases it is possible to suppose that a particular imagined instance was before the mind of the writer as an illustration of the general class of cases.

311. D. Future Supposition with Less Probability.
The relative clause states a supposition which refers to the future, suggesting less probability of its fulfilment than is implied by the Subjunctive with ἄν. It has the Optative without ἄν. The principal clause has the Optative with ἄν. *HA.* 917 ; *G.* 1436.

No instance occurs in the New Testament.

312. E. Present General Supposition.   The relative clause refers to any occurrence of a class of acts in the

general present, and the principal clause states what is
wont to take place in any instance of the act referred to
in the relative clause. The relative clause has the Subjunctive with ἄν, the principal clause the Present Indicative. *HA*. 914, *B*. (1); *G*. 1431, 1.

1 Cor. 11 : 26; ὁσάκις γὰρ ἐὰν ἐσθίητε τὸν ἄρτον τοῦτον καὶ τὸ ποτήριον
πίνητε, τὸν θάνατον τοῦ κυρίου καταγγέλλετε, ἄχρι οὗ ἔλθῃ, *for as
often as ye eat this bread, and drink the cup, ye proclaim the Lord's
death, till he come.* See also Matt. 15 : 2; Mark 10 : 11; Rev. 9 : 5.

REM. Concerning the use of ἐάν for ἄν, see 304.

313. The Present Indicative not infrequently occurs in conditional relative clauses which apparently imply a present
general supposition. *G*.MT. 534. Yet in most such passages
in the New Testament, it is possible that a particular imagined
instance in the present or future is before the mind as an
illustration of the general class of cases. Cf. 301, 309. It is
scarcely possible to decide in each case whether the supposition is particular or general. The difference of meaning is in
any case slight.

Luke 14 : 27; ὅστις οὐ βαστάζει τὸν σταυρὸν ἑαυτοῦ καὶ ἔρχεται ὀπίσω
μου, οὐ δύναται εἶναί μου μαθητής, *whosoever doth not bear his own
cross and come after me, cannot be my disciple.* See also Matt. 10 : 38;
13 : 12 (cf. Luke 8 : 18); Luke 7 : 47; John 3 : 8; Rom. 6 : 16; 9 : 18;
1 Cor. 15 : 36, 37; Heb. 12 : 6.

314. Concerning the similarity of the third and fifth classes of conditional relative clauses, cf. 262. The statements there made respecting
ordinary conditional sentences are applicable also to conditional relative
sentences. See Mark 3 : 28, 29; Luke 9 : 24, 48; 1 John 3 : 22.

315. F. **Past General Supposition.** The relative clause
refers to any occurrence of a certain act or class of acts,
and the principal clause states what was wont to take

place in any instance of the act referred to in the relative clause. In classical Greek, the relative clause has the Optative without ἄν, the principal clause the Imperfect Indicative. *HA*. 914, *B*. (2); *G*. 1431, 2.

In the New Testament, the Optative does not occur in such clauses, the Imperfect or Aorist Indicative with ἄν being used instead. Cf. 26.

Mark 3 : 11; καὶ τὰ πνεύματα τὰ ἀκάθαρτα, ὅταν αὐτὸν ἐθεώρουν, προσέπιπτον αὐτῷ καὶ ἔκραζον, *and the unclean spirits, whensoever they beheld him, were wont to fall down before him and cry out.* See also Mark 6 : 56; 11 : 19; Acts 2 : 45; 4 : 35; 1 Cor. 12 : 2; cf. Gen. 2 : 19; 1 Sam. 2 : 13, 14.

316. In the New Testament, relative clauses conditional in form are sometimes definite in force.

Mark 2 : 20; ἐλεύσονται δὲ ἡμέραι ὅταν ἀπαρθῇ ἀπ αὐτῶν ὁ νυμφίος, *but days will come when the bridegroom shall be taken away from them.* See also Luke 5 : 35; 13 : 28; Rev. 8 : 1.

III. RELATIVE CLAUSES EXPRESSING PURPOSE

317. Relative Clauses of Pure Purpose. Relative clauses expressing purpose take the Future Indicative both in classical and New Testament Greek. *HA*. 911; *G*. 1442; *B*. p. 229; *WM*. p. 386, f. n.

Matt. 21 : 41; τὸν ἀμπελῶνα ἐκδώσεται ἄλλοις γεωργοῖς, οἵτινες ἀποδώσουσιν αὐτῷ τοὺς καρπούς, *he will let out the vineyard unto other husbandmen, which shall render him the fruits.* See also Acts 6 : 3.

318. Complementary relative clauses expressing that for which a person or thing is fitted, or other similar relation, take the Subjunctive or the Future Indicative both in classical and New Testament Greek. *G*.MT. 572; *Hale* in *T.A.P.A.* 1893, pp. 156 ff.

Heb. 8 : 3; ὅθεν ἀναγκαῖον ἔχειν τι καὶ τοῦτον ὃ προσενέγκῃ, *wherefore it is necessary that this high priest also have somewhat to offer.* See also Mark 14 : 14; Luke 11 : 6; 22 : 11. In Luke 7 : 4 a complementary relative clause limiting the adjective ἄξιος has the Future Indicative.

319. The clauses referred to in 318 are to be distinguished from true relative clauses of purpose in that they do not express the purpose with which the action denoted by the principal clause is done, but constitute a complementary limitation of the principal clause. Cf. the clause with ἵνα (215-217) and the Infinitive (368) expressing a similar relation.

The Subjunctive in such clauses is probably in origin a Deliberative Subjunctive. Thus in Mark 14 : 14, ποῦ ἐστὶν τὸ κατάλυμά μου ὅπου τὸ πάσχα μετὰ τῶν μαθητῶν μου φάγω, the relative clause ὅπου . . . φάγω reproduces in dependent construction the thought of the deliberative question ποῦ . . . φάγω. The same explanation doubtless applies, though less obviously, to the Subjunctive in Acts 21 : 16, and to the Future in Luke 7 : 4. In both instances the thought of a deliberative question is reproduced in the relative clause. Cf. the clauses similar in force, but employing an interrogative pronoun, 346. See *Tarbell* in *Cl. Rev.* July 1891, p. 302 (*contra, Earle* in *Cl. Rev.* March 1892, pp. 93-95); *Hale* in *T.A.P.A.*, 1893.

320. The Optative sometimes occurs after a past tense in these deliberative relative clauses in classical Greek. There are, however, no New Testament instances of the Optative so used.

IV. Relative Clauses Introduced by Words Meaning Until, While, and Before

321. Ἕως is properly a relative adverb which marks one action as the temporal limit of another action. It does this in two ways, either (*a*) so that the *beginning* or *simple occurrence* of the action of the verb introduced by ἕως is the limit of the action denoted by the principal verb, or (*b*) so that the *continuance* of the former is the limit of the latter. In the former case ἕως means *until*, in the latter, *while, as long as.*

On the classical use of ἕως and similar words, see *HA.* 920-924; *G.* 1463-1474; *G.MT.* 611-661; *Gild.* in *A.J.P.* IV.

416–418. On ἕως in Hellenistic Greek see *G. W. Gilmore* in *J.B.L.*, 1890, pp. 153–160.

322. Clauses Introduced by ἕως and referring to the Future. When the clause introduced by ἕως depends on a verb of future time, and refers to a future contingency, it takes the Subjunctive with ἄν both in classical and New Testament Greek.

Mark 6 : 10; ἐκεῖ μένετε ἕως ἂν ἐξέλθητε ἐκεῖθεν, *there abide till ye depart thence.* See also Matt. 5 : 18; 12 : 20; Luke 9 : 27; 1 Cor. 4 : 5.

323. In classical Greek, especially in tragic poetry, the Subjunctive without ἄν sometimes occurs with ἕως after a verb of present or future time. *G.*MT. 620. In the New Testament this construction is frequent.

Luke 15 : 4; καὶ πορεύεται ἐπὶ τὸ ἀπολωλὸς ἕως εὕρῃ αὐτό, *and goeth after that which is lost, until he find it.* See also Matt. 10 : 23; Luke 12 : 59; 22 : 34.

324. Clauses Introduced by ἕως and referring to what was in Past Time a Future Contingency. When the clause introduced by ἕως depends on a verb of past time and refers to what was at the time of the principal verb conceived of as a future contingency, it takes the Optative without ἄν in classical Greek. In the New Testament it takes the Subjunctive without ἄν.

Matt. 18 : 30; ἔβαλεν αὐτὸν εἰς φυλακὴν ἕως ἀποδῷ τὸ ὀφειλόμενον, *he cast him into prison till he should pay that which was due.*

325. The Subjunctive after ἕως in the New Testament is always an Aorist, the action denoted being conceived of as a simple event, and ἕως meaning properly *until.* Thus the accurate translation of Mark 14 : 32 (Matt. 26 : 36 is similar), καθίσατε ὧδε ἕως προσεύξωμαι, is, *Sit ye here till*

I pray, or *have prayed* (cf. 98). *While I pray* (R.V.) is slightly para-
phrastic. Cf. Luke 17 : 8.

**326. Clauses Introduced by ἕως (until) and referring
to a Past Fact.** When ἕως means *until* and the clause
introduced by it refers to an actual past occurrence, the
verb of this clause is in a past tense of the Indicative, as in
an ordinary relative clause referring to past time.

Matt. 2 : 9 ; ὁ ἀστήρ . . . προῆγεν αὐτούς, ἕως ἐλθὼν ἐστάθη ἐπάνω οὗ
ἦν τὸ παιδίον, *the star . . . went before them, till it came and stood
over where the young child was.*

**327. Clauses Introduced by ἕως (while) and referring
to a Contemporaneous Event.** When ἕως means *while*
and the clause introduced by it refers to an event contemporaneous with that of the principal verb, it has the construction of an ordinary relative clause. Cf. 293.

John 9 : 4 ; ἡμᾶς δεῖ ἐργάζεσθαι τὰ ἔργα τοῦ πέμψαντός με ἕως ἡμέρα
ἐστίν, *we must work the works of him that sent me, while it is day.*

328. In John 21 : 22, 23 ; 1 Tim. 4 : 13, the exact meaning of ἕως
ἔρχομαι is probably *while I am coming*, the coming being conceived of as
in progress from the time of speaking. Cf. Luke 9 : 13. In 1 Cor. 4 : 5
on the other hand it is thought of as a future event. In Mark 6 : 45 ἕως
ἀπολύει represents ἕως ἀπολύω of the direct form (cf. 347), the original
sentence meaning, *go before me while I am sending away*, etc.

329. When the ἕως clause refers to the future or to what was at the
time of the principal verb the future (322–326), it frequently has the
force of a conditional relative clause. See Matt. 18 : 30 ; Luke 15 : 4.
When it refers to an actual event (327, 328), it is an ordinary temporal
clause (293), requiring special mention here only to distinguish these
usages from those described above.

330. In the New Testament ἕως is sometimes followed by οὗ or ὅτου.
Ἕως is then a preposition governing the genitive of the relative pronoun,

but the phrase ἕως οὗ or ἕως ὅτου is in effect a compound conjunction having the same force as the simple ἕως. The construction following it is also the same, except that ἄν never occurs after ἕως οὗ or ἕως ὅτου. See Matt. 5 : 25 ; 13 : 33 ; John 9 : 18 ; Acts 23 : 12.

331. Clauses introduced by ἄχρι, ἄχρι οὗ, ἄχρι ἧς ἡμέρας, μέχρι and μέχρις οὗ have in general the same construction and force as clauses introduced by ἕως, ἕως οὗ, and ἕως ὅτου.

Mark 13 : 30 ; οὐ μὴ παρέλθῃ ἡ γενεὰ αὕτη μέχρις οὗ ταῦτα πάντα γένηται.

Acts 7 : 18 ; ηὔξησεν ὁ λαὸς καὶ ἐπληθύνθη ἐν Αἰγύπτῳ, ἄχρι οὗ ἀνέστη βασιλεὺς ἕτερος ἐπ' Αἴγυπτον. See also Rev. 15 : 8 ; 20 : 3 ; Luke 17 : 27 ; Acts 27 : 33.

Rev. 7 : 3 ; μὴ ἀδικήσητε τὴν γῆν . . . ἄχρι σφραγίσωμεν τοὺς δούλους τοῦ θεοῦ.

332. Gal. 3 : 19 [*WH. text*] furnishes one instance of ἄχρις ἄν with a word meaning *until* after a verb of past time [*WH. margin, Tisch.,* and *Treg.* read ἄχρις οὗ]; cf. 324. Rev. 2 : 25 contains the combination ἄχρι οὗ ἄν with the Future Indicative ; cf. 330. Rev. 17 : 17 contains a Future Indicative with ἄχρι after a past tense.

333. Clauses introduced by πρίν and employing a finite mood have in general the same construction as clauses introduced by ἕως.

The New Testament, however, contains but two instances of a finite verb after πρίν, Luke 2 : 26 ; Acts 25 : 16. In both cases the clause is in indirect discourse, and expresses what was from the point of view of the original statement a future contingency. In Luke 2 : 26 the Subjunctive with ἄν is retained from the direct discourse. In Acts 25 : 16 the Optative represents a Subjunctive with or without ἄν of the direct discourse. Cf. 341–344.

REM. 1. The employment of a finite mood rather than an Infinitive in these instances is in accordance with classical usage. Cf. 382, and *G.* 1470.

REM. 2. In Acts 25 : 16 ἤ occurs after πρίν, and in Luke 2 : 26 it appears as a strongly attested variant reading. Attic writers used the simple πρίν with the finite moods. Cf. 381.

MOODS IN INDIRECT DISCOURSE

334. When words once uttered or thought are afterward quoted, the quotation may be either direct or indirect. In a direct quotation the original statement is repeated without incorporation into the structure of the sentence in the midst of which it now stands. In an indirect quotation the original sentence is incorporated into a new sentence as a subordinate element dependent upon a verb of *saying, thinking,* or the like, and suffers such modification as this incorporation requires. The following example will illustrate :

> Original sentence (direct discourse), *I will come.*
> Direct quotation, *He said, " I will come."*
> Indirect quotation, *He said that he would come.*

REM. The distinction between direct discourse and indirect is not one of the exactness of the quotation. Direct quotation may be inexact. Indirect quotation may be exact. Suppose, for example, that the original statement was, *There are good reasons why I should act thus.* If one say, *He said, " I have good reasons for acting thus,"* the quotation is direct but inexact. If one say, *He said that there were good reasons why he should act thus,* the quotation is exact though indirect.

335. Direct quotation manifestly requires no special discussion, since the original statement is simply transferred to the new sentence without incorporation into its structure.

336. Indirect quotation, on the other hand, involving a readjustment of the original sentence to a new point of view, calls for a determination of the principles on which this readjustment is made. Its problem is most simply stated in the form of the question, What change does the original form of a sentence undergo when incorporated into a new sentence as an indirect quotation ? All consideration of the principles of indirect discourse must take as its starting point the original form of the words quoted.

For the student of Greek that expresses his own thought in another language, it will also be necessary to compare the idiom of the two languages. See 351 ff.

337. The term indirect discourse is commonly applied only to indirect assertions and indirect questions. Commands, promises, and hopes indirectly quoted might without impropriety be included under the term, but are, in general, excluded because of the difficulty of drawing the line between them and certain similar usages, in which, however, no direct form can be thought of. Thus the Infinitive after a verb of commanding might be considered the representative in indirect discourse of an Imperative in the direct discourse; somewhat less probably the Infinitive after a verb of wishing might be supposed to represent an Optative of the direct; while for the Infinitive after verbs of striving, which in itself can scarcely be regarded as of different force from those after verbs of commanding and wishing, no direct form can be thought of.

338. Concerning commands indirectly quoted, see 204. Concerning the Infinitive after verbs of *promising*, see 391.

339. Indirect assertions in Greek take three forms:

(*a*) A clause introduced by ὅτι or ὡς. In the New Testament, however, ὡς is not so used.

(*b*) An Infinitive with its subject expressed or understood. See 390.

(*c*) A Participle agreeing with the object of a verb of *perceiving*, and the like. See 460.

340. Indirect Questions are introduced by εἰ or other interrogative word; the verb is in a finite mood. *HA.* 930; *G.* 1605.

341. Classical Usage in Indirect Discourse. In indirect assertions after ὅτι and in indirect questions, classical usage is as follows :

(*a*) When the leading verb on which the quotation depends denotes present or future time, the mood and tense of the direct discourse are retained in the indirect.

(*b*) When the leading verb on which the quotation depends denotes past time, the mood and tense of the direct discourse may be retained in the indirect, or the tense may be retained and an Indicative or Subjunctive of the direct discourse may be changed to an Optative. *HA.* 932; *G.* 1497.

342. The above rule applies to all indirect quotations in which the quotation is expressed by a finite verb, and includes indirect quotations of simple sentences and both principal and subordinate clauses of complex sentences indirectly quoted.

The classical grammars enumerate certain constructions in which an Indicative of the original sentence is uniformly retained in the indirect discourse. These cases do not, however, require treatment here, the general rule being sufficient as a basis for the consideration of New Testament usage.

343. New Testament Usage in Indirect Discourse. In indirect assertions after ὅτι and in indirect questions, New Testament usage is in general the same as classical usage. Such peculiarities as exist pertain chiefly to the relative frequency of different usages. See 344–349.

John 11 : 27 ; ἐγὼ πεπίστευκα ὅτι σὺ εἶ ὁ χριστὸς ὁ υἱὸς τοῦ θεοῦ, *I have believed that thou art the Christ, the Son of God.*

Gal. 2 : 14 ; εἶδον ὅτι οὐκ ὀρθοποδοῦσιν, *I saw that they were not walking uprightly.*

Matt. 20 : 10 ; ἐλθόντες οἱ πρῶτοι ἐνόμισαν ὅτι πλεῖον λήμψονται, *when the first came, they supposed that they would receive more.*

Mark 9 : 6 ; οὐ γὰρ ᾔδει τί ἀποκριθῇ, *for he wist not what to answer.*

Luke 8 : 9 ; ἐπηρώτων δὲ αὐτὸν οἱ μαθηταὶ αὐτοῦ τίς αὕτη εἴη ἡ παρα-βολή, *and his disciples asked him what this parable was.*

Luke 24 : 23 ; ἦλθαν λέγουσαι καὶ ὀπτασίαν ἀγγέλων ἑωρακέναι, οἳ λέγουσιν αὐτὸν ζῆν, *they came saying that they had also seen a vision of angels, which said that he was alive.* In this example the principal clause of the direct discourse is expressed in the indirect discourse after a verb of past time by an Infinitive, while the subordinate clause retains the tense and mood of the original.

Acts 5 : 24 ; διηπόρουν περὶ αὐτῶν τί ἂν γένοιτο τοῦτο, *they were per-plexed concerning them whereunto this would grow.* But for ἂν in this sentence, it might be thought that the direct form was a deliberative question having the Subjunctive or Future Indicative. But in the absence of evidence that ἂν was ever added to an Optative arising under the law of indirect discourse, it must be supposed that the indirect discourse has preserved the form of the direct unchanged, and that this was therefore a Potential Optative with protasis omitted. See also Luke 6 : 11; 15 : 26; Acts 10 : 17.

344. The Optative occurs in indirect discourse much less frequently in the New Testament than in classical Greek. It is found only in Luke's writings, and there almost exclusive-ly in indirect questions.

REM. 1. Acts 25 : 16 contains the only New Testament instance of an Optative in the indirect quotation of a declarative sentence. (But cf. 347 and 258.) It here stands in a subordinate clause which in the direct discourse would have had a Subjunctive with or without ἄν. If the ἄν be supposed to have been in the original sentence (cf. Luke 2 : 26), it has been dropped in accordance with regular usage in such cases. *HA.* 934; *G.* 1497, 2.

Rᴇм. 2. The clause μήποτε δῴη [or δώῃ] αὐτοῖς ὁ θεὸς μετάνοιαν in 2 Tim. 2 : 25 is regarded by *B.* p. 256, *Moulton, WM.* pp. 374, 631, foot notes, as an indirect question. But concerning the text and the interpretation, see 225.

345. In quoting declarative sentences the indirect form is comparatively infrequent in the New Testament, the direct form either with or without ὅτι being much more frequent. The presence of ὅτι before a quotation is in the New Testament therefore not even presumptive evidence that the quotation is indirect. The ὅτι is of course redundant.

Luke 7 : 48 ; εἶπεν δὲ αὐτῇ Ἀφέωνταί σου αἱ ἁμαρτίαι, *and he said unto her, Thy sins are forgiven.*

John 9 : 9 ; ἐκεῖνος ἔλεγεν ὅτι Ἐγώ εἰμι, *he said, I am he.*

Rᴇм. The redundant ὅτι sometimes occurs even before a direct question. Mark 4 : 21, *et al.*

346. Indirect deliberative questions are sometimes found after ἔχω and other similar verbs which do not properly take a question as object. The interrogative clause in this case serves the purpose of a relative clause and its antecedent, while retaining the form which shows its origin in a deliberative question.

Mark 6 : 36 ; ἵνα . . . ἀγοράσωσιν ἑαυτοῖς τί φάγωσιν, *that . . . they may buy themselves somewhat to eat.*

Luke 9 : 58 ; ὁ δὲ υἱὸς τοῦ ἀνθρώπου οὐκ ἔχει ποῦ τὴν κεφαλὴν κλίνῃ, *but the Son of man hath not where to lay his head.* See also Matt. 8 : 20 ; Mark 8 : 1, 2 ; Luke 12 : 17.

347. The principles of indirect discourse apply to all subordinate clauses which express indirectly the thoughts of another or of the speaker himself, even when the construction is not strictly that of indirect discourse. *HA.* 937 ; *G.* 1502. See New Testament examples under 258.

348. Both in classical and New Testament Greek, the Imperfect occasionally stands in indirect discourse after a verb of past time as the representative of a Present of the direct discourse, and a Pluperfect as the representative of the Perfect. Thus exceptional Greek usage coincides with regular English usage. *HA.* 936; *G.* 1489.

John 2 : 25; αὐτὸς γὰρ ἐγίνωσκεν τί ἦν ἐν τῷ ἀνθρώπῳ, *for he himself knew what was in man.* See also Acts 19 : 32.

349. In classical Greek, ὅστις is used in introducing indirect questions. *HA.* 1011; *G.* 1600. In the New Testament it is not so employed, but there are a few passages in which it is apparently used as an interrogative pronoun in a direct question.

It is so taken by *Mey.*, *B.*, *WH.*, *et al.* in Mark 9 : 11, 28, and by *WH.* in Mark 2 : 16. See *B.* pp. 252 f. ; *Th.*, ὅστις, 4 ; also (*contra*) *WM.* p. 208, f.n. ; *WT.* p. 167.

350. The simple relative pronouns and adverbs are sometimes used in indirect questions in the New Testament as in classical Greek. *HA.* 1011, a; *G.* 1600; *J.* 877, Obs. 3; *B.* pp. 250 f.

Luke 8 : 47; δι᾽ ἣν αἰτίαν ἥψατο αὐτοῦ ἀπήγγειλεν, *she declared for what cause she had touched him.* See also Mark 5 : 19, 20; Acts 14 : 27; 15 : 14.

351. INDIRECT DISCOURSE IN ENGLISH AND IN GREEK. From what has been said above, it appears that the tense of a verb standing in a clause of indirect discourse in Greek does not express the same relation between the action denoted and the time of speaking as is expressed by a verb of the same tense standing in a principal clause; or, to speak more exactly, does not describe it from the same point of view. A verb in a principal clause views its action from the point of view of the speaker. A verb in an indirect quotation, on the other hand, views its action from the point of view of another person, viz. the original author of the words quoted. It has also appeared that in certain cases the mood of the Greek verb is changed when it is indirectly quoted. Now it is evident that in order to translate the Greek sentence containing a clause of indirect discourse into English correctly and intelligently, we must ascertain what English usage is in respect to the tenses and moods of the verbs of indirect discourse; otherwise we have no principle by which to determine what English tense and mood properly represent a given Greek tense and mood in indirect discourse. Furthermore, since Greek usage has been expressed in terms of the relation between the original utterance and the quotation, it will be expedient to state English usage in the same way. An example will illustrate at the same time the necessity of formulating the law and of formulating it in terms of relation to the direct form.

(1) *He has seen a vision.*　　(2) ὀπτασίαν ἑώρακεν.

(3) *They said that he had seen a vision.*　(4) εἶπον ὅτι ὀπτασίαν ἑώρακεν.

The sentences marked (1) and (2) express the same idea and employ corresponding tenses. The sentences marked (3) and (4) represent respectively the indirect quotation of (1) and (2) after a verb of past time, and express therefore the same meaning. They do not, however, employ corresponding tenses, the Greek using a Perfect, the English a Pluperfect. It is evident therefore that the principle of indirect discourse is not the same in English as in Greek, and that we cannot translate (4) into (3) by the same principle of equivalence of tenses which we employ in direct assertions. To translate (4) we must first restore (2) by the Greek law of indirect discourse, then translate (2) into (1), and finally by the English law of indirect discourse construct (3) from (1) and the translation of the Greek εἶπον. This process requires the formulation of the law of indirect discourse for English as well as for Greek.

352. English usage in indirect discourse is illustrated in the following examples:

Direct form			. .	*I see the city.*
Indirect, after present tense			. .	*He says that he sees the city.*
"	"	future	" . .	*He will say that he sees the city.*
"	"	past	" . .	*He said that he saw the city.*
Direct form				*I saw the city.*
Indirect, after present tense			. .	*He says that he saw the city.*
"	"	future	" . .	*He will say that he saw the city.*
"	"	past	" . .	*He said that he had seen the city.*
Direct form				*I shall see the city.*
Indirect, after present tense			. .	*He says that he shall see the city.*
"	"	future	" . .	*He will say that he shall see the city.*
"	"	past	" . .	*He said that he should see the city.*
Direct form				*I may see the city.*
Indirect, after present tense			. .	*He says that he may see the city.*
"	"	future	" . .	*He will say that he may see the city.*
"	"	past	" . .	*He said that he might see the city.*

From these examples we may deduce the following rule for indirect discourse in English:

(*a*) After verbs of present or future time, the mood and tense of the direct discourse are retained in the indirect discourse.

(*b*) After verbs of past time, the mood of the direct discourse is retained, but the tense is changed to that tense which is past relatively to the time of the direct discourse.

Thus, *see* becomes *saw; saw* becomes *had seen; shall see* becomes *should see* (the change of mood here is only apparent); *may see* becomes *might see*, etc.

REM. In questions and in conditional clauses a Present Indicative of the direct form may become a Past Subjunctive in indirect quotation after a verb of past time. See Luke 3:15; Acts 10:18; 20:17, E.V.

353. Comparing this with the Greek rule, we may deduce the following principles for the translation into English of clauses of indirect discourse in Greek:

(*a*) When the quotation is introduced by a verb of present or future time, translate the verbs of the indirect discourse by the same forms which would be used in ordinary direct discourse.

(*b*) When the quotation is introduced by a verb of past time, if there are Optatives which represent Indicatives or Subjunctives of the direct discourse, first restore in thought these Indicatives or Subjunctives, then translate each Greek verb by that English verb which is relatively past to that which would correctly translate the same verb standing in direct discourse.

354. The statement of English usage in indirect discourse is presented in the form adopted above for the sake of brevity and convenience of application. It is, however, rather a formula than a statement which represents the process of thought. In order to apprehend clearly the difference between English and Greek usage it must be recognized that certain English tenses have, not like the Greek tenses a two-fold function, but a three-fold. They mark (1) the temporal relation of the point of view from which the action is described to the time of speaking; (2) the temporal relation of the action described to this point of view; (3) the conception of the action as respects its progress. Thus in the sentence, *I had been reading,* (1) the point of view from which the act of reading is viewed is past, (2) the action itself is previous to that point of view, and (3) it is viewed as in progress. *He will not go* is a Future from a present point of view presenting the action as a simple event. In the sentence, *When he came, I was reading,* *I was reading* would be more accurately described as a Present progressive from a past point of view, than as a Past progressive from a present point of view. In other instances the same form might be a Past from a present point of view. These triple-function tenses have perhaps their chief use in English in indirect discourse, but are used also in direct discourse. Many of them are derived by the process of composition, out of which so many English tenses have arisen, from verb-forms which originally had only the two-fold function, but their existence in modern English is none the less clearly established. Professor W. G. Hale [1] in *A.J.P.*, vol. VIII. pp. 66 ff., has set forth the similar three-fold function of the Latin tenses in the Indicative Mood. But it should be noticed that the English has developed this three-fold function more clearly even than the Latin. For example, the antecedence of an action to a past point of view is in Latin only implied in the assertion of its completeness at that past point of time. But in English this antecedence may be affirmed without affirming the completeness of the act.

Bearing in mind this three-fold function of certain English tenses, the difference between Greek and English usage in indirect discourse may be stated comprehensively as follows:

The Greek, while adopting in indirect discourse the point of view of the person quoting as respects the person of verbs and pronouns, and while sometimes after a verb of past time marking the dependent character of the statement by the use of the Optative in place of an Indicative or Subjunctive of the original statement, yet as respects tense, regularly carries over into the indirect discourse the point of view of the original statement, treating it as if it were still present. What was present to the original speaker is still treated from his point of view, as present; what was past, as past; what was future, as future.

In English, on the other hand, in quoting a past utterance,

---

[1] Professor Hale's article furnished the suggestion for the view of the English tenses presented here.

the fact that it is past is not only indicated by the past tense of the verb which introduces the quotation, but still further by the employment of a tense in the quotation which marks the point of view from which the act is looked at as past. Thus in Greek a prediction expressed originally by a Future tense, when afterward quoted after a verb of past time, is still expressed by a Future, the act being viewed as future from the assumed point of view, and this point of view being treated as present or its character as past being ignored. But in English such a prediction is expressed by a Past-future, *i.e.* by the English tense which describes an action as future from a past point of view. Thus in quoting ὄψομαι, *I shall see*, in indirect discourse, one says in Greek, εἶπεν ὅτι ὄψεται; but in English, *he said that he should see*. Similarly, a statement made originally by the Perfect tense, when quoted after a verb of past time, is still expressed by a Perfect tense in Greek, but in English by a Pluperfect. Thus ἡμάρτηκα, *I have sinned;* εἶπεν ὅτι ἡμάρτηκεν, *he said that he had sinned.*

When we pass to quotations after verbs of present time, the usages of the two languages naturally coincide, since the difference between the point of view of the original utterance and the quotation, which in English gave rise to a change of tense not however made in Greek, disappears. The point of view of the original statement is in both languages retained and treated as present, because it is present. Thus ἐλεύσομαι, *I shall come*, requires only a change of person in quotation after a verb of present time, λέγει ὅτι ἐλεύσεται, *he says that he shall come.*

It might naturally be anticipated that in quotations after verbs of future time, where again the time of the original statement differs from that of the quotation, there would arise a difference of usage between English and Greek. Such however is not the case. What the Greek does after a verb of

past time, the English as well as the Greek does after a verb
of future time, viz. treats the point of view of the original
utterance as present. Thus let us suppose the case of one
predicting what a person just now departing will say when he
returns. He has not yet seen anything, but it is imagined that
when he returns he will say, *I have seen all things.* The assertion of this by *he will say*, takes the form *he will say that he
has seen all things;* just as in Greek one quoting ἑώρακα πάντα
after ἐρεῖ says ἐρεῖ ὅτι ἑώρακεν πάντα. Thus the person quoting
does not describe the event from his own point of view — this
would require *he will see,* nor does he mark the fact that the
point of view of the utterance is different from his own — this
would require *he will have seen;* but treats the point of view
of the person whose expected language he quotes in advance,
as if it were present. Thus while the Greek is consistent in
simply adopting the conceived point of view of the future
statement, the English departs from the principle which it follows after past tenses, and follows here the same method as
the Greek.

355. These facts enable us to see that it would be incorrect to say
that the tense of the direct discourse is in Greek determined from the
point of view of the original speaker, in English from the point of view of
the person who makes the quotation. The correct statement is that in
both languages the act is looked at from the point of view of the original
speaker, but that the two languages differ somewhat in their method of
indicating the relation of this point of view to the time of the quotation.
This difference, however, pertains only to quotations whose point of view
is past. Its precise nature has already been stated (354). When the
point of view is present or future the usage of the two languages is
identical.

356. The comparison of English and Greek usage may
be reduced to articulated statement as follows: English usage
is like Greek usage in three respects, and different in two
respects.

I. It is like Greek in that,

(*a*) It adapts the person of the pronouns and verbs of the original utterance to the point of view of the quoter.

(*b*) It looks at the act described in the quotation from the point of view of the original statement.

(*c*) After a verb of present or future time this point of view of the original utterance is treated in the quotation as present, as after verbs of present time it is in fact.

II. It differs from Greek in that,

(*a*) While it looks at the act from the point of view of the original statement, if that point of view is past it designates it as past, using a tense which describes the action from a past point of view. A Past of the original utterance becomes in the quotation a Past-past; a Future becomes a Past-future, etc. This the Greek does not do, having in general no tense which has this double temporal power.

(*b*) It does not as a rule change the original mood of the verb in quotation. Most apparent changes of mood, such as *will* to *would*, are changes of tense. But cf. 352, Rem.

CONSTRUCTION AFTER Καὶ ἐγένετο

357. Clause or Infinitive as the Subject of ἐγένετο. By a Hebraism καὶ ἐγένετο and ἐγένετο δέ, Septuagint renderings of וַיְהִי, are used in the New Testament (Matt., Mark, Luke, Acts) to introduce a clause or an Infinitive which is logically the subject of the ἐγένετο. The ἐγένετο is usually followed by a phrase or clause of time; the event to be narrated is then expressed by καί with an Indicative, or by an Indicative without καί, or by an Infinitive. It thus results that the construction takes three forms:

358. (a) Καὶ ἐγένετο, or ἐγένετο δέ, and the phrase of time are followed by καί with an Indicative.

Luke 5 : 1; ἐγένετο δὲ ἐν τῷ τὸν ὄχλον ἐπικεῖσθαι αὐτῷ καὶ ἀκούειν τὸν λόγον τοῦ θεοῦ καὶ αὐτὸς ἦν ἑστὼς παρὰ τὴν λίμνην Γεννησα-ρέτ, *now it came to pass, while the multitude pressed upon him and heard the word of God, that he was standing by the lake of Gennesaret.*

359. (b) Καὶ ἐγένετο, or ἐγένετο δέ, and the phrase of time are followed by an Indicative without καί.

Mark 1 : 9; Καὶ ἐγένετο ἐν ἐκείναις ταῖς ἡμέραις ἦλθεν Ἰησοῦς ἀπὸ Ναζαρὲτ τῆς Γαλιλαίας, *and it came to pass in those days, that Jesus came from Nazareth of Galilee.*

360. (c) καὶ ἐγένετο, or ἐγένετο δέ, and the phrase of time are followed by an Infinitive, the narrative being continued either by an Infinitive or an Indicative.

Acts 9 : 32; ἐγένετο δὲ Πέτρον διερχόμενον διὰ πάντων κατελθεῖν, *and it came to pass, as Peter went throughout all parts, he came down.* See also Mark 2 : 23; Luke 6 : 12. *B.* pp. 276–278.

THE INFINITIVE

361. That the Infinitive in Greek had its origin as respects both form and function in a verbal noun, and chiefly at least in the dative case of such a noun, is now regarded as an assured result of comparative grammar. At the time of the earliest Greek literature, however, the other cases of this verbal noun had passed out of use, and the dative function of the form that remained had become so far obscured that, while it still retained the functions appropriate to the dative, it was also used as an accusative and as a nominative. Beginning with Pindar it appears with the article, at first as a subject-nominative. Later it developed also the other cases, accusative, genitive, and dative. By this process its distinctively dative force was obscured while the scope of its use was enlarged. In Post-

Aristotelian Greek, notably in the Septuagint and the New Testament, another step was taken. The Infinitive with the article in the genitive began to assume some such prominence as at a much earlier time the dative had acquired, and as before, the sense of its case being in some degree lost, this genitive Infinitive came to be used as a nominative or accusative. We mark therefore four stages of development. First, that for which we must go back of the historic period of the Greek language itself, when the Infinitive was distinctly a dative case. Second, that which is found in Homer: the Infinitive begins to be used as subject or object, though the strictly dative functions still have a certain prominence, and the article is not yet used. Third, that of which the beginnings are seen in Pindar and which is more fully developed in classical authors of a later time: the Infinitive without the article, sometimes with dative functions, sometimes with the force of other cases, is used side by side with the articular Infinitive in the nominative, genitive, dative, and accusative singular. Fourth, that which appears in the Septuagint and the New Testament: all the usages found in the third stage still continuing, the Infinitive with the article in the genitive begins to lose the sense of its genitive function and to be employed as a nominative or accusative.

From the earliest historic period of the Greek language the Infinitive partakes of the characteristics both of the verb and the noun. As a verb it has a subject more or less definite, and expressed or implied, and takes the adverbial and objective limitations appropriate to a verb. As a noun it fills the office in the sentence appropriate to its case. Many of these case-functions are identical with those which belong to other substantives; some are peculiar to the Infinitive.

REM. Concerning the history of the Infinitive, see *G*.MT. 742, 788; *Gild.* in *T.A.P.A.* 1878, and in *A.J.P.* III. pp. 193 ff.; IV. pp. 241 ff., pp. 418 ff.; VIII. p. 329; *Birklein,* Entwickelungsgeschichte des sub-stantivierten Infinitivs, in *Schanz,* Beiträge zur historischen Syntax der griechischen Sprache, Heft 7.

362. In the Greek of the classical and later periods, the functions of the Infinitive as an element of the sentence are very various. They may be classified logically as follows:

I. AS A PRINCIPAL VERB (364, 365).

II. AS A SUBSTANTIVE ELEMENT.

    (1) As subject (384, 385, 390, 393, 404).

    (2) As object in indirect discourse (390).

    (3) As object after verbs of *exhorting, striving, promising, hoping,* etc. (387–389, 391, 394, 404).

    (4) As object after verbs that take a genitive (401–403).

III. AS AN ADJECTIVE ELEMENT.

    (1) As appositive (386, 395).

    (2) Expressing other adnominal limitations (378, 379, 400).

IV. AS AN ADVERBIAL ELEMENT, denoting,

    (1) Purpose (366, 367, 370 (d), 371 (d), 372, 397).

    (2) Indirect object (368).

    (3) Result (369–371, 398).

    (4) Measure or degree (after adjectives and adverbs) (376, 399).

    (5) Manner, means, cause, or respect (375, 377, 396).

    (6) A modal modification of an assertion (383).

The articular Infinitive governed by a preposition (406–417) expresses various adverbial relations, the precise nature of which is determined by the meaning of the preposition employed. Similarly πρίν or πρίν ἤ with the Infinitive (380–382) constitutes an adverbial phrase of time, the temporal idea lying in πρίν rather than in the Infinitive.

363. To arrange the treatment of the Infinitive on the basis of such a logical classification as that given above (362) would, however, disregard the historical order of development and to some extent obscure the point of view from which the Greek language looked at the Infinitive. It seems better, therefore, to begin with those uses of the Infinitive which are most evidently connected with the original dative function, and proceed to those in which the dative force is vanishing or lost. This is the general plan pursued in the following sections, though it is by no means affirmed that in details the precise order of historical development has been followed.

THE INFINITIVE WITHOUT THE ARTICLE

364. The Imperative Infinitive. The Infinitive without the article is occasionally used to express a command or exhortation. This is the only use of the Infinitive as a principal verb. It is of ancient origin, being especially frequent in Homer. *HA.* 957 ; *G.* 1536. The New Testament furnishes but one certain instance of this usage.

Phil. 3 : 16 ; πλὴν εἰς ὃ ἐφθάσαμεν, τῷ αὐτῷ στοιχεῖν, *only whereunto we have attained, by the same rule walk.*

365. Rom. 12 : 15 affords another probable instance of the imperative use of the Infinitive. *Buttmann* supposes an ellipsis of λέγω, and *Winer* a change of construction by which the writer returns from the independent Imperatives used in v. 14 to the construction of an Infinitive dependent on λέγω employed in v. 3. This explanation of change of construction probably applies in Mark 6 : 9 (cf. the even more abrupt change in Mark 5 : 23) ; but in Rom. ch. 12 the remoteness of the verb λέγω (in v. 3) from the Infinitive (in v. 15) makes the dependence of the latter upon the former improbable. *B.* pp. 271 f. ; *WM.* pp. 397 f. ; *WT.* 316.

366. The Infinitive of Purpose. The Infinitive is used to express the purpose of the action or state denoted by the principal verb. *HA.* 951 ; *G.* 1532.

Matt. 5 : 17 ; μὴ νομίσητε ὅτι ἦλθον καταλῦσαι τὸν νόμον ἢ τοὺς προφήτας · οὐκ ἦλθον καταλῦσαι ἀλλὰ πληρῶσαι, *think not that I came to destroy the law or the prophets : I came not to destroy, but to fulfil.*

Luke 18 : 10 ; ἄνθρωποι δύο ἀνέβησαν εἰς τὸ ἱερὸν προσεύξασθαι, *two men went up into the temple to pray.*

Acts 10 : 33 ; νῦν οὖν πάντες ἡμεῖς ἐνώπιον τοῦ θεοῦ πάρεσμεν ἀκοῦσαι πάντα τὰ προστεταγμένα σοι ὑπὸ τοῦ κυρίου, *now therefore we are all here present in the sight of God, to hear all things that have been commanded thee of the Lord.*

367. The Infinitive expressing purpose is sometimes introduced by ὥστε or ὡς. See 370 (d), 371 (d), 372.

368. THE INFINITIVE AS AN INDIRECT OBJECT.   Closely akin to the Infinitive of Purpose is the Infinitive of the indirect object.   The former is a supplementary addition to a statement in itself complete, and expresses the purpose had in view in the doing of the action or the maintenance of the state. The Infinitive of the indirect object on the other hand is a complementary limitation of a verb, expressing the direct tendency of the action denoted by the principal verb, or other similar dative relation.   Some of the instances of this usage are scarcely to be distinguished from the Infinitive of Purpose, while in others the distinction is clearly marked.

Luke 10 : 40 ; Κύριε, οὐ μέλει σοι ὅτι ἡ ἀδελφή μου μόνην με κατέλειπεν διακονεῖν, *Lord, dost thou not care that my sister has left me to serve alone?*

Acts 17 : 21 ; 'Αθηναῖοι δὲ πάντες καὶ οἱ ἐπιδημοῦντες ξένοι εἰς οὐδὲν ἕτερον ηὐκαίρουν ἢ λέγειν τι ἢ ἀκούειν τι καινότερον, *now all the Athenians and the strangers sojourning there spent their time in nothing else than either to tell or to hear some new thing.*   See also Mark 4 : 23 ; 6 : 31 ; 10 : 40 ; Luke 7 : 40 ; 12 : 4 ; Acts 4 : 14 ; 7 : 42 ; 23 : 17, 18, 19 ; 25 : 26 ; Tit. 2 : 8.

369. The Infinitive of Result.   The Infinitive may be used to denote the result of the action expressed by the principal verb.   When so used it is usually introduced by ὥστε.   *HA.* 953 ; *G.* 1449.

Mark 4 : 37 ; καὶ τὰ κύματα ἐπέβαλλεν εἰς τὸ πλοῖον, ὥστε ἤδη γεμίζεσθαι τὸ πλοῖον, *and the waves beat into the boat, insomuch that the boat was now filling.*

1 Thess. 1 : 8 ; ἐν παντὶ τόπῳ ἡ πίστις ὑμῶν ἡ πρὸς τὸν θεὸν ἐξελήλυθεν, ὥστε μὴ χρείαν ἔχειν ἡμᾶς λαλεῖν τι, *in every place your faith to God-ward is gone forth, so that we need not to speak anything.*

370.   Under the general head of expressions of result it is necessary to distinguish three different conceptions :

(*a*) Actual result, conceived of and affirmed as actual; in this case classical Greek uses ὥστε with the Indicative.   See 236.

(*b*) Tendency or conceived result which it is implied is an actual result. In this case the result is thought of as that which the action of the principal verb is adapted or sufficient to produce, and it is the context or the nature of the case only which shows that this result is actually produced. In this case classical Greek uses ὥστε with the Infinitive.

(*c*) Tendency or conceived result thought of and affirmed simply as such. In this case the result is one which the action of the principal verb is adapted or sufficient to produce, though the actual production is either left in doubt, or is indicated by the context not to have taken place. Classical Greek employs ὥστε with the Infinitive (in Homer the Infinitive without ὥστε).

To these three may be added as a closely related conception which the Greek also expressed by ὥστε with the Infinitive:

(*d*) Purpose, *i.e.* intended result.

The constructions by which these several shades of meaning are expressed are substantially the same in the New Testament as in classical Greek, except that the construction appropriate to the second meaning has apparently encroached upon the realm of the first meaning, and the line of distinction between them has become correspondingly indistinct. Ὥστε with the Indicative occurs very rarely except with the meaning *therefore*, introducing a principal clause; and this fact, together with the large number of instances in which ὥστε with the Infinitive is used of a result evidently actual, makes it probable that the use of ὥστε with the Infinitive is no longer restricted, as in classical Greek, to instances in which the result is thought of as theoretical, but is used also of result in fact and in thought actual. Cf. *G.*MT. 582–584. There remain, however, instances entirely similar to those found in classical Greek, in which a result shown by the context to be actual is apparently presented simply as one which the event previously expressed tends to produce. Between these two classes it is evidently impossible to draw a sharp line of distinction. Cases of the third class are expressed in the New Testament by the Infinitive with or without ὥστε. Cf. also 218 and 398.

371. The following examples illustrate New Testament usage:

(a) Actual result conceived and affirmed as such.

Indicative after ὥστε.

John 3 : 16; οὕτως γὰρ ἠγάπησεν ὁ θεὸς τὸν κόσμον ὥστε τὸν υἱὸν τὸν μονογενῆ ἔδωκεν, *for God so loved the world that he gave his only begotten Son.*

Infinitive after ὥστε.

Mark 9 : 26; ἐγένετο ὡσεὶ νεκρὸς ὥστε τοὺς πολλοὺς λέγειν ὅτι ἀπέθανεν, *he became as one dead; insomuch that the more part said that he was dead.*

(b) Tendency, by implication realized in actual result. Infinitive, usually after ὥστε.

Luke 12 : 1; ἐν οἷς ἐπισυναχθεισῶν τῶν μυριάδων τοῦ ὄχλου, ὥστε καταπατεῖν ἀλλήλους, *in the meantime, when the many thousands of the multitude were gathered together, so as to tread one upon another.*

Rev. 5 : 5; ἰδοὺ ἐνίκησεν ὁ λέων ὁ ἐκ τῆς φυλῆς Ἰούδα, ἡ ῥίζα Δαυείδ, ἀνοῖξαι τὸ βιβλίον, *behold the lion that is of the tribe of Judah, the Root of David, hath overcome, to open the book.* See also Acts 1 : 25; 2 Cor. 1 : 8; 2 Thess. 2 : 4.

(c) Tendency or conceived result thought of as such. Infinitive, usually after ὥστε.

1 Cor. 13 : 2; κἂν ἔχω πᾶσαν τὴν πίστιν ὥστε ὄρη μεθιστάνειν, *and if I have all faith, so as to remove mountains.*

Matt. 10 : 1; ἔδωκεν αὐτοῖς ἐξουσίαν πνευμάτων ἀκαθάρτων ὥστε ἐκβάλλειν αὐτά, *he gave them authority over unclean spirits to cast them out.* Here probably belongs also Rom. 1 : 10. See also 2 Cor. 2 : 7; Rev. 16 : 9.

REM. The Infinitive in Heb. 6 : 10, οὐ γὰρ ἄδικος ὁ θεὸς ἐπιλαθέσθαι, must also be accounted an Infinitive of conceived result. The origin of this idiom may be an impersonal construction (cf. *G*.MT. 762), but it has departed in meaning as well as in form from its original. The meaning of this sentence is not, *It would not be unjust for God to forget*, but, *God is not unjust so as to forget.*

(*d*) Purpose, *i.e.* intended result.

Luke 4 : 29 ; καὶ ἤγαγον αὐτὸν ἕως ὀφρύος τοῦ ὄρους ὥστε κατακρημνίσαι αὐτόν, *and they led him unto the brow of the hill that they might throw him down headlong.* See also Luke 20 : 20.

REM. In Matt. 27 : 1, ὥστε with the Infinitive stands in definitive apposition with συμβούλιον, defining the content of the plan, rather than expressing the purpose of making it.

372. The Infinitive is used with ὡς in Luke 9 : 52 according to the reading adopted by *WH.* (most editors read ὥστε) and in Acts 20 : 24 according to the generally adopted reading (*WH.* read a Subjunctive). In both cases the phrase denotes purpose. No instance of ὡς with the Infinitive denoting result occurs in the New Testament. See *Th.* ὡς, III., and references cited there, and cf. *G.* 1456. In 2 Cor. 10 : 9 ὡς ἄν is used with the Infinitive. This usage also occurs rarely in classical and later Greek. See *Alf. ad loc.* and *Gr.* p. 230. The phrase is elliptical, the Infinitive most probably expressing purpose and ὡς ἄν modifying it in the sense of *quasi.* *WM.* p. 390 ; *WT.* p. 310.

373. In the New Testament the Infinitive is not used either with ὥστε or ἐφ᾽ ᾧ or ἐφ᾽ ᾧτε in the sense *on condition that.* *HA.* 953, b ; *G.* 1453, 1460.

374. The classical usage of an Infinitive (of conceived result) with ἤ, or ἤ ὥστε, or ἤ ὡς, after a comparative, does not occur in the New Testament. The Infinitive after ἤ in the New Testament is used as the correlative of some preceding word or phrase, and usually as a nominative. See Luke 18 : 25 ; Acts 20 : 35. On Acts 17 : 21 cf. 368.

375. Somewhat akin in force to the Infinitive of (conceived) result, but probably of Hebraistic origin, is the Infinitive used to define more closely the content of the action denoted by a previous verb or noun. Cf. *Hr.* 29, 3, e.

Acts 15:10; νῦν οὖν τί πειράζετε τὸν θεόν, ἐπιθεῖναι ζυγὸν ἐπὶ τὸν τράχηλον τῶν μαθητῶν, *now therefore why tempt ye God, that ye should put* (i.e. *by putting*, or *in that ye put*) *a yoke upon the neck of the disciples?* Cf. Ps. 78:18 (Hebrew).

Heb. 5:5; οὕτως καὶ ὁ χριστὸς οὐχ ἑαυτὸν ἐδόξασεν γενηθῆναι ἀρχιερέα, *so Christ also glorified not himself to be made a high priest.* See also Luke 1:54, 72; cf. 1 Sam. 12:23, ἀνιέναι; 22:13; Ps. Sol. 2:28, 39, 40. See *Ryle and James*, Ps. Sol. p. lxxxiii.

376. The Infinitive limiting Adjectives and Adverbs. The Infinitive is used with adjectives and adverbs of *ability, fitness, readiness,* etc., to denote that which one is or is not *able, fit,* or *ready* to do. *HA.* 952; *G.* 1526.

Mark 1:7; οὗ οὐκ εἰμὶ ἱκανὸς κύψας λῦσαι τὸν ἱμάντα τῶν ὑποδημάτων αὐτοῦ, *the latchet of whose shoes I am not worthy to stoop down and unloose.*

2 Tim. 2:2; οἵτινες ἱκανοὶ ἔσονται καὶ ἑτέρους διδάξαι, *who shall be able to teach others also.*

Rev. 4:11; ἄξιος εἶ, ὁ κύριος καὶ ὁ θεὸς ἡμῶν, λαβεῖν τὴν δόξαν καὶ τὴν τιμὴν καὶ τὴν δύναμιν, *worthy art thou, our Lord and our God, to receive the glory and the honor and the power.* See also Luke 14:31; 2 Cor. 12:14.

377. The Infinitive may be used after any adjective to limit its application to a particular action. *HA.* 952; *G.* 1528.

Heb. 5:11; περὶ οὗ πολὺς ἡμῖν ὁ λόγος καὶ δυσερμήνευτος λέγειν, *of whom we have many things to say, and hard of interpretation* — a felicitous free translation. More literally it would read, *concerning whom our discourse is much, and hard of interpretation to state,* i.e. *hard to state intelligibly.*

378. The Infinitive limiting Nouns. The Infinitive is used with abstract nouns of *ability, authority, need, hope,* etc., to denote that which one has, or has not, *ability, authority, need,* etc., to do. Here may also be included the Infinitive after ὥρα, which implies a necessity. *HA.* 952; *G.* 1521.

Matt. 3 : 14; ἐγὼ χρείαν ἔχω ὑπὸ σοῦ βαπτισθῆναι, *I have need to be baptized of thee.*

John 1 : 12; ἔδωκεν αὐτοῖς ἐξουσίαν τέκνα θεοῦ γενέσθαι, *to them gave he the right to become children of God.*

Rom. 13 : 11; καὶ τοῦτο εἰδότες τὸν καιρόν, ὅτι ὥρα ἤδη ὑμᾶς ἐξ ὕπνου ἐγερθῆναι, *and this, knowing the season, that now it is high time for you to awake out of sleep.* See also 2 Cor. 10 : 15; Rev. 9 : 10.

379. The Infinitive is also occasionally used after concrete nouns cognate with verbs which take an object Infinitive.

Gal. 5 : 3; ὀφειλέτης ἐστὶν ὅλον τὸν νόμον ποιῆσαι, *he is a debtor to do the whole law.*

380. The Infinitive is used after πρίν **or** πρὶν ἤ. *HA.* 955; *G.* 1469–1474.

Mark 14 : 30; πρὶν ἢ δὶς ἀλέκτορα φωνῆσαι τρίς με ἀπαρνήσῃ, *before the cock crow twice, thou shalt deny me thrice.*

John 4 : 49; κύριε, κατάβηθι πρὶν ἀποθανεῖν τὸ παιδίον μου, *Sir, come down ere my child die.*

381. The use of ἤ after πρίν, which occurs twice in the Iliad, frequently in Herodotus, and rarely in Attic writers, is well attested in three of the thirteen instances in the New Testament in which πρίν is used with the Infinitive, and occurs as a variant in other passages. *G.* 1474.

382. As respects the mood which follows πρίν or πρὶν ἤ, New Testament usage is the same as that of Post-Homeric Greek in general, in that the Infinitive is generally (in the New Testament invariably) used when the leading clause is affirmative; the Subjunctive and Optative occur only after a negative leading clause. The Indicative after πρίν which sometimes occurs in classical Greek, chiefly after a negative leading clause, is not found in the New Testament. *HA.* 924, a; *G.* 1470.

383. The Infinitive used absolutely in a parenthetic clause occurs but once in the New Testament. *HA.* 956; *G.* 1534.

Heb. 7 : 9 ; ὡς ἔπος εἰπεῖν, *so to speak.*

384. The Infinitive as Subject. The Infinitive may be used as the subject of a finite verb. *HA.* 949, 959 ; *G.* 1517.

Matt. 3 : 15 ; οὕτω γὰρ πρέπον ἐστὶν ἡμῖν πληρῶσαι πᾶσαν δικαιοσύνην, *for thus it becometh us to fulfil all righteousness.*

Luke 18 : 25 ; εὐκοπώτερον γάρ ἐστιν κάμηλον διὰ τρήματος βελόνης εἰσελθεῖν, *for it is easier for a camel to enter in through a needle's eye.* See also Mark 3 : 4 ; Luke 16 : 17 ; 20 : 22 ; Gal. 4 : 18.

385. The Infinitive with subject accusative sometimes stands as the subject of an impersonal verb (δοκεῖ, etc.). Frequently, however, the personal construction is employed, that which is properly the subject of the Infinitive being put in the nominative as the subject of the principal verb. But the logical relation is the same in either case. *HA.* 944.

In the New Testament the personal construction is regularly employed with δοκεῖ.

Acts 17 : 18 ; ξένων δαιμονίων δοκεῖ καταγγελεὺς εἶναι, *he seemeth to be a setter forth of strange gods.* See also Gal. 2 : 9 ; Jas. 1 : 26, etc.

Rem. Concerning the Infinitive as subject of ἐγένετο, see 357, 360.

386. The Infinitive as Appositive. The Infinitive may stand in apposition with a noun or pronoun. *HA.* 950 ; *G.* 1517.

Jas. 1 : 27 ; θρησκεία καθαρὰ καὶ ἀμίαντος . . . αὕτη ἐστίν, ἐπισκέπτεσθαι ὀρφανοὺς καὶ χήρας ἐν τῇ θλίψει αὐτῶν, *pure religion and undefiled . . . is this, to visit orphans and widows in their affliction.* See also Acts 15 : 28 ; 1 Thess. 4 : 3.

387. The Infinitive as Object. The Infinitive may be used as the object of a verb. The verbs which are thus limited by an Infinitive are in part such as take a noun or pronoun in the accusative as object, in part such as take a noun or pronoun in the genitive as object, in part verbs which cannot take a noun or pronoun as object but require an Infinitive to complete their meaning. *HA.* 948; *G.* 1518, 1519.

Matt. 19 : 14; ἄφετε τὰ παιδία καὶ μὴ κωλύετε αὐτὰ ἐλθεῖν πρός με, *suffer the little children, and forbid them not, to come unto me.*

Mark 12 : 12; καὶ ἐζήτουν αὐτὸν κρατῆσαι, *and they sought to lay hold on him.*

Luke 16 : 3; σκάπτειν οὐκ ἰσχύω, ἐπαιτεῖν αἰσχύνομαι, *I have not strength to dig; to beg I am ashamed.*

Heb. 7 : 25; ὅθεν καὶ σώζειν εἰς τὸ παντελὲς δύναται, *wherefore also he is able to save to the uttermost.* See also Matt. 1 : 19; John 5 : 18; Rom. 14 : 2; Gal. 3 : 2, *et freq.*

388. The Infinitive χαίρειν in salutations is to be regarded as the object of an unexpressed verb of bidding.

Acts 23 : 26; Κλαύδιος Λυσίας τῷ κρατίστῳ ἡγεμόνι Φήλικι χαίρειν, *Claudius Lysias unto the most excellent governor Felix, greeting.*

Jas. 1 : 1; Ἰάκωβος . . . ταῖς δώδεκα φυλαῖς ταῖς ἐν τῇ διασπορᾷ χαίρειν, *James . . . to the twelve tribes which are of the Dispersion, greeting.*

389. The verbal idea governing the Infinitive is sometimes implied rather than expressed. The Infinitive τεκεῖν in Rev. 12 : 2 is doubtless an object Infinitive governed by the idea of *desire* implied in the preceding participles. The Infinitive ψεύσασθαι in Acts 5 : 3 may be regarded as an object Infinitive governed by the idea of *persuading* implied in ἐπλήρωσεν τὴν καρδίαν, or as an Infinitive of conceived result. Cf. 370 (c).

390. The Infinitive in Indirect Discourse. The Infinitive is frequently used in the indirect quotation of assertions. It is usually the object of a verb of saying or of thinking, or the subject of such a verb in the passive voice. *HA.* 946; *G.* 1522.

Mark 12 : 18 ; οἵτινες λέγουσιν ἀνάστασιν μὴ εἶναι, *which say that there is no resurrection.*

John 21 : 25 ; οὐδ᾽ αὐτὸν οἶμαι τὸν κόσμον χωρήσειν τὰ γραφόμενα βιβλία, *I suppose that even the world itself will not contain the books that will be written.*

Heb. 11 : 5 ; πρὸ γὰρ τῆς μεταθέσεως μεμαρτύρηται εὐαρεστηκέναι τῷ θεῷ, *for before his translation he had witness borne to him that he had been well-pleasing unto God.* See also Luke 2 : 26 ; 22 : 34 ; 24 : 46 (?) ; John 12 : 29 ; Acts 16 : 27 ; Rom. 15 : 8 ; 2 Tim. 2 : 18 ; 1 John 2 : 9.

Rem. 1. Respecting the force of the tenses of the Infinitive in indirect discourse, see 110–114.

Rem. 2. Respecting the use of negatives with the Infinitive in indirect discourse, see 480–482.

391. The Infinitive occurs frequently as object after verbs *of hoping, promising, swearing,* and *commanding,* with a force closely akin to that of the Infinitive in indirect discourse. Such instances are not, however, usually included under that head. Cf. 337, and *G.*MT. 684.

THE INFINITIVE WITH THE ARTICLE

392. The prefixing of the article to the Infinitive tends to the obscuring of its original dative force, while it emphasizes its new substantive character as a noun which can be used in any case. Some of the uses of the Infinitive with the article differ from those without the article only by the greater emphasis on the substantive character of the form. This is the case with its use as subject and object. Others express nearly the same relations which were expressed by the Infinitive without the article, but with a different thought of the case-relation involved. Thus the use of the Infinitive without the article after adjectives of *fitness, worthiness,* etc., doubtless sprang originally from the thought of the Infinitive as a dative. The Infinitive with the article after such adjectives is thought of as a genitive, as is evident from the use of the article τοῦ. The difference in meaning is, however, very slight. Compare the English *worthy to receive* and *worthy of receiving*. Still other uses of the Infinitive with the article are wholly new, being developed only after the Infinitive had begun to be used with the article. To this class belongs the use of the Infinitive after prepositions.

REM. The Infinitive with the article being by means of that article practically a declinable noun, the various uses are grouped in the following sections according to cases.

393. The Infinitive with τό as Subject. The Infinitive with the article τό is used as the subject of a finite verb. *HA.* 959; *G.* 1542.

Matt. 15 : 20; τὸ δὲ ἀνίπτοις χερσὶν φαγεῖν οὐ κοινοῖ τὸν ἄνθρωπον, *but to eat with unwashen hands defileth not the man.* See also Matt. 20 : 23; Mark 9 : 10; 12 : 33; Rom. 14 : 21.

394. The Infinitive with τό as Object. The Infinitive with the article τό is used as the object of a transitive verb. This usage is far less common than the object Infinitive without the article. *HA.* 959; *G.* 1543.

Acts 25 : 11; οὐ παραιτοῦμαι τὸ ἀποθανεῖν, *I refuse not to die.* See also 2 Cor. 8 : 11; Phil. 2 : 6.

395. The Infinitive with the Article, in Apposition. The Infinitive with the article may stand in apposition with a preceding noun or pronoun.

Rom. 4 : 13; οὐ γὰρ διὰ νόμου ἡ ἐπαγγελία τῷ Ἀβραὰμ ἢ τῷ σπέρματι αὐτοῦ, τὸ κληρονόμον αὐτὸν εἶναι κόσμου, *for not through the law was the promise to Abraham or to his seed, that he should be heir of the world.*

2 Cor. 2 : 1; ἔκρινα γὰρ ἐμαυτῷ τοῦτο, τὸ μὴ πάλιν ἐν λύπῃ πρὸς ὑμᾶς ἐλθεῖν, *for I determined this for myself, that I would not come again to you with sorrow.* See also Rom. 14 : 13.

396. The Infinitive with τῷ. The Infinitive with the article τῷ is used in classical Greek to express cause, manner, means. In the New Testament it is used to express cause. Its only other use is after the preposition ἐν. *HA.* 959 ; *G.* 1547.

2 Cor. 2 : 13; τῷ μὴ εὑρεῖν με Τίτον τὸν ἀδελφόν μου, *because I found not Titus my brother.*

397. The Infinitive of Purpose with τοῦ. The Infinitive with the article τοῦ is used to express the purpose of the action or state denoted by the principal verb. *HA.* 960 ; *G.* 1548.

Matt. 2 : 13; μέλλει γὰρ Ἡρῴδης ζητεῖν τὸ παιδίον τοῦ ἀπολέσαι αὐτό, *for Herod will seek the young child to destroy him.* See also Matt. 24 : 45; Luke 2 : 24, 27; Acts 26 : 18; Phil. 3 : 10.

Rem. That the Infinitive with τοῦ expresses purpose with substantially the same force as the simple Infinitive appears from the joining of the two together by καί.

Luke 2 : 22, 24; ἀνήγαγον αὐτὸν εἰς Ἱεροσόλυμα παραστῆσαι τῷ κυρίῳ, . . . καὶ τοῦ δοῦναι θυσίαν, *they brought him up to Jerusalem, to present him to the Lord, and to offer a sacrifice.* Cf. also Luke 1 : 76, 77; 1 : 79.

398. The Infinitive of Result with τοῦ. The Infinitive with the article τοῦ is occasionally used in the New Testament to express conceived result. Cf. 218 and 369–371.

Matt. 21 : 32; ὑμεῖς δὲ ἰδόντες οὐδὲ μετεμελήθητε ὕστερον τοῦ πιστεῦσαι αὐτῷ, *and ye, when ye saw it, did not even repent afterward, so as to believe him.* See also Acts 7 : 19; Rom. 7 : 3; probably also Acts 18 : 10; cf. Gen. 3 : 22; 19 : 21; 34 : 17, 22; Isa. 5 : 14.

REM. Meyer takes the Infinitive phrase τοῦ μὴ εἶναι in Rom. 7 : 3 as expressing a divine purpose, and adds that τοῦ with the Infinitive never expresses result, not even in Acts 7 : 19. But this is grammatical purism not justified by the evidence. The uniformly telic force of τοῦ with the Infinitive can be maintained only by evasive definition or forced interpretation.

399. The Infinitive with τοῦ after Adjectives. The Infinitive with the article τοῦ is used with such adjectives as may be limited by a simple Infinitive. *HA.* 959; *G.* 1547. Cf. 376.

Acts 23 : 15; ἕτοιμοί ἐσμεν τοῦ ἀνελεῖν αὐτόν, *we are ready to slay him.* See also Luke 24 : 25.

400. The Infinitive with τοῦ after Nouns. The Infinitive with the article τοῦ is used to limit nouns. The relations thus expressed are very various and are not always easy to define exactly. Instances occur not only, as in classical Greek, of the objective genitive, but also of the genitive of characteristic, the genitive of connection, and the appositional genitive. *HA.* 959; *G.* 1547.

Heb. 5 : 12; πάλιν χρείαν ἔχετε τοῦ διδάσκειν ὑμᾶς, *ye have need again that some one teach you.*

Luke 2 : 21; καὶ ὅτε ἐπλήσθησαν ἡμέραι ὀκτὼ τοῦ περιτεμεῖν αὐτόν, *and when eight days were fulfilled for circumcising him.*

Rom. 11 : 8; ἔδωκεν αὐτοῖς ὁ θεὸς πνεῦμα κατανύξεως, ὀφθαλμοὺς τοῦ μὴ βλέπειν καὶ ὦτα τοῦ μὴ ἀκούειν, *God gave them a spirit of stupor, eyes that see not, and ears that hear not.* See also Luke 1 : 57, 74; 2 : 6; 10 : 19; 21 : 22; 22 : 6; Acts 14 : 9; 20 : 3; Rom. 1 : 24; 1 Cor. 9 : 10; 2 Cor. 8 : 11; 1 Pet. 4 : 17; cf. Gen. 16 : 3; 1 Sam. 2 : 24.

401. The Infinitive with τοῦ after Verbs that take the Genitive. The Infinitive with τοῦ is used as the object of verbs which take a noun in the genitive as object, especially of verbs of *hindering*, etc. *HA.* 959, 963; *G.* 1547, 1549.

Luke 1 : 9 ; ἔλαχε τοῦ θυμιᾶσαι, *it was his lot* (prop. *he obtained by lot*)
to burn incense.

2 Cor. 1 : 8 ; ὥστε ἐξαπορηθῆναι ἡμᾶς καὶ τοῦ ζῆν, *insomuch that we de-*
spaired even of life.

Rom. 15 : 22 ; διὸ καὶ ἐνεκοπτόμην τὰ πολλὰ τοῦ ἐλθεῖν πρὸς ὑμᾶς,
wherefore also I was hindered these many times from coming to you.
Cf. Gen. 34 : 19 ; Ps. Sol. 2 : 28, 29.

402. In classical Greek, verbs of *hindering* are followed by
three constructions, (*a*) Infinitive without the article, (*b*) In-
finitive with τοῦ, (*c*) Infinitive with τό. Μή may be used or
omitted with the Infinitive without difference of meaning.
HA. 963 ; *G.* 1549, 1551 ; *G.*MT. 791 (exx.). In the New
Testament, all these constructions occur except that with τὸ μή.
See Matt. 19 : 14 ; Rom. 15 : 22 ; 1 Cor. 14 : 39 ; Gal. 5 : 7 ;
Acts 10 : 47.

403. The Infinitive with τοῦ μή after verbs of *hindering* is closely akin
to the Infinitive of Result. Cf. Luke 24 : 16 ; Acts 14 : 18.

Rem. Meyer's interpretation of τοῦ μὴ ἐπιγνῶναι αὐτόν in Luke 24 : 16
as expressing a divine purpose (the English translation does not correctly
represent the meaning of the German original), is not required by New
Testament usage. The Greek most naturally means, *Their eyes were*
held from knowing him. Cf. 398, Rem.

404. The Infinitive with τοῦ as Subject or Object.
The Infinitive with τοῦ is used even as the subject of a
finite verb or as the object of transitive verbs which regularly take a direct object. This is a wide departure from
classical usage, and indicates that the sense of the genitive
character of the article τοῦ before the Infinitive was partly
lost in later Greek. *B.* p. 270 ; *WM.* pp. 411 f. ; *WT.* pp. 327 f.

Acts 27 : 1 ; ἐκρίθη τοῦ ἀποπλεῖν ἡμᾶς εἰς τὴν Ἰταλίαν, *it was determined*
that we should sail for Italy. See also Luke 4 : 10 ; 5 : 7 ; Acts 3 : 12 ;
10 : 25 ; 15 : 20 ; 21 : 12 ; 23 : 20 ; 1 Sam. 12 : 23 ; Eccl. 4 : 13, 17 ;
1 Macc. 3 : 15.

405. The origin of this use of the Infinitive with τοῦ is perhaps in such usages as appear in Luke 17 : 1 ; 1 Cor. 16 : 4 ; and still more in such as that in Luke 4 : 10. In Luke 17 : 1 the genitive is apparently suggested by the idea of *hindering* or *avoiding* in the adjective ἀνένδεκτον ; in 1 Cor. 16 : 4 it is the adjective ἄξιον which gives occasion to the genitive ; but in both cases the Infinitive seems to be logically the subject of the copulative verb, the adjective being the predicate. Whether this construction represents the thought in the mind of the writer, or whether the expression is rather to be regarded as an impersonal one, the Infinitive being dependent on the predicate adjective, cannot with confidence be decided. Such usages as Luke 4 : 10 and 5 : 7 doubtless owe their origin to the same mental process by which a clause introduced by ἵνα came to stand as the object of a verb of *exhorting*. Ps. Sol. 2 : 28 compared with Luke 12 : 45 is also suggestive. It is doubtless the idea of hindering in χρονίζω that gives rise to the genitive in the former passage ; in the latter the Infinitive is a direct object.

406. The Infinitive with the Article governed by Prepositions. The Infinitive with the article τό, τοῦ, τῷ is governed by prepositions. *HA.* 959; *G.* 1546.

The prepositions so used in the New Testament are : with the accusative, διά, εἰς, μετά, πρός ; with the genitive, ἀντί, διά, ἐκ, ἕνεκεν, ἕως, πρό ; with the dative, ἐν.

Mark 4 : 6 ; καὶ διὰ τὸ μὴ ἔχειν ῥίζαν ἐξηράνθη, *and because it had no root, it withered away.*

1 Thess. 3 : 5 ; ἔπεμψα εἰς τὸ γνῶναι τὴν πίστιν ὑμῶν, *I sent that I might know your faith.*

Mark 14 : 28 ; ἀλλὰ μετὰ τὸ ἐγερθῆναί με προάξω ὑμᾶς εἰς τὴν Γαλιλαίαν, *howbeit, after I am raised up, I will go before you into Galilee.*

Matt. 6 : 1 ; προσέχετε [δὲ] τὴν δικαιοσύνην ὑμῶν μὴ ποιεῖν ἔμπροσθεν τῶν ἀνθρώπων πρὸς τὸ θεαθῆναι αὐτοῖς, *take heed that ye do not your righteousness before men, to be seen of them.*

Gal. 3 : 23 ; πρὸ τοῦ δὲ ἐλθεῖν τὴν πίστιν ὑπὸ νόμον ἐφρουρούμεθα, *but before faith came, we were kept in ward under the law.*

Luke 24 : 51 ; καὶ ἐγένετο ἐν τῷ εὐλογεῖν αὐτὸν αὐτοὺς διέστη ἀπ᾽ αὐτῶν, *and it came to pass, while he blessed them, he parted from them.*

407. These prepositions vary greatly in frequency in the New Testament. Εἰς occurs with the Infinitive 63 times

(Infinitives 72); ἐν 52 times (Infinitives 56); διά with the Accusative 27 times (Infinitives 31); μετά 15 times; πρός 12 times; πρό 9 times; each of the others once (*WH. text*). See *Votaw*, Infinitive in Biblical Greek, p. 20; cf. *G.*MT. 800–802.

408. Διά governing the Infinitive with τό denotes cause, and is nearly equivalent to ὅτι or διότι with the Indicative, differing in that the Infinitive gives in itself no indication of the time of the action.

Jas. 4 : 2, 3; οὐκ ἔχετε διὰ τὸ μὴ αἰτεῖσθαι ὑμᾶς· αἰτεῖτε καὶ οὐ λαμβάνετε, διότι κακῶς αἰτεῖσθε, *ye have not, because ye ask not. Ye ask, and receive not, because ye ask amiss.*

In Mark 5 : 4 διά with the Infinitive expresses the evidence rather than the cause strictly so called.

409. Εἰς governing the Infinitive with τό most commonly expresses purpose. It is employed with special frequency by Paul, but occurs also in Heb., 1 Pet., and Jas.

Rom. 8 : 29; ὅτι οὓς προέγνω, καὶ προώρισεν συμμόρφους τῆς εἰκόνος τοῦ υἱοῦ αὐτοῦ, εἰς τὸ εἶναι αὐτὸν πρωτότοκον ἐν πολλοῖς ἀδελφοῖς, *for whom he foreknew, he also foreordained to be conformed to the image of his Son, that he might be the first-born among many brethren.* See also Rom. 1 : 11; 3 : 26; 7 : 4; Eph. 1 : 12; Phil. 1 : 10; Heb. 2 : 17; Jas. 1 : 18; 1 Pet. 3 : 7.

410. Εἰς with the Infinitive is also used, like the simple Infinitive, to represent an indirect object. Cf. 368.

1 Cor. 11 : 22; μὴ γὰρ οἰκίας οὐκ ἔχετε εἰς τὸ ἐσθίειν καὶ πίνειν, *what? have ye not houses to eat and to drink in?* See also Matt. 20 : 19; 26 : 2.

411. Εἰς with the Infinitive also expresses tendency, measure of effect, or result, conceived or actual.

Heb. 11 : 3; πίστει νοοῦμεν κατηρτίσθαι τοὺς αἰῶνας ῥήματι θεοῦ, εἰς τὸ μὴ ἐκ φαινομένων τὸ βλεπόμενον γεγονέναι, *by faith we understand that the worlds have been framed by the word of God, so that what is seen hath not been made out of things which do appear.* See also Rom. 12 : 3; 2 Cor. 8 : 6; Gal. 3 : 17; 1 Thess. 2 : 16.

Εἰς τὸ ἐσθίειν in 1 Cor. 8 : 10 either expresses measure of effect or is the indirect object of οἰκοδομηθήσεται. Εἰς τὸ εἶναι αὐτοὺς ἀναπολογήτους in Rom. 1 : 20 might appropriately be interpreted as expressing purpose but for the causal clause which follows. This clause could be joined to an expression of purpose only by supposing an ellipsis of some such expression as καὶ οὕτως εἰσίν, and seems therefore to require that εἰς τὸ εἶναι be interpreted as expressing result.

Rem.　Meyer's dictum (see on Rom. 1 : 20) that εἰς with the articular Infinitive is always telic, is, like his similar dictum respecting τοῦ with the Infinitive, a case of grammatical purism, not justified by the evidence.

412. Εἰς with the Infinitive is also used, like ἵνα with the Subjunctive, or the simple Infinitive, as the direct object of verbs of *exhorting*, etc. 1 Thess. 2 : 12; 3 : 10; 2 Thess. 2 : 2.

413. Εἰς with the Infinitive is still further used, like the simple Infinitive, to limit an adjective, as in Jas. 1 : 19, or a noun, as in Phil. 1 : 23.

414. Πρός governing the Infinitive with τό usually expresses purpose; it is occasionally used with the sense, *with reference to*.

Matt. 6 : 1; προσέχετε [δὲ] τὴν δικαιοσύνην ὑμῶν μὴ ποιεῖν ἔμπροσθεν τῶν ἀνθρώπων πρὸς τὸ θεαθῆναι αὐτοῖς, *but take heed that ye do not your righteousness before men, to be seen of them.*

Matt. 26 : 12; βαλοῦσα γὰρ αὕτη τὸ μύρον τοῦτο ἐπὶ τοῦ σώματός μου πρὸς τὸ ἐνταφιάσαι με ἐποίησεν, *for in that she poured this ointment upon my body, she did it to prepare me for burial.* See also Matt. 5 : 28; 13 : 30; 2 Cor. 3 : 13; Eph. 6 : 11, etc. (purpose); Luke 18 : 1 (reference).

415. Ἐν governing the Infinitive with τῷ is most commonly temporal, but occasionally expresses other relations, such as manner, means, or content. This construction is especially frequent in Luke and Acts.

Luke 8 : 5; καὶ ἐν τῷ σπείρειν αὐτὸν ὃ μὲν ἔπεσεν παρὰ τὴν ὁδόν, *and as he sowed, some fell by the way side.*

Acts 3 : 26; ὑμῖν πρῶτον ἀναστήσας ὁ θεὸς τὸν παῖδα αὐτοῦ ἀπέστειλεν αὐτὸν εὐλογοῦντα ὑμᾶς ἐν τῷ ἀποστρέφειν ἕκαστον ἀπὸ τῶν πονηριῶν [ὑμῶν], *unto you first God, having raised up his Servant, sent him to bless you, in turning away every one of you from your iniquities.* See also Luke 1 : 8; Acts 9 : 3; 11 : 15; Ps. Sol. 1 : 1 (temporal); Luke 12 : 15; Acts 4 : 30; Heb. 2 : 8; 3 : 12, 15; Ps. Sol. 1 : 3; Gen. 19 : 16; 34 : 15.

416. The force of the other prepositions used with the Infinitive scarcely needs special definition, the meaning of each being in general the same as that of the same preposition governing nouns. Respecting the force of the tenses after prepositions, see 104–109.

417. Concerning the Infinitive without the article governed by prepositions, see *G.*MT. 803, and cf. Gen. 10 : 19. The Infinitive γίνεσθαι in Acts 4 : 30, which is by R.V. taken as the object of δός is more probably governed by the preposition ἐν. It is however not strictly without the article, the τῷ which precedes ἐκτείνειν belonging in effect also to γίνεσθαι.

THE PARTICIPLE

418. The Participle is a verbal adjective, sharing in part the characteristics of both the verb and the adjective. As a verb it has both tense functions and functions which may be designated as modal functions, being analogous to those which in the case of verbs in the Indicative, Subjunctive, or Optative belong to the mood. For the proper understanding of a participle, therefore, it is necessary to consider (*a*) The grammatical agreement, (*b*) The use of the tense, and (*c*) The logical force or modal function. The first and second of these have already been treated, grammatical agreement in 116, the uses of the tenses in 118–156. It remains to consider the logical force or modal function of the participle. From the point of view of the interpreter this is usually the matter of most importance.

419. In respect to logical force, participles may be classified as Adjective, Adverbial, and Substantive.

REM. 1. The terminology here employed for the classification of participles differs somewhat from that commonly employed. It is adopted substantially from the article of Professor *Wm. Arnold Stevens*, " On the Substantive Use of the Greek Participle " in *T.A.P.A.* 1872. The Adjective Participle corresponds nearly to the Attributive Participle

as treated in *G.* and *HA.*, the Adverbial Participle to the Circum-
stantial Participle, and the Substantive Participle to the Supplementary
Participle.

REM. 2.   Respecting the use of the negatives μή and οὐ with participles, see 485.

THE ADJECTIVE PARTICIPLE

420. The Adjective Participle limits its subject directly
and exclusively.   It attributes the action which it denotes
to the subject as a quality or characteristic, or assigns the
subject to the class marked by that action.   *HA.* 965; *G.*
1559.

Acts 10 : 1, 2 ; ἀνὴρ δέ τις ἐν Καισαρίᾳ ὀνόματι Κορνήλιος, ἑκατοντάρχης ἐκ σπείρης τῆς καλουμένης Ἰταλικῆς, εὐσεβὴς καὶ φοβούμενος
τὸν θεὸν σὺν παντὶ τῷ οἴκῳ αὐτοῦ, ποιῶν ἐλεημοσύνας πολλὰς τῷ
λαῷ καὶ δεόμενος τοῦ θεοῦ διὰ παντός, *now there was a certain man
in Cæsarea, Cornelius by name, a centurion of a band called the
Italian band, a devout man and one that feared God with all his house,
who gave much alms to the people and prayed to God alway.*   The
four participles in this sentence are all Adjective Participles, describing their subject.   This is especially clear in the case of φοβούμενος, which is joined by καί to the adjective εὐσεβής.   For other
similar examples see Col. 1 : 21 ; Jas. 2 : 15 ; see also examples
under the following sections.

421. The Adjective Participle may be used attributively or
predicatively.   When used attributively it may be either restrictive or explanatory.

422. The Restrictive Attributive Participle.   An attributive Adjective Participle may be used to define or
identify its subject, pointing out what person or thing is
meant.   It is then equivalent to a restrictive relative clause.
Cf. 295.

John 6 : 50 ; οὗτός ἐστιν ὁ ἄρτος ὁ ἐκ τοῦ οὐρανοῦ καταβαίνων, *this is the bread which cometh down out of heaven.*

Jude 17 ; μνήσθητε τῶν ῥημάτων τῶν προειρημένων ὑπὸ τῶν ἀποστόλων τοῦ κυρίου ἡμῶν Ἰησοῦ Χριστοῦ, *remember the words which have been spoken before by the apostles of our Lord Jesus Christ.*

423. The subject of the Restrictive Attributive Participle is often omitted. The participle is then an Adjective Participle used substantively. Such a participle usually has the article, but not invariably. *HA.* 966 ; *G.* 1560.

Matt. 10 : 37 ; ὁ φιλῶν πατέρα ἢ μητέρα ὑπὲρ ἐμὲ οὐκ ἔστιν μου ἄξιος, *he that loveth father or mother more than me is not worthy of me.*

Acts 5 : 14 ; προσετίθεντο πιστεύοντες τῷ κυρίῳ πλήθη ἀνδρῶν τε καὶ γυναικῶν, *believers were added to the Lord, multitudes both of men and women.*

Acts 10 : 35 ; ἀλλ' ἐν παντὶ ἔθνει ὁ φοβούμενος αὐτὸν καὶ ἐργαζόμενος δικαιοσύνην δεκτὸς αὐτῷ ἐστίν, *but in every nation he that feareth him, and worketh righteousness, is acceptable to him.*

Rev. 1 : 3 ; μακάριος ὁ ἀναγινώσκων καὶ οἱ ἀκούοντες τοὺς λόγους τῆς προφητείας καὶ τηροῦντες τὰ ἐν αὐτῇ γεγραμμένα, *blessed is he that readeth, and they that hear the words of the prophecy, and keep the things which are written therein.*

424. A noun without the article, or an indefinite pronoun, is sometimes limited by a participle with the article. The article in this case does not make the noun strictly definite. The person or thing referred to is placed within the class characterized by the action denoted by the participle, and the attention is directed to some one or to certain ones of that class, who are not, however, more specifically identified. Nearly the same meaning is expressed by a participle without the article, or on the other hand by a relative clause limiting an indefinite substantive. For classical examples of this usage see *WM.* p. 136 ; *WT.* pp. 109 f.

Col. 2 : 8 ; βλέπετε μή τις ὑμᾶς ἔσται ὁ συλαγαγῶν διὰ τῆς φιλοσοφίας, *take heed lest there shall be any one that maketh spoil of you through his philosophy.* See also Acts 5 : 17 ; 10 : 41 ; Gal. 1 : 7.

425. A neuter participle with the article is sometimes equivalent to an abstract noun. It is then limited by a genitive like any other abstract noun. *HA.* 966, b. ; *G.* 1562.

Phil. 3 : 8 ; διὰ τὸ ὑπερέχον τῆς γνώσεως Χριστοῦ Ἰησοῦ τοῦ κυρίου μου, *because of the excellency [superiority] of the knowledge of Christ Jesus my Lord.* See also the similar use of neuter adjectives in Rom. 2 : 4 ; 1 Cor. 1 : 25 ; Phil. 4 : 5 ; Heb. 6 : 17. *WM.* pp. 294 f. ; *WT.* pp. 234 f.

426. The Explanatory Attributive Participle. An attributive Adjective Participle may be used to describe a person or thing already known or identified. It is then equivalent to an explanatory relative clause. Cf. 295.

2 Tim. 1 : 8, 9 ; κατὰ δύναμιν θεοῦ, τοῦ σώσαντος ἡμᾶς καὶ καλέσαντος κλήσει ἁγίᾳ, *according to the power of God ; who saved us, and called us with a holy calling.*
1 Thess. 1 : 10 ; Ἰησοῦν τὸν ῥυόμενον ἡμᾶς ἐκ τῆς ὀργῆς τῆς ἐρχομένης, *Jesus, which delivereth us from the wrath to come.* In this example ῥυόμενον is explanatory, ἐρχομένης is restrictive. See also Acts 20 : 32 ; Heb. 7 : 9.

427. An Attributive Participle when used to limit a noun which has the article, stands in the so-called attributive position, *i.e.* between the article and the noun, or after an article following the noun ; but when the participle is limited by an adverbial phrase, this phrase may stand between the article and the noun, and the participle without the article follow the noun. It thus results that all the following orders are possible :

(1) article, participle, modifier of the participle, noun ;
(2) art., mod., part., noun ;
(3) art., mod., noun, part. ;
(4) art., part., noun, mod. ;
(5) art., noun, art., mod., part. ;

(6) art., noun, art., part., mod. See Professor *Charles Short's*
essay on The Order of Words in Attic Greek Prose, in *Yonge's*
English-Greek Lexicon, pp. xlix. f. ; *K.* 464, 8 ; *HA.* 667, a.

Acts 13 : 32 ; καὶ ἡμεῖς ὑμᾶς εὐαγγελιζόμεθα τὴν πρὸς τοὺς πατέρας
ἐπαγγελίαν γενομένην, *and we bring you good tidings of the promise
made unto the fathers.* See also Acts 12 : 10 ; 26 : 4, 6 ; Heb. 2 : 2 ;
and especially Rom. 2 : 27, where ἡ ἐκ φύσεως ἀκροβυστία τὸν νόμον
τελοῦσα should doubtless be rendered, *the uncircumcision which
by nature fulfils the law* (cf. v. 14).

428. An Attributive Participle equivalent to a relative
clause, may like a relative clause convey a subsidiary idea of
cause, purpose, condition, or concession (cf. 294, 296 ff., 317
ff.). It then partakes of the nature of both the Adjective
Participle and the Adverbial Participle. Cf. 434.

Rom. 3 : 5 ; μὴ ἄδικος ὁ θεὸς ὁ ἐπιφέρων τὴν ὀργήν, *is God unright-
eous, who [because he] visiteth with wrath?*
Matt. 10 : 39 ; ὁ εὑρὼν τὴν ψυχὴν αὐτοῦ ἀπολέσει αὐτήν, καὶ ὁ ἀπολέ-
σας τὴν ψυχὴν αὐτοῦ ἕνεκεν ἐμοῦ εὑρήσει αὐτήν, *he that findeth his
life shall lose it, and he that loseth his life for my sake shall find it.*
See also vss. 37, 40, 41 ; cf. vss. 38, 42, and Luke 14 : 26.

429. The Predicative Adjective Participle. A participle may be used as the predicate of the verb εἰμί or other
copulative verb.

Matt. 3 : 15 ; οὕτω γὰρ πρέπον ἐστὶν ἡμῖν πληρῶσαι πᾶσαν δικαιοσύνην,
for thus it is becoming for us to fulfil all righteousness.
Gal. 1 : 22 ; ἤμην δὲ ἀγνοούμενος τῷ προσώπῳ ταῖς ἐκκλησίαις τῆς
Ἰουδαίας, *and I was unknown by face unto the churches of Judea.*
Rev. 1 : 18 ; καὶ ἐγενόμην νεκρὸς καὶ ἰδοὺ ζῶν εἰμι εἰς τοὺς αἰῶνας τῶν
αἰώνων, *and I became dead, and behold, I am alive for evermore.*

430. The Predicative Participle always stands in the so-
called predicative position, *i.e.* not in attributive position,
which is between the article and its noun or after an article
following the noun. Cf. 427.

431. Under the head of the Predicative Participle belong those Present and Perfect Participles which, with the Present, Imperfect, and Future of the verb, form periphrastic Presents, Imperfects, Perfects, Pluperfects, Futures, and Future Perfects. Cf. 20, 34, 71, 84, 91, 97 ; *G*.MT. 45, 830, 831 ; *B.* pp. 308–313 ; *S.* pp. 131 ff. See Rev. 1 : 18 ; Matt. 27 : 33 ; Mark 2 : 18 ; Luke 1 : 21 ; 13 : 10 ; Jas. 5 : 15 ; 2 Cor. 9 : 3 ; Luke 2 : 26 ; John 13 : 5 ; Matt. 18 : 18.

432. To the Greek mind there was doubtless a distinction of thought between the participle which retained its adjective force and its distinctness from the copula, and that which was so joined with the copula as to be felt as an element of a compound tense-form. This distinction can usually be perceived by us ; yet in the nature of the case there will occur instances which it will be difficult to assign with certainty to one class or the other. Since, moreover, an Adjective Participle used substantively without the article may stand in the predicate, this gives rise to a third possibility. A participle without the article standing in the predicate is therefore capable of three explanations :

(*a*) It may be an Attributive Participle used substantively. So probably

Mark 10 : 22 ; ἦν γὰρ ἔχων κτήματα πολλά, *for he was one that had great possessions.* See also John 18 : 30.

(*b*) It may be a Predicative Participle retaining its adjective force. So probably the examples under 429, especially Gal. 1 : 22.

(*c*) It may form with the copula a periphrastic verb-form.

Luke 5 : 17 ; καὶ ἐγένετο ἐν μιᾷ τῶν ἡμερῶν καὶ αὐτὸς ἦν διδάσκων, *and it came to pass on one of those days that he was teaching.*

433. An Adjective Participle used substantively with the article may of course occur as a predicate with a copula. This, however, is not properly a Predicative Participle. The presence of the article makes its use as a noun easily evident. The participle without the article may be as really substantive (432, a), but is not so easily distinguished as such.

Luke 7 : 19 ; σὺ εἶ ὁ ἐρχόμενος ; *art thou he that cometh?* See also Luke 16 : 15 ; 22 : 28.

THE ADVERBIAL PARTICIPLE

434. The Adverbial Participle logically modifies some other verb of the sentence in which it stands, being equivalent to an adverbial phrase or clause denoting time, condition, concession, cause, purpose, means, manner, or attendant circumstance. *HA.* 969 ; *G.* 1563. Thus we find:

435. The Adverbial Participle of Time, equivalent to a temporal clause.

Luke 24 : 36 ; ταῦτα δὲ αὐτῶν λαλούντων αὐτὸς ἔστη ἐν μέσῳ αὐτῶν, *and as they spake these things, he himself stood in the midst of them.*
John 16 : 8 ; καὶ ἐλθὼν ἐκεῖνος ἐλέγξει τὸν κόσμον, *and he, when he is come, will convict the world.*

436. The Adverbial Participle of Condition, equivalent to a conditional clause.

Heb. 2 : 3 ; πῶς ἡμεῖς ἐκφευξόμεθα τηλικαύτης ἀμελήσαντες σωτηρίας, *how shall we escape, if we neglect so great salvation?*
1 Tim. 4 : 4 ; ὅτι πᾶν κτίσμα θεοῦ καλόν, καὶ οὐδὲν ἀπόβλητον μετὰ εὐχαριστίας λαμβανόμενον, *for every creature of God is good, and nothing is to be rejected, if it be received with thanksgiving.* See also 1 Cor. 11 : 29 ; Gal. 6 : 9.

437. The Adverbial Participle of Concession, equivalent to a concessive clause. The concessive force is sometimes emphasized by prefixing καίπερ or καί γε to the participle.

Acts 13 : 28; καὶ μηδεμίαν αἰτίαν θανάτου εὑρόντες ᾐτήσαντο Πειλᾶτον ἀναιρεθῆναι αὐτόν, *and though they found no cause of death in him, yet asked they of Pilate that he should be slain.*
Heb. 5 : 8; καίπερ ὢν υἱός, ἔμαθεν ἀφ' ὧν ἔπαθεν τὴν ὑπακοήν, *though he was a Son, yet he learned obedience by the things which he suffered.* See also Matt. 14 : 9; Mark 4 : 31; Acts 17 : 27.

438. A concessive participle refers to a fact which is unfavorable to the occurrence of the event denoted by the principal verb. Cf. 278. It should be distinguished from the participle which is merely antithetical. A participle denoting accompanying circumstance, or even condition or cause, may be antithetical. See 1 Cor. 4 : 12, διωκόμενοι ἀνεχόμεθα; 2 Cor. 8 : 9; Gal. 2 : 3.

439. The Adverbial Participle of Cause, equivalent to a causal clause.

Col. 1 : 3, 4; εὐχαριστοῦμεν τῷ θεῷ . . . ἀκούσαντες τὴν πίστιν ὑμῶν ἐν Χριστῷ Ἰησοῦ, *we give thanks to God . . . having heard (because we have heard) of your faith in Christ Jesus.*
1 Tim. 4 : 8; ἡ δὲ εὐσέβεια πρὸς πάντα ὠφέλιμός ἐστιν, ἐπαγγελίαν ἔχουσα ζωῆς τῆς νῦν καὶ τῆς μελλούσης, *but godliness is profitable for all things, having promise of the life which now is, and of that which is to come.* See also Matt. 2 : 3, 10; Acts 9 : 26.

440. Ὡς prefixed to a Participle of Cause implies that the action denoted by the participle is supposed, asserted, or professed by some one, usually the subject of the principal verb, to be the cause of the action of the principal verb. The speaker does not say whether the supposed or alleged cause actually exists. *HA.* 978; *G.* 1574.

1 Cor. 4 : 18 ; ὡς μὴ ἐρχομένου δέ μου πρὸς ὑμᾶς ἐφυσιώθησάν τινες, *but some are puffed up, as though I were not coming to you*, i.e. *because (as they suppose) I am not coming*. See also Acts 23 : 15, 20 ; 27 : 30 ; 28 : 19 ; 1 Pet. 4 : 12.

441. The origin of this idiom is probably in a clause of manner consisting of ὡς and a finite verb, the latter modified by a Participle of Cause. Thus κολάζεις με ὡς κακοποιήσαντα, *you punish me as having done evil*, i.e. *you punish me because, as you allege, I have done evil*, may have its origin in such a sentence as κολάζεις με ὡς κολάζεις τινὰ κακοποιήσαντα, *you punish me, as you punish one who has* (or *because he has*) *done evil*. Yet it is not to be supposed that the Greek any more than the English required the supplying of a finite verb after ὡς. Such phrases in classical Greek or in the New Testament are, as they stand and without the addition of other words, expressions of cause, the use of ὡς indicating that the phrase describes the opinion or assertion of the subject of the sentence rather than of the speaker.

442. The Adverbial Participle of Purpose, equivalent to a final clause. This is usually, but not invariably, in the Future tense.

Acts 8 : 27 ; [ὃς] ἐληλύθει προσκυνήσων εἰς Ἰερουσαλήμ, *who had come to Jerusalem to worship*.

Acts 3 : 26 ; ἀπέστειλεν αὐτὸν εὐλογοῦντα ὑμᾶς, *he sent him to bless you*.

443. The Adverbial Participle of Means. This cannot usually be resolved into a clause.

Matt. 6 : 27 ; τίς δὲ ἐξ ὑμῶν μεριμνῶν δύναται προσθεῖναι ἐπὶ τὴν ἡλικίαν αὐτοῦ πῆχυν ἕνα, *and which of you by being anxious can add one cubit unto his stature?* See also Acts 16 : 16 ; Heb. 2 : 18.

444. The Adverbial Participle of Manner, describing the manner in which the action denoted by the verb is done.

Acts 2 : 13 ; ἕτεροι δὲ διαχλευάζοντες ἔλεγον, *but others mocking said*. See also Luke 19 : 48.

445. The manner of an action is frequently expressed by
ὡς with the participle.

Mark 1 : 22 ; ἦν γὰρ διδάσκων αὐτοὺς ὡς ἐξουσίαν ἔχων καὶ οὐχ ὡς οἱ
γραμματεῖς, *for he taught them as one having authority, and not as the
scribes.*
1 Cor. 9 : 26 ; οὕτως πυκτεύω ὡς οὐκ ἀέρα δέρων, *so fight I as not beat-
ing the air.*
2 Cor. 5 : 20 ; ὑπὲρ Χριστοῦ οὖν πρεσβεύομεν ὡς τοῦ θεοῦ παρακαλοῦν-
τος δι' ἡμῶν, *we are ambassadors therefore on behalf of Christ, as
though God were intreating by us.*

446. When ὡς with the participle is used to express manner, the participle itself may be either an Adjective Participle used substantively or an
Adverbial Participle of Manner.   The origin of such expressions is doubtless, in either case, in a clause of manner consisting of ὡς and a finite verb
similar to the principal verb, the participle being either the subject of
such a verb or an adverbial (or other) limitation of it.   Thus διδάσκει ὡς
ἔχων ἐξουσίαν is equivalent to διδάσκει ὡς ἔχων ἐξουσίαν διδάσκει, *he teaches
as one having authority teaches,* or διδάσκει ὡς τις διδάσκει ἔχων ἐξουσίαν, *he
teaches as one teaches having authority.*   Yet in neither case is it to be
supposed that the Greek, any more than the English, required the supplying of a finite verb after ὡς.   The phrase as it stood was an expression of manner.   That the participle, however, was in some cases still
felt as a substantive (Adjective Participle used substantively) seems
probable from its being used correlatively with an adjective or noun and
from the occasional use of the participle with the article.   See Mark 1 : 22
above ; also 1 Cor. 7 : 25 ; 2 Cor. 6 : 9, 10 ; 1 Pet. 2 : 16 ; and cf. Mark
6 : 34 ; Luke 22 : 26, 27.   That this is not always the case, but that the
participle itself is sometimes adverbial is evident from such cases as 2 Cor.
5 : 20 (see above, 445).

447. The participle expressing manner or means often
denotes the same action as that of the principal verb, describing it from a different point of view.   In this case the participle
is as respects its tense a (Present or Aorist) Participle of
Identical Action (cf. 120, 139), while as respects its modal
function it is a participle of manner or means.

Acts 5:30; ὁ θεὸς τῶν πατέρων ἡμῶν ἤγειρεν Ἰησοῦν, ὃν ὑμεῖς διεχειρίσασθε κρεμάσαντες ἐπὶ ξύλου, *the God of our fathers raised up Jesus, whom ye slew by hanging him on a tree.* See also Acts 9:22; 10:33; 1 Tim. 5:21.

448. In quotations from the Old Testament a participle is sometimes placed before a personal form of the same verb. The idiom arises from an imitation of the Hebrew construction with the Infinitive Absolute. The force of the participle is in general intensive. *Hr.* 28, 3, a; *B.* pp. 313 f.; *WM.* pp. 445 f.; *WT.* pp. 354 f.

Heb. 6:14; εὐλογῶν εὐλογήσω σε καὶ πληθύνων πληθυνῶ σε, *blessing I will bless thee, and multiplying I will multiply thee.*

449. The Adverbial Participle of Attendant Circumstance.

Mark 16:20; ἐκεῖνοι δὲ ἐξελθόντες ἐκήρυξαν πανταχοῦ, τοῦ κυρίου συνεργοῦντος καὶ τὸν λόγον βεβαιοῦντος, *and they went forth and preached everywhere, the Lord working with them and confirming the word.*

Luke 4:15; καὶ αὐτὸς ἐδίδασκεν ἐν ταῖς συναγωγαῖς αὐτῶν, δοξαζό-μενος ὑπὸ πάντων, *and he taught in their synagogues, being glorified of all.*

Acts 15:22; τότε ἔδοξε τοῖς ἀποστόλοις καὶ τοῖς πρεσβυτέροις . . . ἐκλεξαμένους ἄνδρας ἐξ αὐτῶν πέμψαι εἰς Ἀντιόχειαν, *then it seemed good to the apostles and the elders . . . to choose men out of their company and send them to Antioch.*

Acts 18:18; ὁ δὲ Παῦλος . . . ἐξέπλει εἰς τὴν Συρίαν, καὶ σὺν αὐτῷ Πρίσκιλλα καὶ Ἀκύλας, κειράμενος ἐν Κενχρεαῖς τὴν κεφαλήν, *and Paul . . . sailed thence for Syria, and with him Priscilla and Aquila; having shorn his head in Cenchreæ.*

2 Tim. 4:11; Μάρκον ἀναλαβὼν ἄγε μετὰ σεαυτοῦ, *take Mark and bring him with thee.* See also Luke 5:7; 11:7.

450. The term "attendant" as used above does not define the temporal relation of the participle to the verb, but the logical relation. The action of a Participle of Attendant Circumstance may precede the action of the principal verb, accompany it, or even follow it. But as respects logical relation, it is presented merely as an accompaniment of the action of the verb. It does not, *e.g.*, define the time or the cause, or the means of the action of the principal verb, but simply prefixes or adds an associated fact or conception. It is thus often equivalent to a coördinate verb with καί. Though grammatically not an independent element of the sentence, the participle in such cases becomes in thought assertive, hortatory, optative, imperative, etc., according to the function of the principal verb.

The position of the Participle of Attendant Circumstance with reference to the verb is not determined by any fixed rules, but by the order of the writer's thought, this being in turn governed of course to a certain extent by the order of the events. If the action of the participle is antecedent to that of the verb, the participle most commonly precedes the verb, but not invariably. Such a participle is usually in the Aorist tense (134), but occasionally in the Present (127). If the action of the participle is simultaneous with that of the verb, it may either precede or follow the verb, more frequently the latter. It is of course in the Present tense (119). If the action of the participle is subsequent to that of the principal verb, it almost invariably follows the verb, the tense of the participle being determined by the conception of the action as respects its progress. The instances of this last-named class are not frequent in the New Testament and are perhaps due to Aramaic influence. Cf. 119, Rem.; 145.

451. The various relations of time, cause, manner, etc., being not expressed, but implied by the participle, cases arise in which it is impossible to assign the participle unquestionably to any one of the above heads. Indeed, more than one of these relations may be implied by the same participle.

452. THE GENITIVE ABSOLUTE. An Adverbial Participle may stand in agreement with a noun or pronoun in the genitive without grammatical dependence upon any other part of the sentence, the two constituting a genitive absolute phrase and expressing any of the adverbial relations enumerated in 435–449. *HA.* 970, 971; *G.* 1568.

Rom. 9 : 1; ἀλήθειαν λέγω ἐν Χριστῷ, οὐ ψεύδομαι, συνμαρτυρούσης μοι τῆς συνειδήσεώς μου ἐν πνεύματι ἁγίῳ, *I say the truth in Christ, I lie not, my conscience bearing witness with me in the Holy Ghost.* See also John 8 : 30; Acts 12 : 18; 18 : 20.

453. The noun or pronoun of the genitive absolute phrase regularly refers to a person or thing not otherwise mentioned in the sentence. Occasionally, however, this principle is violated, and the genitive phrase may even refer to the subject of the sentence. This irregularity is somewhat more frequent in the New Testament than in classical Greek. *HA.* 972, d.; *G.*MT. 850. See Matt. 1: 18; Acts 22 : 17, and other examples in *B.* pp. 315 f.

454. A participle in the genitive absolute occasionally stands alone without an accompanying noun or pronoun, when the person or thing referred to is easily perceived from the context. *HA.* 972, a.; *G.* 1568; *G.*MT. 848. See Luke 12 : 36 ; Rom. 9 : 11.

455. The Adverbial Participle always stands in the so-called predicative position, *i.e.* not in attributive position, which is between the article and its noun or after an article following the noun. Cf. 427.

THE SUBSTANTIVE PARTICIPLE

456. The Substantive Participle is employed as itself the name of an action. It thus performs a function which is more commonly discharged by the Infinitive. *HA.* 980–984; *G.* 1578–1593.

457. The Substantive Participle as Subject. The Substantive Participle may be used as an integral part of the subject of a verb, the action which it denotes being itself an essential part of that of which the predicate is affirmed.

Matt. 6 : 16 ; ὅπως φανῶσιν τοῖς ἀνθρώποις νηστεύοντες, *that they may be seen of men to fast.* (Not only *they*, but *their fasting*, is to be seen.)
Acts 5 : 42 ; οὐκ ἐπαύοντο διδάσκοντες καὶ εὐαγγελιζόμενοι τὸν χριστὸν Ἰησοῦν, *they ceased not teaching and preaching Jesus as the Christ.* See also Matt. 1 : 18, ἔχουσα; Mark 6 : 2, γινόμεναι; Luke 5 : 4, λαλῶν.

458. The Substantive Participle as Object. The Substantive Participle may be used as an integral part of the object of a transitive verb. This occurs especially after verbs of perception, the action denoted by the participle being itself that which one perceives.

Luke 8 : 46 ; ἐγὼ γὰρ ἔγνων δύναμιν ἐξεληλυθυῖαν ἀπ᾽ ἐμοῦ, *for I perceived power to have gone out of me.*

John 7 : 32 ; ἤκουσαν οἱ Φαρισαῖοι τοῦ ὄχλου γογγύζοντος, *the Pharisees heard the multitude murmuring.*

459. With verbs of *finishing, ceasing,* etc., the Substantive Participle agrees grammatically with the subject of the verb. Since, however, certain of these verbs are transitive, the action denoted by the participle must in these cases be regarded as logically the object of the verb.

Matt. 11 : 1 ; ὅτε ἐτέλεσεν ὁ Ἰησοῦς διατάσσων τοῖς δώδεκα μαθηταῖς αὐτοῦ, *when Jesus had finished commanding his twelve disciples.* Cf. Matt. 13 : 53 ; see also Luke 7 : 45.

460. THE SUBSTANTIVE PARTICIPLE IN INDIRECT DISCOURSE. A Substantive Participle forming a part of the object of a verb is sometimes equivalent to a clause of indirect discourse.

1 John 4 : 2 ; πᾶν πνεῦμα ὃ ὁμολογεῖ Ἰησοῦν Χριστὸν ἐν σαρκὶ ἐληλυθότα ἐκ τοῦ θεοῦ ἐστίν, *every spirit which confesseth that Jesus Christ has come in the flesh is of God.* See also Luke 4 : 23 ; Acts 7 : 12 ; 8 : 23 ; 3 John 4.

461. The Substantive Participle as a Limiting Genitive. The Substantive Participle may be used as an integral part of a genitive limiting phrase.

John 4 : 39 ; πολλοὶ ἐπίστευσαν εἰς αὐτὸν τῶν Σαμαρειτῶν διὰ τὸν λόγον τῆς γυναικὸς μαρτυρούσης, *many of the Samaritans believed on him because of the word of the woman testifying,* i.e. *of the woman's testimony.* See also Heb. 8 : 9 ; and cf. Jos. Ant. 10. 4. 2, where a Substantive Participle occurs after a preposition.

462. The Substantive Participle, like the Adverbial Participle, always stands in the so-called predicative position. Cf. 455, and 427.

463. The Substantive Participle must be carefully distinguished from the Adjective Participle used substantively. The latter designates the doer of an action, the former the action itself. "In the one it is the adjective force of the word which is substantivized, in the other, the verbal force." See *Stevens, u.s.*, 419, Rem. 1.

THE USE OF NEGATIVES WITH VERBS

464. In the use of the simple negatives οὐ and μή and their compounds, οὐδέ, οὐδείς, οὔτε, οὐκέτι, μηδέ, μηδείς, μήτε, μηκέτι, etc., as also of the double negatives οὐ μή and μὴ οὐ, New Testament Greek conforms in the main to classical usage, yet exhibits several important variations. The following sections exhibit the essential features of New Testament usage in comparison with that of classical writers; rarer and more delicate classical usages which have no analogies in New Testament usage are not mentioned; statements which are not restricted to classical or New Testament usage are to be understood as referring to both. What is said respecting the simple negatives οὐ and μή applies in general also to their respective compounds when standing alone.

NEGATIVES WITH THE INDICATIVE

465. The Indicative in an independent declaratory sentence regularly takes οὐ as its negative. *HA.* 1020; *G.* 1608.

John 1 : 11; εἰς τὰ ἴδια ἦλθεν, καὶ οἱ ἴδιοι αὐτὸν οὐ παρέλαβον, *he came unto his own, and they that were his own received him not.*

Rem. On the use of negatives in later Greek, see *Gild.*, Encroachments of μή on οὐ in later Greek, in *A.J.P.* I. pp. 45 ff.

178

466. In classical Greek, the Future Indicative used to express a prohibition sometimes has οὐ, sometimes μή. *HA.* 844; *G.*MT. 69, 70.

In the New Testament a Prohibitory Future takes οὐ.

Matt. 6 : 5; καὶ ὅταν προσεύχησθε, οὐκ ἔσεσθε ὡς οἱ ὑποκριταί, *and when ye pray, ye shall not be as the hypocrites.*

467. In questions that can be answered affirmatively or negatively, οὐ is used with the Indicative to imply that an affirmative answer is expected; μή to imply that a negative answer is expected. *HA.* 1015; *G.* 1603.

Matt. 13 : 55; οὐχ οὗτός ἐστιν ὁ τοῦ τέκτονος υἱός, *is not this the carpenter's son?*
John 7 : 51; μὴ ὁ νόμος ἡμῶν κρίνει τὸν ἄνθρωπον ἐὰν μὴ ἀκούσῃ πρῶτον παρ᾽ αὐτοῦ, *doth our law judge a man, except it first hear from himself?*

468. In Rom. 10 : 18, 19; 1 Cor. 9 : 4, 5; 11 : 22, μὴ οὐ is used in rhetorical questions equivalent to affirmative statements. Each negative has, however, its own proper force, οὐ making the verb negative, and μή implying that a negative answer is expected to the question thus made negative.

469. In classical Greek, the Indicative in conditional and conditional relative clauses is regularly negatived by μή. But οὐ sometimes occurs in conditions of the first class. In this case οὐ negatives the verb of the clause or other single element rather than the supposition as such. *HA.* 1021; *G.* 1610, 1383.

In the New Testament, conditional clauses of the second class (248) are regularly negatived by μή. In other conditional clauses and in conditional relative clauses, the Indicative usually takes οὐ as its negative, occasionally μή. In concessive clauses the Indicative takes οὐ.

John 9 : 33 ; εἰ μὴ ἦν οὗτος παρὰ θεοῦ, οὐκ ἠδύνατο ποιεῖν οὐδέν, *if this man were not from God, he could do nothing.*   See also Matt. 24 : 22.

Rom. 8 : 9 ; εἰ δέ τις πνεῦμα Χριστοῦ οὐκ ἔχει, οὗτος οὐκ ἔστιν αὐτοῦ, *but if any man hath not the Spirit of Christ, he is none of his.*   See also Luke 14 : 26.

Matt. 10 : 38 ; καὶ ὃς οὐ λαμβάνει τὸν σταυρὸν αὐτοῦ καὶ ἀκολουθεῖ ὀπίσω μου, οὐκ ἔστιν μου ἄξιος, *and he that does not take his cross and follow after me, is not worthy of me.*   See also Luke 9 : 50; 14 : 33; cf. 2 Pet. 1 : 9; 1 John 4 : 3.

Luke 18 : 4, 5 ; εἰ καὶ τὸν θεὸν οὐ φοβοῦμαι οὐδὲ ἄνθρωπον ἐντρέπομαι, διά γε τὸ παρέχειν μοι κόπον τὴν χήραν ταύτην ἐκδικήσω αὐτήν, *though I fear not God nor regard man, yet because this widow troubleth me, I will avenge her.*

2 Cor. 13 : 5 ; ἢ οὐκ ἐπιγινώσκετε ἑαυτοὺς ὅτι Ἰησοῦς Χριστὸς ἐν ὑμῖν ; εἰ μήτι ἀδόκιμοί ἐστε, *or know ye not as to your own selves that Jesus Christ is in you? unless indeed ye are reprobate.*   See also 1 Tim. 6 : 3 ; Tit. 1 : 6.

REM. In Matt. 26 : 24; Mark 14 : 21, οὐ occurs in the protasis of a conditional sentence of the second class.

470. It is possible that οὐ in conditional and conditional relative sentences in the New Testament is usually to be explained as negativing the predicate directly (cf. *G.* 1383. 2 ; *Th. εἰ,* III. 11.), μή on the other hand as negativing the supposition as such. Yet the evidence does not clearly establish this distinction; to press it in every case is certainly an over-refinement. Cf., *e.g.,* 1 John 4 : 3, πᾶν πνεῦμα ὃ μὴ ὁμολογεῖ τὸν Ἰησοῦν ἐκ τοῦ θεοῦ οὐκ ἔστιν, and 1 John 4 : 6, ὃς οὐκ ἔστιν ἐκ τοῦ θεοῦ οὐκ ἀκούει ἡμῶν. See also 1 Tim. 6 : 3 and Tit. 1 : 6, where μή is used after εἰ, yet quite evidently belongs to the verb rather than to the supposition as such.

471. Εἰ μή in the sense of *except* is used as a fixed phrase, without reference to the mood which would follow it if the ellipsis were supplied. Cf. 274.

Matt. 17 : 8 ; οὐδένα εἶδον εἰ μὴ αὐτὸν Ἰησοῦν μόνον, *they saw no one save Jesus only.*

Mark 9 : 9 ; διεστείλατο αὐτοῖς ἵνα μηδενὶ ἃ εἶδον διηγήσωνται, εἰ μὴ ὅταν ὁ υἱὸς τοῦ ἀνθρώπου ἐκ νεκρῶν ἀναστῇ, *he charged them that they should tell no man what things they had seen, save when the Son of man should have arisen from the dead.*

472. In clauses introduced by μή as a conjunction, **the** Indicative takes οὐ as its negative.   After other final particles its negative is μή.   *HA.* 1021, 1033;   *G.* 1610.

Rev. 9 : 4;   καὶ ἐρρέθη αὐταῖς ἵνα μὴ ἀδικήσουσιν τὸν χόρτον τῆς γῆς, *and it was said unto them that they should not hurt the grass of the earth.*   The continuation of this sentence by οὐδέ . . . οὐδέ is a syntactical irregularity.   Col. 2 : 8 illustrates the rule.

473. In indirect discourse the negative of the direct form is retained.   *HA.* 1022;   *G.* 1608.

Matt. 16 : 11;   πῶς οὐ νοεῖτε ὅτι οὐ περὶ ἄρτων εἶπον ὑμῖν, *how is it that ye do not perceive that I spake not to you concerning bread?*

REM.   In 1 John 2 : 22 a clause of indirect discourse depending on a verb meaning *to deny* contains a redundant οὐ.   Cf. 482, and *B.* p. 355.

474. In causal clauses, and in simple relative clauses not expressing purpose or condition, the Indicative is regularly negatived by οὐ.   *HA.* 1021;   *G.* 1608.

John 8 : 20;   καὶ οὐδεὶς ἐπίασεν αὐτόν, ὅτι οὔπω ἐληλύθει ἡ ὥρα αὐτοῦ, *and no man took him; because his hour was not yet come.*
Mark 2 : 24;   ἴδε τί ποιοῦσιν τοῖς σάββασιν ὃ οὐκ ἔξεστιν, *behold, why do they on the sabbath day that which is not lawful?*

REM. 1.   In John 3 : 18 a causal clause has an Indicative with μή.   This is quite exceptional in the New Testament, but similar instances occur in later Greek.   *B.* p. 349, *Gild. u.s.* p. 53.

REM. 2.   Tit. 1 : 11, διδάσκοντες ἃ μὴ δεῖ is an exception to the general rule for relative clauses, unless indeed the relative clause is to be taken as conditional.   Cf. 469.

NEGATIVES WITH THE SUBJUNCTIVE, OPTATIVE, AND IMPERATIVE

475. The negative of the Subjunctive both in principal and in subordinate clauses is μή, except in clauses introduced by the conjunction μή, *lest.* In these the negative is οὐ. Concerning οὐ μή with the Subjunctive see 487, 488.   *HA.* 1019, 1033 ; *G.* 1610.

1 John 3 : 18 ; μὴ ἀγαπῶμεν λόγῳ, *let us not love in word.*
Heb. 4 : 7 ; μὴ σκληρύνητε τὰς καρδίας ὑμῶν, *harden not your hearts.*
2 Cor. 12 : 20 ; φοβοῦμαι γὰρ μή πως ἐλθὼν οὐχ οἵους θέλω εὕρω ὑμᾶς, *for I fear, lest by any means, when I come, I should find you not such as I would.* See also Acts 20 : 16 ; Rom. 10 : 15 ; 1 Cor. 2 : 5.

REM. 1. In Matt. 25 : 9 a Subjunctive after the conjunction μή is negatived by οὐ (*WH. margin*), or, according to other MSS., followed by *WH.* (*text*) by the strong negative οὐ μή.

REM. 2. In Rom. 5 : 11 οὐ μόνον limits a verb understood which is probably to be taken as a Subjunctive. Cf. 479, 481.

476. In classical Greek, οὐ is used with the Potential Optative ; μή with the Optative of Wishing.   In the New Testament, no instance of a negatived Potential Optative occurs.   With the Optative of Wishing μή is used as in classical Greek. *HA.* 1020 ; *G.* 1608.

Gal. 6 : 14 ; ἐμοὶ δὲ μὴ γένοιτο καυχᾶσθαι, *but far be it from me to glory.* See also Mark 11 : 14 ; Rom. 3 : 4, 6, 31, etc.

477. In classical Greek, the Optative in subordinate clauses takes μή as its negative except in indirect discourse and after μή, *lest.* *HA.* 1021, 1022 ; *G.* 1610.

In the New Testament, no instance of a negatived Optative in a subordinate clause occurs.

478. The negative of the Imperative is μή. *HA.* 1019 ; *G.* 1610.

This rule holds in the New Testament with very rare exceptions.

Luke 12 : 11 ; μὴ μεριμνήσητε πῶς [ἢ τι] ἀπολογήσησθε, *be not anxious how or what ye shall answer.* See also under 165.

479. Of the apparent exceptions to the rule stated above (478), some are to be explained as parenthetic non-imperative phrases in the midst of imperative sentences. So, clearly, in 1 Cor. 5:10, [*I meant*] *not* [*that you should have no company*] *at all, with the fornicators of this world*, etc. So also 2 Tim. 2:14, *that they strive not about words*, [*a thing which is*] *profitable for nothing*. The use of οὐχ rather than μή in 1 Pet. 3:3 seems to indicate that the following words, ὁ . . . κόσμος, are excluded from the injunction rather than included in a prohibition. In 1 Pet. 2:18 οὐ μόνον occurs, perhaps as a fixed phrase, after a participle with Imperative of the verb εἶναι understood. On the other hand, it is noticeable that elsewhere limitations of the Imperative when negatived regularly take μή. Thus μὴ μόνον occurs in John 13:9; Phil. 2:12; Jas. 1:22. Cf. 481.

NEGATIVES WITH THE INFINITIVE AND PARTICIPLE

480. In classical Greek, the Infinitive usually takes οὐ as its negative in indirect discourse; elsewhere μή. *HA.* 1023, 1024; *G.* 1611; but see also *Gild. u.s.* (465, Rem.) pp. 48 ff. on the use of μή with the Infinitive in indirect discourse.

In the New Testament, the Infinitive regularly takes μή as its negative in all constructions.

Matt. 22:23; λέγοντες μὴ εἶναι ἀνάστασιν, *saying that there is no resurrection.*
Luke 11:42; ταῦτα δὲ ἔδει ποιῆσαι κἀκεῖνα μὴ παρεῖναι, *but these ought ye to have done, and not to leave the other undone.*

481. When a limitation of an Infinitive or of its subject is to be negatived rather than the Infinitive itself, the negative οὐ is sometimes used instead of μή. See Rom. 7:6; 1 Cor. 1:17; Heb. 7:11; 13:9. This principle applies especially in the case of the adverb μόνον. In the New Testament at least, οὐ μόνον rather than μὴ μόνον occurs regularly with the Infinitive, and this both when the phrase as a whole belongs to the Infinitive itself, and when it applies rather to some limitation of the Infinitive. See John 11:52; Acts 21:13; 26:29; 27:10; Rom. 4:12, 16; 13:5; 2 Cor. 8:10; Phil.

1 : 29; 1 Thess. 2 : 8. Μὴ μόνον is found with the Infinitive only in Gal. 4 : 18. It is perhaps as a fixed phrase, unaffected by the Infinitive, that εἰς οὐθέν limits λογισθῆναι in Acts 19 : 27.

482. A compound of οὐ may occur with an Infinitive dependent on a principal verb limited by οὐ, in accordance with the principle of 488.

John 5 : 30; οὐ δύναμαι ἐγὼ ποιεῖν ἀπ᾽ ἐμαυτοῦ οὐδέν, *I can of myself do nothing.* See also Mark 7 : 12; Luke 20 : 40; John 3 : 27, etc. Probably Acts 26 : 26 should be translated, *I am not persuaded* (i.e. *I cannot believe*) *that any of these things was hidden from him.* B. p. 350.

483. The Infinitive after verbs of *hindering, denying,* etc., may take μή without change of meaning. Such a negative cannot be translated into English. *HA.* 1029; *G.* 1615.

Acts 14 : 18; καὶ ταῦτα λέγοντες μόλις κατέπαυσαν τοὺς ὄχλους τοῦ μὴ θύειν αὐτοῖς, *and with these sayings scarce restrained they the multitudes from doing sacrifice unto them.* See also under 402.

484. In classical Greek, an Infinitive which would regularly take μή, usually takes μὴ οὐ when it depends on a verb which is itself negatived by οὐ. *HA.* 1034; *G.* 1616.

In the New Testament, the simple negative μή is retained in such a case.

Acts 4 : 20; οὐ δυνάμεθα γὰρ ἡμεῖς ἃ εἴδαμεν καὶ ἠκούσαμεν μὴ λαλεῖν, *for we cannot but speak the things which we saw and heard.*

485. In classical Greek, the participle takes μή if it is equivalent to a conditional, or conditional relative clause; otherwise it takes οὐ. *HA.* 1025; *G.* 1612; *Gild. u.s.* (465, Rem.) pp. 55 ff.

In the New Testament, participles in all relations usually take μή as the negative. But participles not conditional in force occasionally take οὐ, there being in all some seventeen instances in the New Testament.

Acts 13 : 28; καὶ μηδεμίαν αἰτίαν θανάτου εὑρόντες ᾐτήσαντο Πειλᾶτον ἀναιρεθῆναι αὐτόν, *and though they found no cause of death in him, yet asked they of Pilate that he should be slain.*

Luke 12 : 33; ποιήσατε ἑαυτοῖς βαλλάντια μὴ παλαιούμενα, *make for yourself purses which wax not old.*

John 5 : 23; ὁ μὴ τιμῶν τὸν υἱὸν οὐ τιμᾷ τὸν πατέρα, *he that honoreth not the Son honoreth not the Father.*

Matt. 22 : 11; εἶδεν ἐκεῖ ἄνθρωπον οὐκ ἐνδεδυμένον ἔνδυμα γάμου, *he saw there a man which had not on a wedding-garment.*

Acts 17 : 6; μὴ εὑρόντες δὲ αὐτοὺς ἔσυρον Ἰάσονα καί τινας ἀδελφοὺς ἐπὶ τοὺς πολιτάρχας, *and not finding them they dragged Jason and certain brethren before the rulers of the city.* See also Matt. 22 : 29; Luke 6 : 42; 9 : 33; John 10 : 12; Acts 7 : 5; 13 : 28; 26 : 22; Gal. 4 : 8.

SUCCESSIVE AND DOUBLE NEGATIVES

486. When two simple negatives not constituting a double negative, or a compound negative followed by a simple negative, occur in the same clause, each has its own independent force.   The same is also true of course when the negatives occur in successive clauses.   *HA.* 1031; *G.* 1618.

1 Cor. 12 :15; οὐ παρὰ τοῦτο οὐκ ἔστιν ἐκ τοῦ σώματος, *it is not therefore not of the body.* See also 1 John 3 : 10; 5 : 12.

Matt. 10 : 26; οὐδὲν γάρ ἐστιν κεκαλυμμένον ὃ οὐκ ἀποκαλυφθήσεται, *for there is nothing covered, that shall not be revealed.* See also 1 John 2 : 21.

REM. Concerning μὴ οὐ in questions, see 468.

487. The double negative οὐ μή is used with the Subjunctive, and more rarely with the Future Indicative, in emphatic negative assertions referring to the future. Cf. 172, 66. *HA.* 1032; *G.* 1360, 1361.

Mark 13 : 2 ; οὐ μὴ ἀφεθῇ ὧδε λίθος ἐπὶ λίθον ὅς οὐ μὴ καταλυθῇ, *there shall not be left here one stone upon another, which shall not be thrown down.*

Rev. 2 : 11 ; ὁ νικῶν οὐ μὴ ἀδικηθῇ ἐκ τοῦ θανάτου τοῦ δευτέρου, *he that overcometh shall not be hurt of the second death.*

Rev. 7 : 16 ; οὐ πεινάσουσιν ἔτι οὐδὲ διψήσουσιν ἔτι, οὐδὲ μὴ πέσῃ ἐπ᾽ αὐτοὺς ὁ ἥλιος, *they shall hunger no more, neither thirst any more, neither shall the sun strike upon them at all.* On Matt. 25 : 9 see 475, Rem. 1.

488. Οὐ μή is occasionally used with the Subjunctive or Future Indicative expressing a prohibition. Cf. 167, 67, Rem. 2.

489. When a negative is followed by one or more similar compound negatives or by the double negative οὐ μή the effect is a strengthened negation. *HA.* 1030; *G.* 1619.

Luke 23 : 53 ; οὗ οὐκ ἦν οὐδεὶς οὔπω κείμενος, *where never man had yet lain.*

Heb. 13 : 5 ; οὐ μή σε ἀνῶ οὐδ᾽ οὐ μή σε ἐγκαταλίπω, *I will in no wise fail thee, neither will I in any wise forsake thee.*

Rom. 13 : 8 ; μηδενὶ μηδὲν ὀφείλετε, *owe no man anything.*

INDEX OF SUBJECTS

——◇——

[The Numbers refer to Sections.]

Adjective Participle, 420–433, see under Participle.

Adjectives of *ability, fitness, readiness,* etc., followed by clause with ἵνα, 216 ; followed by Infinitive, 376 ; followed by εἰς with the articular Infinitive, 413.

Adverbial Participle, 434–455, see under Participle.

Adverbs, limited by Infinitive, 376.

Aoristic Present, 13 ; Aoristic Future, 59, 62 ; Aoristic Perfect, 80.

Aorist : constant characteristic, 35 ; Indefinite, Inceptive, Resultative, 35, 37.

Indicative : Historical, 38 ; momentary, comprehensive, collective, 39, 40, 54 ; Inceptive, 41 ; Resultative, 42, 87 ; Gnomic, 43 ; Epistolary, 44 ; Dramatic, 45 ; for English Perfect, 46, 52, 54 ; with force of Greek Perfect, 47 ; for English Pluperfect, 48, 52–54 ; in indirect discourse, 49 ; used proleptically, 50 ; in condition contrary to fact, 248 ; in apodosis of such condition, 248, 249 ; with ἄν in past general supposition, 26, 315 ; expressing an unattained wish, 27 ; English equivalents, 52, 53 ; distinction between Aorist and Imperfect, 56, 57 ; between Aorist and Perfect, 86, 87.

Dependent Moods, 98 ; Subjunctive in prohibitions, 162–164,

166, 167 ; Optative in indirect discourse, 110, 111 ; Imperative in commands and prohibitions, 163, 184 ; Infinitive after prepositions, 104–109 ; Infinitive after verbs signifying *to hope,* etc., 113 ; Infinitive in indirect discourse, 110, 114.

Participle : properly expresses not time but action conceived of as a simple event, 132, 133 ; used of antecedent action, 134–138 ; of identical action, 139–141 ; of subsequent action, 142–145 ; as integral part of the object of a verb of perception, 146 ; with λανθάνω, 147 ; leaving time-relation undefined, 148 ; denoting action in general simultaneous with that of principal verb, 149 ; with the article, equivalent to relative clause with verb in Indicative or Subjunctive, 135, 144, 150, 151.

Apodosis : defined, 238 ; force and form of, after simple present and past particular suppositions, 242, 243 ; after supposition contrary to fact, 248, 249 ; after future supposition more probable, 250, 263 ; after (implied) future supposition with less probability, 259 ; after present general supposition, 260, 263 ; after past general supposition, 265 ; may have two protases, 268 ; may be omitted, 271 ; its

187

object of desire, 276 ; in concessive clauses referring to the future, 285 (a) ; in conditional relative clauses, 308 ; in relative clauses of purpose, 317 ; in complementary relative clauses, 318 ; in relative clauses introduced by ἄχρι, 332 ; negatives with Future Indicative, 465, 466.

Dependent moods, 99 ; periphrastic form made from μέλλειν, 100.

Participle : represents action relatively future, 152 ; of later origin than other participles, 152, Rem. ; periphrastic form made from μέλλων and Infinitive, 153.

Future Perfect Indicative, in New Testament only in periphrastic form, 93, 94.

General and particular suppositions: expressed, 239, 240 ; implied in relative clause, 298, 299.

General Present: Indicative, 12 ; Participle, 123–126.

Genitive absolute, 452–454.

Gnomic tenses : Present, 12 ; Aorist, 43 ; Future, 69 ; Perfect, 79.

Grammar, relation of, to interpretation, 2.

Hebraisms in the New Testament: Εἰ with Future Indicative with force of an emphatic assertion, 272 ; clause or Infinitive as subject of ἐγένετο, 357 ; Infinitive defining content of action of a previous verb or noun, 375 ; intensive participle, 448.

Historical grammar, relation to exegetical grammar, 2.

Historical Present, 14 ; Historical Aorist, 38 ; Historical Perfect, 78.

Hortatory Subjunctive, 160, 161 ; introduced by ὥστε, 237.

Imperative : in commands and exhortations, 180 ; in entreaties and petitions, 181 ; expressing consent or hypothesis, 182, 183 ; force of tenses, 184, 163, 165; introduced by ὥστε, 237 ; negative of, 478, 479.

Imperative Future, 67.

Imperfect Indicative : Progressive, 21, 22 ; Conative, 23 ; of repeated action, 24 ; expressing an unattained wish, 27 ; translated by English Perfect, 28 ; translated by English Pluperfect, 29 ; Imperfect of verbs of obligation, etc., 30–32 ; of verbs of wishing, 33 ; in condition contrary to fact, 248 ; in apodosis of such condition, 248, 249 ; with ἄν in conditional relative clauses, past general supposition, 315 ; in indirect discourse for Present Indicative, 348 ; periphrastic form, 34 ; distinction between Imperfect and Aorist, 56, 57.

Inceptive Aorist, 35, 37 ; Indicative, 41 ; dependent moods, 98 ; participle, 137.

Indefinite Aorist, 35, 98.

Indicative :

In principal clauses : in unqualified assertions, etc., 157 ; in qualified assertions, 158, 159.

In subordinate clauses : in final clauses and clauses introduced by final particles, 198, 199, 205, 211, 215, 224, Rem. 2, 227 ; in clauses of cause, 229, 230 ; in clauses of result, 235, 236 ; in conditional clauses, 242, 248, 254–256, 261 ; in concessive clauses, 284, 285 (a) ; in definite relative clauses, 293, 294 ; in conditional relative clauses, 301, 308, 309, 313 ; with ἄν, 315 ; in relative clauses of pur-

without the article, 366 ; by Infinitive with ὥστε, 370(*d*), 371(*d*); by Infinitive with ὡς, 372 ; by Infinitive with τοῦ, 397 ; by articular Infinitive after εἰς, 409 ; after πρός, 414.

Questions: various classes of, 169 ; negatives with, 467, 468. See also Indirect Questions.

Relative clauses: classification, 289–291 ; distinction between definite and indefinite relative clauses, 289, 290.

Definite Relative clauses: introduced by relative pronouns and adverbs, 292 ; use of moods and tenses, 293 ; may imply relation of cause, result, or concession, 294 ; classified as restrictive and explanatory, 295 ; conditional in form, 316.

Conditional Relative sentences: defined, 289, 290, 296 ; imply particular or general supposition, 298, 299 ; six classes, 300–315 ; clauses conditional in form but definite in thought, 316 ; introduced by ἕως, 329.

Relative clauses expressing purpose, 317–319.

Relative clauses introduced by words meaning *until*, etc., 321–333 ; introduced by ἕως, and referring to the future, 322, 323, 325, 326 ; referring to what was in past time a future contingency, 324, 326 ; referring to a past fact, 327 ; referring to a contemporaneous event, 328 ; introduced by ἕως οὗ or ἕως ὅτου, 330 ; introduced by ἄχρι, ἄχρι οὗ, etc., 331, 332 ; introduced by πρίν, 333.

Negatives in relative clauses, 469, 470, 474.

Restrictive Relative clauses, 295.

Result: several conceptions of, 370 ; methods of expressing, 371 ; actual result expressed by ὥστε with Infinitive or Indicative, 235, 236, 369, 370 (*a*) (*b*), 371 (*a*) (*b*); by articular Infinitive with εἰς, 411 ; conceived result expressed by clause introduced by ἵνα, 218, 219, cf. 222 ; by Infinitive usually with ὥστε, 369, 370 (*c*), 371 (*c*) ; by Infinitive with τοῦ, 398 ; by articular Infinitive with εἰς, 411 ; intended result (purpose), 370 (*d*), 371 (*d*).

Resultative Aorist, 35, 37, 42, 87.

Shall and *will* in translating the Greek Future, 65.

Subjunctive:

In principal clauses : Hortatory, 160, 161 ; with ἄφες or δεῦρο prefixed, 161 ; Prohibitory, 162–164, 166, 167 ; Deliberative, 168–171 ; with θέλεις etc. prefixed, 171 ; in negative assertions referring to the future, 172, 173.

In subordinate clauses : in pure final clauses, 197 ; in object clauses after verbs of *exhorting*, etc., 200 ; after θέλω, 203 ; in clauses after verbs of *striving*, etc., 205–207, 209 ; in subject, predicate, and appositive clauses introduced by ἵνα, 211–214 ; in complementary and epexegetic clauses introduced by ἵνα, 215–217 ; in clauses of conceived result introduced by ἵνα, 218–220 ; in object clauses after verbs of *fear* and *danger* (expressed), 224 ; (implied), 225 ; after ἐάν in conditional clauses, future supposition, 250 ; after εἰ in conditional clauses, future supposition, 252, 253 ; with εἰ, expressing an object of desire, 276 ; changed to Opta-

INDEX OF GREEK WORDS

[The Numbers refer to Sections.]

Ἀκούω, Present with force of Perfect, 16.

Ἄν:

With Indicative: with Imperfect and Aorist to denote a customary past action, 26; in past general supposition, 315; in apodosis of condition contrary to fact, 248; omitted in such apodosis, 31, 249; cases in which it is not to be regarded as having been omitted, 30 (cf. 32, 33); with Future Indicative in future supposition, 308; with Present Indicative in future supposition, 309.

With Subjunctive: in conditional relative clauses, implying future supposition, 303; implying present general supposition, 312; relative clauses introduced by ἔως, 322; after ἄχρι, 332; after ὅπως in final clauses, 195; for ἐάν in conditional clauses, 250.

With Potential Optative, 178, 179.

With Infinitive, 372.

In definite relative clauses conditional in form, 316; retained in indirect discourse with Subjunctive retained unchanged, 305; omitted when Subjunctive is changed to Optative, 344, Rem. 1.

Ἀντί with τοῦ and the Infinitive, 406, 407.

Ἀπέθανον with force of Perfect, 47.

Ἄφες and ἄφετε prefixed to Hortatory Subjunctive, 161.

Ἄχρι, 331, 332.

Βούλεσθε prefixed to Deliberative Subjunctive, 171.

Γέγονα, Aoristic Perfect in Matthew (Mark?) only, 88.

Δεῦρο or δεῦτε prefixed to Hortatory Subjunctive, 161.

Διά with τό and the Infinitive, 108, 406–408.

Διότι as a causal particle, 228.

Δοκεῖ with Infinitive as subject, 385.

Ἐάν:

Conditional: with Present Indicative in present particular supposition, 247; with Future Indicative in future supposition, 254; with Subjunctive in future supposition, 250; in present general supposition, 260; in conditional relative clauses for ἄν, 304, 312, Rem.

Concessive, 279–281, 285 (b).

Ἐὰν καί, concessive, 279, 280, 285 (b), 287; conditional, 282.

Ἐβουλόμην without ἄν, 33.

Ἐγένετο δέ, construction after, 357–360.

Ἔγνων with force of Perfect, 47.

Ἔδει with Infinitive denoting present obligation, 32.

Εἰ:

Conditional: with present or past tense of the Indicative, in

195

INDEX OF PASSAGES REFERRED TO

[The numbers refer to sections. Passages referred to in Remarks are cited by the number of the section to which the Remark is appended.]

I. New Testament Passages

II. Old Testament